P9-DVX-727

Get the eBooks FREE!
(PDF, ePub, Kindle, and liveBook all included)

We believe that once you buy a book from us, you should be able to read it in any format we have available. To get electronic versions of this book at no additional cost to you, purchase and then register this book at the Manning website.

Go to https://www.manning.com/freebook and follow the instructions to complete your pBook registration.

That's it!
Thanks from Manning!

Get Programming

Learn to Code
with Python

Ana Bell

MANNING
Shelter Island

Manning Publications Co.　　Development editor:　Elesha Hyde
    20 Baldwin Road　Tecchnical development editor:　Frances Buontempo
    PO Box 761　　　　　Review editor:　Aleksandar Dragosavljević
    Shelter Island, NY 11964　　Project editor:　David Novak
                         Copy editor:　Sharon Wilkey
                         Proofreader:　Melody Dolab
           Technical proofreader:　Ignacio Beltran Torres
                      Typesetter:　Dottie Marsico
                Cover designer:　Monica Kamsvaag

ISBN 9781617293788
Printed in the United States of America
1 2 3 4 5 6 7 8 9 10 – EBM – 23 22 21 20 19 18

To my sons, James and Thomas

Contents

Preface

I wanted to write this book for two main reasons. I aimed to fill a need for a book that truly taught programming from scratch, and that presented programming as an activity that can help you with daily tasks.

A common misconception people have is that programing has to be a big endeavor every time you do it, where you're trying to write a program that can solve a world problem. But that's not so. Learning to program can improve your day-to-day life! I write short programs all the time, whether it's to solve puzzles or to help me make decisions. I wanted to capture this sentiment in this book by making programming as accessible to everyone as I can, showing how with even a little bit of programming knowledge, you can write useful programs customized to your needs.

I teach an introductory Python computer science course for undergraduates. For the most part, many students taking the class have no prior programming experience, in any language. The course is fast-paced, and many students ask if there are any resources online for people who have never programmed before. Almost all the resources I point them to require prior knowledge of programming, which adds another level of indirection to their learning: they have to first grasp the idea of programming and then understand how to apply that to Python. I try not to forget what it's like to start learning to program from scratch, no matter how many times I teach the course. I want this book to be a gentle introduction to programming in one of the most popular languages at this time, that also shows how approachable coding can be.

Acknowledgments

I'm so glad I had the opportunity to write this book, so I can help others who are just starting out in the wide world of programming.

First, I'd like to thank my husband, CJ. His support throughout the writing of this book was unwavering, from offering suggestions to watching our son while I wrote on weekends.

Next, I'd like to thank my parents and sister. My dad taught me programming when I was 12, and I'll never forget how many times he had to explain object-oriented programming to me before it finally clicked. My sister and mom travelled across the country a few times a year to help watch my sons while I got more writing done. My mom, especially, was my "secret weapon." She has never programmed before and was the perfect target audience, working through the exercises and reviewing the chapters as I was writing them.

I'd also like to thank my development editors at Manning: Kristen Watterson, Dan Maharry, and Elesha Hyde. The book underwent many transformations to become what it is, and I thank them all for their patience while I wrote and rewrote lessons. Their suggestions were much appreciated and made the book that much stronger. A big thanks also goes to my technical development editor, Frances Buontempo, and technical proofreader, Ignacio Beltran Torres, who carefully read the lessons and pointed out corrections and had wonderful suggestions on how to improve the book. Also thanks to everyone else at Manning who helped produce and promote the book. Of course, thank you to all the reviewers who offered their time to read and comment on the book at all stages of development. They are Alexandria Webb, Ana Pop, Andru Estes, Angelo Costa, Ariana Duncan, Artiom Plugachev, Carlie Cornell, David Heller, David Moravec, Adnan Masood, Drew Leon, George Joseph, Gerald Mack, Grace Kacenjar, Ivo Stimac, James Gwaltney, Jeon-Young Kang, Jim Arthur, John Lehto, Joseph M. Morgan, Juston Lantrip, Keith Donaldson, Marci Kenneda, Matt Lemke, Mike Cuddy, Nestor Narvaez, Nicole E. Kogan, Nigel John, Pavol Král', Potito Colluccelli, Prabhuti Prakash, Randy Coffland, R. Udendhran Mudaliyar, Rob Morrison, Rujiraporn Pitaksalee, Sam Johnson, Shawn Bolan, Sowmy Vajjala-Balakrishna, Steven Parr, Thomas Ballinger, Tom Northwood, Vester Thacker, Warren Rust, Yan Guo, and Yves Dorfsman.

About this Book

Who should read this book

Get Programming: Learn to Code with Python is intended for anyone who is curious about programming but doesn't necessarily want to pursue a career in it. It doesn't assume any programming experience. You should be familiar with the following ideas:

- *Variables*—Readers who have taken a math course that deals with introductory algebra know what a variable is. This book explains how variables in a programming setting are different.

- *Assigning truth values (true/false) to statements*—Statements are sentences that can be determined as true or false. For example, "It is raining" is a statement that's either true or false. You should know how to invert statements to take the opposite truth value by using the word *not*. For example, if "It is raining" is true, then "It is not raining" is false.

- *Connecting statements*—When there's more than one statement, they can be connected by using the words *and* or *or*. For example, "It's raining" and "I'm happy" can become "It's raining and I'm happy."

- *Making decisions*—With multiple statements, you can make a decision based on whether one statement is true by using "if…then…." For example, "If it is raining then the ground is wet" is made up of two statements: "It is raining" and "the ground is wet." The statement "the ground is wet" is a consequence of the statement "it is raining."

- *Following instructions by doing any of the following activities or similar*—Playing a game of 20 Questions, following a recipe, completing a read-your-own-adventure book or understanding an algorithm (following a set of instructions and making branching decisions).

How this book is organized: a roadmap

This book has eight units that cover 38 lessons. Every unit ends with a capstone project. Each unit is meant to teach you about one important concept in programming, through a series of short lessons:

- Unit 0 provides a bit of motivation to nudge you into the world of computer programming. You'll see how programming can be compared to other tasks that you might sometimes do.
- Unit 1 introduces you to the basics behind programming and the building blocks of every computer program. You'll download a programming environment and set it up so you can write programs.
- Unit 2 gets you to start writing code that interacts with the user by getting input from them and showing them results.
- Unit 3 shows you how to write programs that make decisions for you. You'll write code that branches off into different directions. When run, programs will decide which branches to take, depending on values at decision points.
- Unit 4 builds on the idea that computers are good at doing tasks quickly. You'll write code that takes advantage of the power of computers by repeating certain commands many times by writing code that automatically repeats a set of commands many times.
- Unit 5 introduces you to one way to write organized code: using functions as modules that can contain reusable code.
- Unit 6 shows you advanced types of objects that you can program with. After this unit, you'll be able to write some incredibly useful and versatile programs.
- Unit 7 introduces you to making your own types of objects. This is a capability that not all programming languages have, but most of the ones being used today do have.
- Unit 8 wraps up the book by showing you code libraries written by others that you can use in your own programs. This lesson brings together abstract ideas that show you how to organize your code and take advantage of previously written code.

About the code

The content and code in this book are presented using Python version 3.5, the most up-to-date version at the time of writing.

The code examples in this book show how to apply the concepts learned in each lesson to perform a task you may have to do in your day-to-day life. Toward the end of the book, the code becomes a bit longer, and the same task is revisited in a couple of different scenarios.

At the end of each unit, a capstone project summarizes key ideas learned in the lessons. A problem is described, and you'll be walked through one possible solution. You'll discover how to "translate" the English description of the task outlined into code.

This book contains many examples of source code both in numbered listings and in line with normal text. In both cases, source code is formatted in a `fixed-width font like this` to separate it from ordinary text. Sometimes code is also set **in bold** to highlight code that has changed from previous steps in the chapter, such as when a new feature adds to an existing line of code.

In many cases, the original source code has been reformatted; we've added line breaks and reworked indentation to accommodate the available page space in the book. In rare cases, even this was not enough, and listings include line-continuation markers (➡). Additionally, comments in the source code have often been removed from the listings when the code is described in the text. Code annotations accompany many of the listings, highlighting important concepts.

Book forum

Purchase of *Get Programming: Learn to Code with Python* includes free access to a private web forum run by Manning Publications where you can make comments about the book, ask technical questions, and receive help from the author and from other users. To access the forum, go to https://forums.manning.com/forums/get-programming. You can also learn more about Manning's forums and the rules of conduct at https://forums .manning.com/forums/about.

Manning's commitment to our readers is to provide a venue where a meaningful dialogue between individual readers and between readers and the author can take place. It is not a commitment to any specific amount of participation on the part of the author, whose contribution to the forum remains voluntary (and unpaid). We suggest you try asking the author some challenging questions lest her interest stray! The forum and the archives of previous discussions will be accessible from the publisher's website as long as the book is in print.

About the author

 Dr. Ana Bell is a lecturer at the Massachusetts Institute of Technology in the Electrical Engineering and Computer Science department. She has co-lectured two introductory computer science courses in Python for the past five years: one aimed at students who have no prior programming experience, and one intended to expand on what students learn in the first course. She enjoys introducing others to programming and watching them gain confidence in themselves as they progress. It's an extremely rewarding feeling to explain the same concept in different ways and watch it suddenly click with a student.

She was first introduced to Python in graduate school at Princeton University, where she started using it to parse and reformat large files in her research and found it to be an intuitive language to learn and use.

Learning how to program

This unit begins with a bit of motivation on why learning to program is beneficial no matter who you are; you can even use programming in your daily life to make certain tasks easier. You'll briefly be introduced to ideas you should be familiar with before starting to program, and you'll get an idea of the kinds of things you'll be able to do by the end of this book.

The unit ends by drawing a parallel with baking so that you can see programming as a skill requiring practice and creativity. This unit also serves as an overview of what you should expect as you go through this journey: lots and lots of practice! Learning to program seems like a big undertaking, but it's best to take small steps every day rather than giant occasional leaps. It's a challenging but rewarding path.

Let's begin!

WHY SHOULD YOU LEARN HOW TO PROGRAM?

After reading lesson 1, you'll be able to

- Understand why programming matters
- Set up a plan for learning how to program

1.1 Why programming matters

Programming is universal. No matter who you are or what you do, you can learn to write programs that can help make your life easier.

1.1.1 Programming isn't just for professionals

A misconception, both for veteran programmers and for people who have never programmed before, is that after you start to learn how to program, you'll have to continue until you become a professional programmer. Likely, this misconception stems from associating programming with incredibly complex systems: your operating system, car/aviation software, artificial intelligence that learns, and many others.

I think of programming as a skill, like reading/writing, math, or cooking. You don't have to become a best-selling author, a world-class mathematician, or a Michelin star chef.

Your life significantly improves with a little bit of knowledge in each of those subjects: if you know how to read and write, you can communicate with others; if you know how to do basic calculations, you can tip appropriately at a restaurant; if you know how to follow a recipe, you can make a meal in a pinch. Knowing a little bit of programming will enable you to avoid having to rely on others to help you and will enable you to finish tasks you may want to do in a specific way more efficiently.

1.1.2   Improve your life

If you learn to program, your skill can be used as you effectively build your own personal toolbox of utilities. The more you try to integrate programming into your daily life, the more you'll be able to solve personal tasks more efficiently.

To keep up with your skill, you can write custom programs that fit your daily needs. The benefit of writing your own programs instead of using ones that already exist is that you can customize them to your exact needs. For example:

- Do you keep track of the checks that you write in the paper logbook that came with your checkbook? Consider typing them in a file and writing a program that reads the file and organizes the information. With programming, after the data is read, you can calculate sums, separate the checks by date ranges, or whatever else you want.
- Have you taken pictures and downloaded them to your computer, but the names given by the camera software aren't what you want? Instead of manually renaming everything by hand for a thousand pictures, you can write a short program that renames all files automatically.
- Are you a student preparing for the SAT and want to make sure your solution for the quadratic equation is correct? You can write a program that takes in missing parameters and solves the equation for you, so that when you do it by hand, you can be sure that the calculations were done correctly.
- Are you a teacher who would like to send a personalized email to each student with that student's grade for a test? Instead of copying and pasting text and filling in the values manually, you can write a program that reads the student name, email address, and score from a file, and then effectively fills in the blank automatically for each student, and sends out the email.

These are just a few situations in which programming can help you to be more organized and self-reliant.

1.1.3   Challenge yourself

At first glance, programming feels technical. At the beginning, it is, especially as you're learning all the basic concepts. Perhaps unintuitively, programming is also creative. After you become familiar with a few ways to do one task in programming, you get to make decisions about which way would be best to apply. For example, if you're reading a file, do you want to read all the data at once, store it, and then do some analysis, or do you want to read the data one piece at a time and analyze as you go along?

By making these kinds of decisions with the knowledge you gain, you challenge yourself to think critically about what you want to achieve and how to do it most efficiently.

1.2   Where you are now and where you'll be

This book doesn't assume that you've programmed before. Having said that, you should be familiar with the following:

- *Understanding a variable*—If you took a math course that covers introductory algebra, you should know what a variable is. In the next unit, you'll see how variables in a programming setting are different.
- *Understanding true/false statements*—You can think of statements as sentences that can be determined to be true or false. For example, "it is raining" is a statement that's either true or false. You can also invert statements to take the opposite truth value by using the word *not*. For example, if "it is raining" is true, then "it is not raining" is false.
- *Connecting statements*—When you have more than one statement, you can connect them by using the words *and* or *or*. For example, if "it is raining" is true and "I am hungry" is false, then "it is raining and I am hungry" is false because both parts need to be true. But "it is raining or I am hungry" is true because at least one of the parts is true.
- *Making decisions*—When you have multiple statements, you can make decisions based on whether one statement is true by using *if…then*. For example, "if it is raining, then the ground is wet" is made up of two statements: "it is raining" and "the ground is wet." The statement "the ground is wet" is a consequence of the statement "it is raining."
- *Following flowcharts*—You won't need to know flowcharts to understand this book, but understanding them requires the same skills as understanding basic programming. Other ideas that use the same skill set are playing the game of 20 Questions, following a recipe, reading a choose-your-own-adventure book, or

understanding algorithms. You should be familiar with following a set of instructions and making branching decisions. Flowcharts show a list of instructions that flow from one to the next and allow you to make decisions, which lead to different paths. In a flowchart, you're asked a series of questions, whose answer is one of two choices: yes or no. Depending on your answer, you follow certain paths through the flowchart and will eventually end up at a final answer. Figure 1.1 is an example of a flowchart.

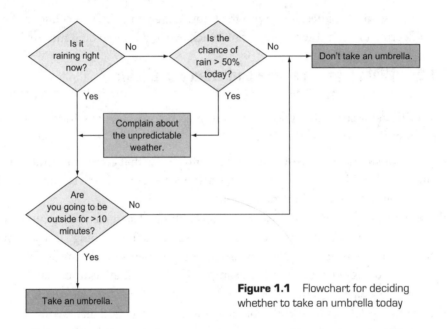

Figure 1.1   Flowchart for deciding whether to take an umbrella today

Knowing the preceding skills is all you need to begin your programming journey. After reading this book, you'll know the basics of programming. The basic concepts you'll learn that can apply to any programming language are as follows:

- Using variables, expressions, and statements in programming
- Getting the program to make decisions based on conditions
- Getting the program to automatically repeat tasks under some conditions
- Reusing operations built into the language to help you be more efficient
- Making your code more readable and easy to maintain by breaking a larger task into smaller ones
- Knowing which data structure (a structure already created that can store information in a certain format) is appropriate to use in different situations

You'll be learning how to program by using a language called Python (version 3.5). Any knowledge gained about programming concepts will be easily translatable to any other programming language; the basics are going to be the same between different languages. More specifically, at the end of this book, you'll be familiar with the details of the Python programming language. You'll know the following:

- How to use the syntax of the language (in English, the equivalent is how to form valid sentences).
- How to write more-complex programs with different blocks of code working together in harmony (in English, the equivalent is writing a short story).
- How to use code that other programmers wrote (in English, the equivalent is referencing someone else's work so you don't have to rewrite it).
- How to effectively check that your program works, including testing and debugging (in English, the equivalent is checking for spelling and grammar errors).
- How to write programs that interact with the keyboard and mouse.
- How to write more data-centric or mathematical programs.

1.3   Our plan for learning how to program

Individual motivation is one of the greatest make-or-break factors when learning a programming language. Taking things slow, getting a lot of practice, and allowing time to absorb the material will make the road to success less bumpy.

1.3.1   First steps

If you've never programmed before, this book is for you. This book is separated into units. A *unit* is a set of lessons that all deal with one particular concept in programming. The first lesson in the unit is usually a motivating lesson. The last lesson in a unit is a capstone project, which introduces a real-life problem or task. You can attempt the capstone on your own or you can read the walk-through of the solution; it's intended to make sure that you're on track with understanding the concepts.

You'll have many opportunities to practice what you read. At the beginning of each lesson, you'll see a simple exercise, called *Consider this,* that will get you thinking about the world around you and the way you interact with it; this exercise introduces you to the main idea of the lesson. It's described without code jargon and hints at the kinds of programming ideas you'll learn in the lesson. Throughout the lesson, you'll discover how to "translate" the English description of the outlined exercise into code. Each lesson contains many exercises to help you understand the concepts; doing all the exercises will help the concepts click. Answers to these exercises will be found in Appendix A so that you can check your work.

Being hands-on with the exercises is important in the first few lessons, as you'll be learning the basics of programming using Python. In the last few lessons, you'll see packages that other programmers wrote, and you'll have an opportunity to learn how to use those packages to build more-complex programs. One of the packages will get you to build programs that you can interact with visually, by mouse click or keyboard input, and you'll see your program update an image on the screen. Another package will show you how to deal with data as input. You'll learn how to read files that have a certain structure, how to analyze the data gathered, and how to write data to another file.

1.3.2   Practice, practice, practice, practice

Each lesson has short exercises with solutions. With Python, and programming in general, lots of practice is essential to truly understand the concepts—this is especially true if you've never programmed before. Don't be frustrated by errors when writing a program; you'll improve your understanding by correcting unexpected mistakes.

You can think of these exercises as checkpoints to help you understand how much you understand. Programming isn't a passive activity. You should be actively engaged with the material presented and the concepts shown by constantly trying things out on your own. The checkpoint exercises touch upon the important ideas presented in the lesson, and you should attempt them all to cover the breadth of the material. If you feel adventurous, you can even come up with variations on the exercises presented and attempt to write new programs for problems you come up with!

1.3.3   Think like a programmer

This book is intended to be a unique learning experience. I don't just want to teach you programming in Python. I also want to teach you how to think like a programmer.

To understand this, consider the following metaphor. There are two people: an author of fiction and a journalist. The author of fiction is someone who comes up with a plot, characters, dialogue, and interactions and then puts these ideas together in interesting ways by using the rules of the English language. The author writes a story for people to enjoy. The journalist doesn't need to employ their creative side but rather hunts down stories based on fact. The journalist then puts the facts on paper, also using the rules of the English language, for people to be informed.

I compare an author of fiction and a journalist to demonstrate the difference between a computer scientist and a programmer, respectively. Both a computer scientist and a programmer know how to write computer code, and both adhere to the rules of a programming language in order to create programs that do certain tasks. In the same way that an author thinks about a unique story and how to best pace it, a computer scientist may put more effort into coming up with ideas rather than putting their ideas into words. A computer scientist thinks about brand-new algorithms or studies theoretical questions, such as what a computer can and can't do. On the other hand, a programmer implements programs based on preexisting algorithms or a set of requirements to which they must adhere. A programmer knows the details of a language well and can implement code quickly, efficiently, and correctly. In practice, the roles of a programmer and computer scientist often overlap, and there isn't always a clear distinction.

This book will show you how to implement tasks on a computer by giving the computer detailed instructions and will help you become proficient at doing this.

Thinking like a programmer

Be on the lookout throughout the rest of the book for this box.

You'll get useful tips on which principles of thinking like a computer programmer apply to the ideas being discussed. These principles tie the book together, and I hope that revisiting these ideas will help you get into the mindset of a programmer.

The next lesson outlines several principles that get at what it means to think like a programmer. Throughout each lesson, you'll be reminded of these principles whenever possible, and I hope that you'll start to think about these principles on your own as you progress through the book.

 ## Summary

In this lesson, my objective was to inspire you to learn to program. You don't have to become a professional programmer. Use basic programming ideas and concepts to improve your personal life, even in simple ways. Programming is a skill, and you'll get better at it the more you practice. As you read this book, try to think of tedious tasks that you're doing manually that can be solved more effectively with programming, and try to do it.

Let's begin!

BASIC PRINCIPLES OF LEARNING A PROGRAMMING LANGUAGE

After reading lesson 2, you'll be able to

- Understand the process of writing a computer program
- Get a big-picture view of the think-code-test-debug-repeat paradigm
- Understand how to approach a programming problem
- Understand what it means to write readable code

 ## 2.1 Programming as a skill

Like reading, counting, playing piano, or playing tennis, programming is a skill. As with any skill, you have to nurture it through lots of practice. Practice requires dedication, perseverance, and self-discipline on your part. At the beginning of your programming career, I highly recommend that you write out as much code as possible. Open your code editor and type up every piece of code that you see. Try to type it out instead of relying on copying and pasting. At this point, the goal is to make programming become second nature, not to program quickly.

This lesson serves as motivation to get you in the mindset of a programmer. The first lesson introduced you to the "Thinking like a programmer" boxes that will be scattered throughout this book. The following sections offer a big-picture view encapsulating the main ideas of those boxes.

Consider this   You want to teach a cave dweller how to get dressed to go to a job interview. Assume the clothes are already laid out and that the dweller is familiar with clothes, just not the process of dressing up. What steps do you tell him to take? Be as specific as possible.

Answer:

1   Pick up underwear, put left foot in one hole, put right foot in the other hole, and pull them up.
2   Pick up shirt, put one arm through one sleeve, and then put your other arm in the other sleeve. The buttons should be on your chest. Close shirt by inserting the little buttons into the holes.
3   Pick up pants, put one foot on one pant leg, and the other foot in the other pant leg. The pant opening should be in the front. Pull zipper up and button the pants.
4   Take one sock and put it on one foot. Then put a shoe on. Pull the laces of the shoes and tie them. Repeat with the other sock and shoe.

2.2   A parallel with baking

Suppose I ask you to bake me a loaf of bread. What is the process you go through—from the time I give you the task, to when you give me the finished loaf?

2.2.1   Understand the task "bake a loaf of bread"

The first step is to make sure you understand the given task. "Bake a loaf of bread" is a bit vague. Here are some questions you may want to ask to clarify the task:

- What size loaf of bread?
- Should it be a simple bread or flavored bread? Are there any specific ingredients you have to use or not use? Are there any ingredients you don't have?
- What equipment do you need? Is the equipment supplied to you, or do you need to get your own?
- Is there a time limit?
- Are there any recipes that you can look up and use, or do you have to make one up on your own?

It's important that you get these details right in order to avoid having to start over on the task. If no further details on the task are provided, the solution you come up with should be as simple as possible and should be as little work for you as possible. For example, you should look up a simple recipe instead of trying to come up with the correct combination of ingredients on your own. As another example, first try to bake a small loaf of bread, don't add any flavors or spices, and use a bread machine (if you have one) to save time.

2.2.2   Find a recipe

After you clarify any questions or misconceptions about the task, you can look up a recipe or come up with one on your own. The recipe tells you how to do the task. Coming up with a recipe on your own is the hardest part of doing the task. When you have a recipe to follow, putting everything together shouldn't be difficult.

Take a quick look at any recipe right now. Figure 2.1 shows a sample recipe. A recipe may include the following:

- The steps you should take and in what order
- Specific measurements
- Instructions on when and how many times to repeat a task
- The substitutions you can make for certain ingredients
- Any finishing touches on the dish and how to serve it

Quantity	Ingredient
1/4 ounce	Active dry yeast
1 tablespoon	Salt
2 tablespoons	Butter (or canola oil)
3 tablespoons	Sugar
2-1/4 cups	Warm water
6-1/2 cups	All-purpose flour

1. In a large bowl, dissolve yeast in warm water. Add the sugar, salt, oil and 3 cups flour. Beat until smooth.
2. Stir in enough remaining flour to form a soft dough.
3. Turn onto a floured surface.
4. Knead until smooth and elastic.
5. Put in a greased bowl, turning once to grease the top.
6. Cover and let rise in a warm place until doubled, about 1-1/2 hours.
7. Punch dough down. Turn onto a lightly floured surface.
8. Divide dough in half. Shape each into a loaf. Place in two greased 9x5-inch loaf pans.
9. Cover and let rise until doubled, about 30–45 minutes.
10. Bake at 375° for 30 minutes or until golden brown.
11. Move breads from pans to wire racks to cool.
12. Slice and enjoy!

Figure 2.1   A sample recipe for bread

The recipe is a sequence of steps that you must follow to bake bread. The steps are sequential; for example, you can't take the loaf out of the oven without first putting the dough in the pan. At certain steps, you can choose to put in one item instead of another; for example, you can put in either butter or canola oil, but not both. And some steps may be repeated, such as occasionally checking for the crust color before declaring that the bread is done.

2.2.3   Visualize the recipe with flowcharts

When you read a recipe, the sequence of steps is likely outlined in words. To prepare you for understanding how to be a programmer, you should start to think about visualizing recipes with flowcharts, as discussed briefly in lesson 1. Figure 2.2 shows how to represent baking bread with a flowchart. In this scenario, you're using a bread machine, and the ingredients differ slightly than the ones shown in figure 2.1. In the flowchart, steps are entered in rectangular boxes. If a recipe allows for a possible substitution, represent that with a diamond box. If a recipe has you repeating a task, draw an arrow going back up to the first step in the repeated sequence.

2.2.4   Use an existing recipe or make one up?

There are many recipes for bread out there. How do you know which one to use? With a vague problem statement such as "Bake a loaf of bread," all are good to use because they all accomplish the task. In that sense, a more general problem statement is easier for you when you have a set of recipes to pick from, because any of the recipes will work.

But if you have a picky eater and are asked to bake something for which there's no recipe, you'll have a hard time accomplishing the task. You'll have to experiment with various ingredient combinations and quantities, and with various temperatures and baking times. Likely, you'll have to start over a few times.

The most common type of problem you'll be given is a specific task for which you have some information, such as "Bake me a two-pound rosemary loaf of bread using 4 cups of flour, 1 tablespoon of sugar, 1 tablespoon of butter, 1 teaspoon of salt, and 1 teaspoon of yeast." You may not find a recipe that accomplishes this task exactly, but you're given a lot of critical information already in the task; in this example, you have all the ingredient measurements except for the rosemary amount. The hardest part is experimenting with ways of putting the ingredients together and determining how much rosemary to add. If this isn't your first time baking, you come to the task with some intuition for how much rosemary is just right. The more practice you have, the easier it'll be.

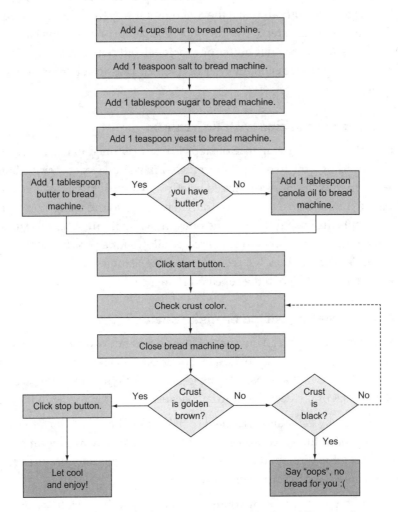

Figure 2.2   A flowchart of a simple recipe for baking bread. Rectangular boxes represent taking an action. Diamonds represent a decision point. The line going back up to a previous step represents a sequence repetition. Follow the arrows to trace paths through various implementations of the recipe.

The main idea to come away with from this baking example is that there's more to baking than following a recipe. First you have to understand what you're being asked to bake. Then you must determine whether you have any existing recipes that you can follow. If not, you have to come up with your own recipe and experiment until you have a final product that matches what is being asked of you. In the next section, you'll see how the baking example translates into programming.

 ## 2.3   Think, code, test, debug, repeat

In this book, you'll write both simple and complicated programs. No matter what the complexity of the program, it's important to approach every problem in an organized and structured manner. I suggest using the think-code-test-debug-repeat paradigm shown in figure 2.3 until you're satisfied that your code works according to the problem specification.

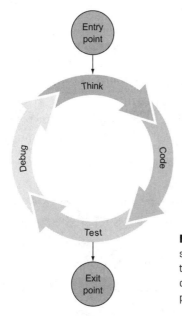

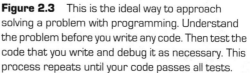

Figure 2.3   This is the ideal way to approach solving a problem with programming. Understand the problem before you write any code. Then test the code that you write and debug it as necessary. This process repeats until your code passes all tests.

The Think step is equivalent to making sure you understand what kind of baked good you're being asked to make. Think about the problem asked of you and decide whether you have any recipes that might work or if you need to come up with one on your own. In programming, recipes are *algorithms*.

The Code step is equivalent to getting your hands dirty and experimenting with possible combinations of ingredients, any substitutions, and any repetitive parts (for example, check the crust every five minutes). In programming, you're coding up an *implementation* of an algorithm.

The Test step is equivalent to determining whether the final product matches what the task was expecting you to produce. For example, is the baked good that came out of the oven a loaf of bread? In programming, you run a program with different inputs and check whether the *actual output* matches the *expected output*.

The Debug step is equivalent to tweaking your recipe. For example, if it's too salty, reduce the amount of salt you add. In programming, you *debug* a program to figure out which lines of code are causing incorrect behavior. This is a rough process if you don't follow best practices. Some are outlined later in this lesson, and unit 7 also contains some debugging techniques.

These four steps repeat as many times as necessary until your code passes all tests.

2.3.1   Understanding the task

When you're given a problem that you need to solve using programming, you should never begin to write code right away. If you start by writing code, you enter the cycle directly at the Code leg shown in figure 2.3. It's unlikely that you'll write your code correctly the first time. You'll have to cycle through until you think about the given problem, because you didn't correctly solve it the first time. By thinking about the problem at the start, you minimize the number of times you'll go through the programming cycle.

As you tackle harder and harder problems, it's also important that you try to break them into smaller problems with a simpler and smaller set of steps. You can focus on solving the smaller problems first. For example, instead of baking a loaf of bread with exotic ingredients, try a few small rolls to get the proportions just right without wasting too many resources or too much time.

When you're given a problem, you should ask yourself the following:

- What is this program supposed to accomplish? For example, "Find the area of a circle."
- Are there any interactions with the user? For example, "The user will enter a number" and "You show the user the area of a circle with that radius."
- What type of input is the user giving you? For example, "The user will give you a number representing the radius of a circle."
- What does the user want from the program and in what form? For example, you might show the user "12.57," you might be more verbose and show "The area of a circle with radius 2 is 12.57," or you might draw a picture for the user.

I suggest that you organize your thoughts on the problem by redescribing the problem in two ways:

- Visualize the problem.
- Write down a few sample inputs and then the outputs that you expect.

Quick check 2.1 Find any recipe (in a box or look one up on the internet). Write a problem statement for what the recipe is trying to achieve. Write a vague problem statement. Write a more specific problem statement.

2.3.2 Visualizing the task

When you're given a task to solve using programming, think of the task as a black box. At first, don't worry about the *implementation*.

> **DEFINITION** An implementation is the way you write the code to solve a task.

Instead of worrying about the details of the implementation, think about what's being asked: Are there any interactions with the user? Is there any input your program might need? Is there any output your program might show? Is your program just supposed to be doing calculations behind the scenes?

It's helpful to draw a diagram showing possible interactions between your program and the user of the program. Go back to the bread example. A possible black box visualization is shown in figure 2.4. The inputs are represented to the left of the black box and the outputs to the right.

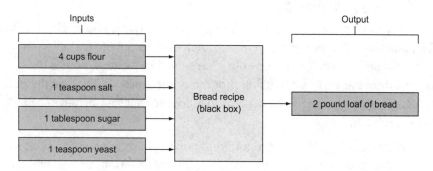

Figure 2.4 A black box visualization of baking a loaf of bread with a given set of ingredients.

When you have an idea of the inputs and outputs of your black box, think about any special behaviors that you may need to take into account. Will the program behave differently in different situations? In the bread example, can you substitute something for sugar if you don't have any? Will you get a different type of bread if you add sugar instead of salt? You should write out what the program will do in these situations.

All these specific interactions can be visualized in a flowchart. You can trace many routes through your flowchart, each route representing a different possible implementation and outcome, as in figure 2.2.

> **Quick check 2.2**   You need to clean up after your baking adventure. You need to do two things: wash the dishes and take out the trash, in that order. Organize the following steps and decision points into a flowchart as in figure 2.2. Use as many steps/decisions as possible, but you don't have to use them all.
>
> Step: Rinse dish   Decision: Anything else to put in the trash bag?
>
> Step: Sing a song   Decision: Am I happy with my baking skills?
>
> Step: Tie up trash bag   Decision: Any more dirty dishes left?
>
> Step: Take trash outside   Decision: Should I watch a movie tonight?
>
> Step: Pick up a dirty dish
>
> Step: Scrub dirty dish with soap
>
> Step: Put clean dish in drying rack
>
> Step: Dump out trash bag on the floor
>
> Step: Put a piece of trash in the trash bag

2.3.3   Writing pseudocode

At this point, you've come up with test cases, special behaviors you might have to be careful of, and a visual representation of a sequence of steps that you believe will accomplish the task given. If you drew out your sequence of steps, now is the time to convert your drawing into words, using programming concepts. To solve the problem, you must come up with a sequence of steps to follow so that they achieve the task outlined in the problem.

Pseudocode is a mix of English and programming on paper or in your code editor. It helps you get the structure of the program looking right at various points: when you get input from the user, when you show output, when you need to make a decision, and when you need to repeat a set of steps.

Putting the sequence of steps into words is like writing down and trying out your recipe. You must use what you know about how ingredients taste and what they're used for to decide the best way to arrange them together. In programming, you must use everything you know about various techniques and constructs to put the code together, and this is the hardest part of programming.

In pseudocode, finding the area of a circle might look like this:

1 Get a radius from the user.
2 Apply a formula.
3 Show the result.
4 Repeat steps 1–3 until the user says to stop.

Throughout this book, you'll see examples where certain programming concepts are useful. The only way to know which concept to use and when to use it is through intuition, which comes with a lot of practice.

Of course, there are many ways to achieve a task with programming. It's not a bad thing to go down one path and find yourself stuck; then you'll have a better understanding of why a particular method doesn't work in that case. With time and experience, you'll develop intuition for when one concept is better to use than another.

> **Quick check 2.3** Here's a problem statement. The Pythagorean theorem is $a^2 + b^2 = c^2$. Solve for c. Write a sequence of steps, in pseudocode, that you might take to solve for c.
> Hint: $\sqrt{(x^2)} = x$

 ## 2.4   Writing readable code

As you learn more about programming, and specifically Python programming in this book, you'll see language specifics that Python offers to help you achieve this principle. I don't discuss those in this lesson. What's important to remember at this point, before you even start writing code, is that any code you write should be with the intent that someone else will read it, including yourself in a few weeks' time!

2.4.1   Using descriptive and meaningful names

Here's a short snippet of code in Python, which you don't need to understand right now. It consists of three lines of code, evaluated in order, top to bottom. Notice that it looks similar to something you may write in a math class:

```
a = 3.1
b = 2.2
c = a * b * b
```

Can you tell, at a high level, what the code is supposed to calculate? Not really. Suppose I rewrite the code:

```
pi = 3.1
radius = 2.2
# use the formula to calculate the area of a circle
circle_area = pi * radius * radius
```

Now can you tell, at a high level, what the code is supposed to do? Yes! It calculates—or rather, estimates—the area of a circle with radius 2.2. As in math, programming languages use *variables* to store data. A key idea behind writing readable code when programming is using descriptive and meaningful variable names. In the preceding code, pi is a variable name, and you can use it to refer to the value 3.1. Similarly, radius and circle_area are variable names.

2.4.2   Commenting your code

Also notice that the preceding code includes a line that starts with the # character. That line is called a *comment*. In Python, a comment starts with the # character, but in other languages, it can start with different special characters. A comment line isn't part of the code that runs when the program runs. Instead, comments are used in code to describe important parts of the code.

> **DEFINITION**   A comment is a line in a Python program that starts with a #. These lines are ignored by Python when running a program.

Comments should help others, and yourself, understand why you wrote code in that way. They shouldn't just put into words what the code implements. A comment that says "Use the formula to calculate the area of a circle" is much better than one that says "Multiply pi times the radius times the radius." Notice that the former explains why the code is correct to use, but the latter simply puts into words what the code is implementing. In this example, someone else reading the code already knows that you're multiplying the three values (because they know how to read code!), but they might not know why you're doing the multiplication.

Comments are useful when they describe the rationale behind a larger chunk of code, particularly when you come up with a unique way to compute or implement something. A comment should describe the big idea behind the implementation of that particular chunk of code, because it might not be obvious to others. When someone reading the code understands the big picture, they can then go into the specifics of the code by reading each line to see exactly what calculations you're doing.

Quick check 2.4 Here's a short piece of Python code implementing a solution to the following problem. Fill in the comments. "You're filling a pool and have two hoses. The green hose fills it in 1.5 hours, and the blue hose fills it in 1.2 hours. You want to speed up the process by using both hoses. How long will it take using both hoses, in minutes?"

```python
# Your comment here
time_green = 1.5
time_blue = 1.2

# Your comment here
minutes_green = 60 * time_green
minutes_blue = 60 * time_blue

# Your comment here
rate_hose_green = 1 / minutes_green
rate_hose_blue = 1 / minutes_blue

# Your comment here
rate_host_combined = rate_hose_green + rate_hose_blue

# Your comment here
time = 1 / rate_host_combined
```

Summary

In this lesson, my objective was to teach you

- The think-code-test-debug-repeat cycle of events that a good programmer should follow.
- To think about the problem you're given and understand what's being asked.
- To draw out what the inputs and outputs are based on the problem description before beginning to code.
- That a problem statement won't necessarily outline the series of steps you should take to solve the task. It may be up to you to come up with a recipe—a series of steps to achieve the task.
- To write code with the intent of it being read. You should use descriptive and meaningful names, and write comments that describe in words the problem and coded solution.

Variables, types, expressions, and statements

In this unit, you'll download software that includes the Python 3.5 version and a special text editor to help you write and run your Python programs. You'll set up your programming environment and try out a little Python code to make sure everything is set up right. Then, you'll get an introduction to the basics of any programming language: various types of objects, variables, statements, and expressions. These are the building blocks of programs— as letters, words, and sentences are to the English language.

This unit ends with a capstone project: your first Python program! I'll guide you through each step. There are many ways to solve a programming problem, and I'll show you two. If you feel adventurous, feel free to attempt the problem before seeing the full solutions.

INTRODUCING PYTHON: A PROGRAMMING LANGUAGE

After reading lesson 3, you'll be able to

- Understand Python,the programming language you'll be using
- Use a program to write your programs
- Understand the components of a programming development environment

3.1   Installing Python

The Python programming language is, at the time of this writing, the most popular language for teaching introductory computer science. The language is used by top universities to expose students to programming, and many students are citing Python as a language they're familiar with upon entering college. Broadly, Python is used to build applications and websites, and is being used behind the scenes by companies such as NASA, Google, Facebook, and Pinterest to maintain features and analyze collected data.

Python is a great general-purpose language that can be used to write quick and simple programs. After you set up a working environment, writing a program in Python doesn't require much setup.

3.1.1   What is Python?

Python is a programming language created by Guido van Rossum at Centrum Wiskunde & Informatica in the Netherlands. But the name *Python* is also used to refer to the interpreter.

> **DEFINITION**   A Python interpreter is a program used to run programs written in the Python programming language.

In the Python programming language, every *thing*, called an *object*, has characteristics (data) associated with it and ways to interact with it. For example, any word is a thing, or object, in Python. The data associated with the word *summer* is the letter characters in that sequence. One way that you can interact with the word is to change every letter to be uppercase. An example of a more complicated object is a bicycle. The data associated with a bicycle could be the number of wheels, its height, its length, and its color. The actions that a bike can do might be that it can fall over, a person can ride it, and you can repaint it.

In this book, you'll be writing programs in the latest Python version at the time of this writing, version 3.5.

3.1.2   Downloading Python version 3.5

You can download Python version 3.5 in various ways; you can get it from the official Python website, www.python.org, or through any third-party programs that offer the Python language as well as extra packages preinstalled. In this book, I recommend that you download a specific third-party program called the *Anaconda Python Distribution*.

3.1.3   Anaconda Python Distribution

You can download the Anaconda Python Distribution from www.anaconda.com. This free Python distribution offers various versions of Python and includes more than 400 of the most popular packages for science, math, engineering, and data analysis. There's also a lighter version, without any of the extra packages, called *Miniconda*.

Go to the downloads page, www.anaconda.com/downloads, and choose the Python 3.5 download link for your appropriate operating system. Follow the installation instructions with the default values to install the distribution on your computer. Note that the latest version might be different than Python 3.5, and that's fine. For our purposes, changes between subversions of Python 3 won't make a difference.

3.1.4   Integrated development environments

After the installation is complete, open Spyder, a program part of Anaconda. Spyder is an integrated development environment (IDE) that you'll use to write and run your programs in this book.

> **DEFINITION**   An integrated development environment (IDE) is a complete programming environment that helps make your program writing experience a lot nicer.

Open Spyder

In Windows only, you can open Spyder from the Anaconda folder in the Start menu, shown in figure 3.1.

Figure 3.1   Anaconda folder in the Start menu

Some of the important features that the Spyder IDE offers, shown in figure 3.2, are as follows:

- An editor to write your Python programs
- A way to see lines of code, before running your program, that may contain potential errors or inefficiencies
- A console to interact with the user of your programs, through input and output
- A way to see values of variables in your program
- A way to step through your code line by line

Figure 3.2 shows the entire Spyder IDE and some code written in the code editor. You don't have to understand the code.

3. A space to indicate any potential lines that may contain errors before running the code

2. The program editor window, in which you can have multiple files open

5. The Debug menu that contains options to run your program step-by-step

4. A variable explorer that shows you values of objects in your programs

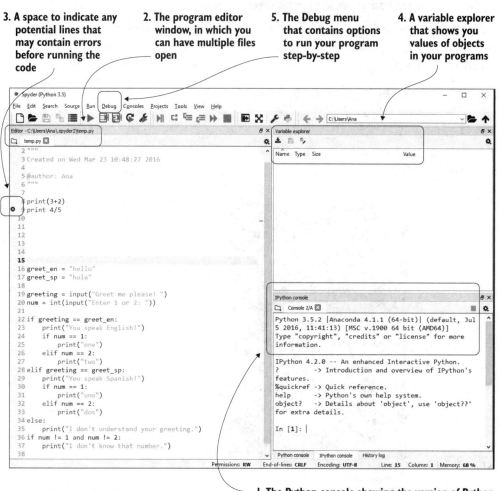

I. The Python console showing the version of Python and any output your program shows to the user

Figure 3.2   The Spyder IDE with the code editor, console, and variable explorer windows

3.2   Setting up your workspace

When you open Spyder, as shown in figure 3.2, you see that the program window is separated into three window panes:

- The left pane is the editor, originally containing no code, only a few lines of text. You'll notice that this text is green, meaning that this is a multi-line comment—not code that will be run.
- The top-right pane might contain the object inspector, variable explorer, or file explorer. You won't be using this window pane, but the variable explorer, for example, shows you the values for each variable in your program after the program is finished.
- The bottom-right pane is, by default, the IPython console. In this lesson, you'll see some basics regarding the IPython console and the file editor.

The next two sections will guide you through simple computations in Spyder. You'll see how to enter the computations directly in the console and how to write more-complicated programs in the code editor. At the end of the next two sections, your Spyder session should look like figure 3.3.

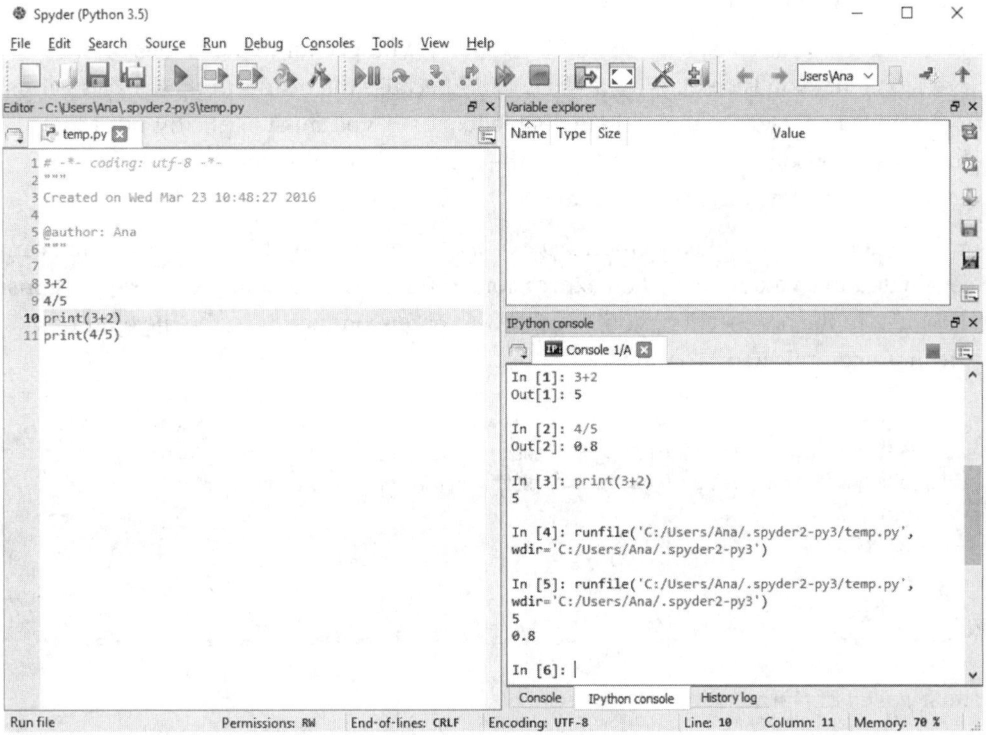

Figure 3.3 Spyder session after entering expressions in the IPython console and the code editor

3.2.1   The IPython console

The IPython console is the primary way that you can quickly test commands to see what they do. More important, users will be using the console to interact with your programs. The *I* in *IPython* stands for *interactive*. The IPython console is an advanced console that gives its users neat features including autocompletion, a history of previous commands typed in, and color highlighting of special words.

Writing commands directly into the console

You can write single commands directly in the IPython console to try things and see what they do. If you're just beginning to program, you should be trying things out a lot. That's the best way to start gaining intuition about what statements do and what expressions evaluate to.

Type `3 + 2` in the console and hit Enter to perform this addition. You'll see the result `5` preceded by the text `Out[]`. Now type `4 / 5` to perform this division and you'll see the result `0.8` preceded by the text `Out[]`.

You can think of this console as something that lets you peek into the values of the expressions that you type in. Why do I say *peek*? Because the results of these expressions aren't visible to a user. To make them visible to a user, you must explicitly print their values to the console. Type `print(3 + 2)` in the console. The number `5` is printed again, except that there's no `Out[]` right before it.

Both `3 + 2` and `4 / 5` are called Python *expressions*. In general, anything in Python that can be evaluated to a value is called an expression. You'll see more examples of expressions in lesson 4. In the next section, you'll see how to enter commands in the file editor to write more-complicated programs.

> **Quick check 3.1**   Will the following expressions show output to the user, or are they just letting you peek into their value? Type the expressions in the console to check yourself!
>
>   1   `6 < 7`
>   2   `print(0)`
>   3   `7 * 0 + 4`
>   4   `print("hello")`

Primary uses of the console

Few programmers can write a perfect program on the first go. Even experienced programmers make mistakes. Your first try to write a program will be a little unsteady, and you'll have *bugs* (errors) that will show up when you try to run your program.

DEFINITION A bug is an error in a program.

If a program has bugs, big or small, you have to try to fix them. You can learn a lot from the debugging process. As you start to write more-complicated programs, you can think of using the console from the point of view of two roles: you as a programmer, and as a person interacting with your program (the user). Figure 3.4 shows the dual role the console lets you play. A programmer primarily uses the console to test commands and debug programs. A user uses the console to interact with a program that's running by typing in input and seeing what the program outputs.

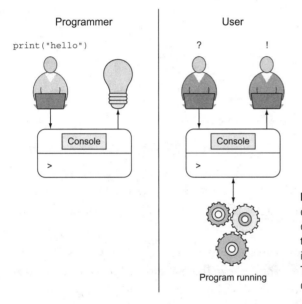

Figure 3.4 Programmers use the console for their own testing and debugging. They type commands directly in the console and look at the output. Users interact with a program via the console. They type input to a program and view the output from a program in the console.

The majority of the programs you'll see in this book don't have a visual interface. Instead, you'll write programs that interact with users via text in the console; users will be given the opportunity to enter text/numbers/symbols when prompted in the console, and your program will display results in the console. Figure 3.5 shows an example of how the user may interact with the programs you write.

As a programmer, you'll be using the console to take on the role of a user of your program. This is most useful when debugging programs (when you're trying to figure out why your program isn't working as expected). When you use the file editor to write more-complicated programs, it's often useful to have the console print values of any computations or objects in your programs, not just the final value. Doing so can help

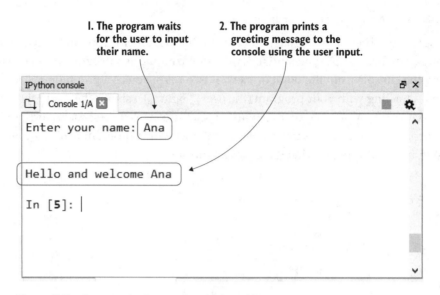

1. The program waits for the user to input their name.

2. The program prints a greeting message to the console using the user input.

Figure 3.5   An example of a user interacting with a program

you determine intermediary values in your programs and help you debug. If running your program is like trying out a recipe, printing intermediary values is like tasting items in your recipe to make sure everything is going well. Debugging is covered in a lot more detail in unit 7.

The console is useful for trying out single expressions and seeing their values. You can retype expressions in the console if you want to run them again, or you can use the up arrow to see expressions you previously typed and hit Enter to run them again. A file editor saves your expressions to a file so you don't need to retype them. This saves a lot of time when you want to write programs that are longer than one line.

3.2.2   The file editor

When you write more-complicated Python programs containing more than just a couple of lines, you should use the file editor pane. Here, you can type the commands (in programming, called *statements*), one on each line, as in figure 3.3. After you finish writing a set of commands, you can run the program by clicking the green arrow in the toolbar at the top of Spyder, shown in figure 3.6. Editing and running files is the same for all operating systems that Anaconda supports: PC, Mac, and Linux. This book shows screenshots from a Windows operating system.

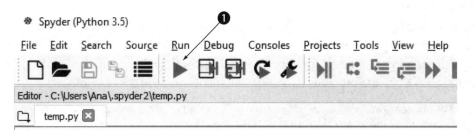

Figure 3.6 Click the green arrow button to run the program.

Not all lines of code produce output visible to the user

In the empty file, type 3 + 2 on line 8, as shown previously in figure 3.3. On the next line, type 4 / 5. Don't type anything else yet. Now click the green arrow to run the program. The first time you click the arrow, you may get a pop-up that asks you for the working directory; it's OK to accept the default values. What happens? Your console at the bottom right shows some red text, similar to the following:

```
runfile('C:/Users/Ana/.spyder2-py3/temp.py',
wdir='C:/Users/Ana/.spyder2-py3')
```

That line indicates that your program ran, but nothing was shown to the user.

Now make the following additions. On line 10, type print(3 + 2). And on the following line, type print(4 / 5). Run the program again. Now what happens? You should see the same thing as in figure 3.3. The console shows the results of the calculations to the user, each on a different line.

How does that work? The Python interpreter executes each line in the file. It first runs the statement 3 + 2 and internally calculates the result of this expression. Then it internally calculates 4 / 5. Because these two statements don't tell Python to show the output of the calculations, their values don't show up on the console.

A keyword in Python, print, is reserved for when you want to output the value of whatever is in the parentheses following print to the console. In this case, you show the result of evaluating the expressions 3 + 2 and 4 / 5, in that order.

> **Quick check 3.2** Which of these expressions will the user see on the console? Type the expressions in the file editor and click Run to check!
>
> 1 print(4 - 4 * 4)
> 2 print(19)
> 3 19 - 10

Saving files

You should save every program you write in a separate file to keep you organized. The file in which you wrote the previous code is a temporary file, saved in some location in the Anaconda installation folder. Open a new file from the Spyder menu bar, as shown in figure 3.7. Type the previous two `print` statements again in the new file.

> **TIP** I strongly encourage you to type the commands again instead of copying and pasting. Repetition is a great way to help you get the hang of programming. Forcing yourself, especially at the beginning of your programming career, to type commands will help speed up your learning process and make writing code second nature.

Now save the file in a directory of your choosing. You must save it with a .py extension. If you don't save it with this extension, you won't be able to run the program (the green Run button will be gray). After you save the file, click the green Run button. The same output as before should show up in the console.

```
Spyder (Python 3.5)

File   Edit   Search   Source   Run   Debug   Consoles   Tools   View   Help

Editor - C:\Users\Ana\Documents\ch2.py

  temp.py        ch2.py

1 # -*- coding: utf-8 -*-
2 """
3 Created on Wed Mar 23 18:24:18 2016
4
5 @author: Ana
6 """
7
8 print(3+2)
9 print(4/5)
10
```

Figure 3.7   Multiple files open in Spyder; each one has its own tab in the file editor pane.

If you close the file you just saved, your program isn't lost. You can reopen the file from the File menu. All the code is still there, and you can run the program as if you just wrote it.

 ## Summary

In this lesson, my objective was to teach you

- How to install a Python distribution called Anaconda, using Python version 3.5 and an IDE called Spyder

- How to open a new file, write a simple program in the file, save the file, and run a program
- How to write code in the file editor and open many files in the editor pane
- That the console allows you to peek into values of variables or to show output to the user
- How to use `print` statements to print expression values to the console

VARIABLES AND EXPRESSIONS: GIVING NAMES AND VALUES TO THINGS

After reading lesson 4, you'll be able to

- Write code that creates Python objects
- Write code that assigns objects to variables

In your everyday life, you encounter many physical objects, or *things*. Each of these things has a name. They have names because it's much easier to refer to them using a name rather than a description.

Using names is a great help when you're always manipulating things, or objects. Some things are simple, such as the number 9. Some are more complicated, such as a dictionary. I can give the name *Nana* to the number 9, and the name *Bill* to my dictionary. You can give things (almost) any name you want. You can even give names to combinations of things. For example, if I glue a banana to my laptop cover to create a new thing, I can name that new trendy creation Banalaptop. Individual things can be named as well; if I have two apples, I can name one Allie and the other one Ollie.

After you name things, you can refer to them later without any confusion. The benefit of using names is that you don't have to re-create (in programming, *recalculate*) values. When you name a thing, you inherently remember every detail about it.

Consider this

Scan the room you're in right now for a few things. Then take these steps:

1 Write the items down. (I saw my phone, a chair, a carpet, papers, and a water bottle.)
2 Write a sentence using some or all of these objects. You can use an object more than once. (My water bottle spilled on my phone and papers, and now my phone is broken and my papers are ruined.)
3 Write a description of each object without using its name.
4 Now rewrite the sentence you came up with using only the descriptions.
5 Is the sentence you wrote easier to read using the item names or descriptions?

Answers:

1 A phone, papers, and a water bottle.
2 My water bottle spilled on my phone and papers, and now my phone is broken and my papers are ruined.
3 Descriptions:
   - *Water bottle*—Thing that holds clear liquid
   - *Phone*—Rectangular device I use to call/text/watch cat videos
   - *Papers*—Stack of thin, white, flimsy things with black-and-white text on them
4 A thing that holds clear liquid spilled on a rectangular device I use to call/text/watch cat videos and on a stack of thin, white, flimsy things with black-and-white text on them, and now my rectangular device is broken, and my things with black-and-white text are ruined.
5 The sentence is easier to read with the item names, not the descriptions.

4.1 Giving names to things

Everything you use has a name, which makes it easier to reference in conversation. Writing a computer program is like writing a detailed description of the events you want to happen and the things involved. In programming, you reference things by using variables, which are discussed in the context of programming in section 4.2.

4.1.1 Math vs. programming

When you hear the word *variable*, it may remind you of math class, where you did calculations with equations and were asked to "solve for *x*." Programming also uses variables, but in a different way.

In math, lines of equations state an equivalence. For example, "$x = 1$" stands for "x is equivalent to 1," and "$2 * x = 3 * y$" stands for "2 times x is equivalent to 3 times y."

In programming, lines of code with an equal sign stand for an *assignment*. Figure 4.1 shows an assignment in Python.

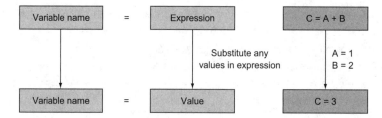

Figure 4.1 Assignment to a name in Python. Any expression on the right side gets converted to a single value and given a name.

You use the equal sign to assign variables to values. For example, a = 1 or c = a + b. The thing to the right of the equal sign is an *expression* with a *value*.

> **DEFINITION** An expression is a line of code that can be reduced to a value.

To get the value, you substitute the values for all other known variables in the expression and do the calculation. For example, if a = 1 and b = 2, then c = a + b = 1 + 2 = 3. In programming, the only thing you're allowed to have to the left of the equal sign is the name of a variable.

4.1.2   What the computer can and can't do

An important point is worth coming back to: a computer needs to be told what to do. A computer can't spontaneously solve an equation on its own. If you tell the computer that a = 2, b = 2, and that a + x = b, it doesn't know what to do with this information or how to solve for x on its own. The line a + x = b doesn't tell the computer how to calculate anything; it just states an equivalence.

The computer needs to be told a recipe for solving something. Recall that when you're following a recipe for baking bread, you need to know the steps. You, as the programmer, have to come up with the recipe and tell the computer what to do. To come up with the recipe, you need to go off-computer and on-paper and do the calculation on your own. Then you can tell the computer what steps it needs to calculate a value.

4.2   Introducing variables

With that bit of intuition for how variables work in programming, you can now dive in and start learning about how variables work.

4.2.1   Objects are things that can be manipulated

In the previous section, we talked about things. In Python, everything is an object. This means that every *thing* that you can create in Python has the following:

- A type
- A set of operations

The *type* of an object tells you the data/values/attributes/properties associated with it. The *operations* are commands that you can tell the object to do; these commands might work only on the object itself, or they might be ways that the object can interact with other objects.

4.2.2   Objects have names

Every *thing* that you create in a program can be given a name so you can refer to it later. The names are *variables* and are used to refer to objects.

> **DEFINITION**   A variable is used to bind a name to an object. A variable name refers to a particular object.

For example:

- If `a = 1`, then the object named `a` has the value `1`, and you can do mathematical operations with it.
- If `greeting = "hello"`, then the object named `greeting` has a value of `"hello"` (a sequence of characters). Operations you can do on this object include "tell me how many characters it has" or "tell me if it has the letter *a* in it" or "tell me at which position the first *e* occurs."

In both of these examples, the item to the left of the equal sign is a variable name that you can use to refer to an object, and the thing to the right of the equal sign is the object itself, which has a value and some operations you can do on it. In Python, you bind a variable name to an object.

The object to the right of the equal sign doesn't have to be only one object. It can be a calculation that can be simplified to give a value. With that final value, you get an object. For example, `a = 1 + 2` is a calculation on two objects (`1` and `2`) that can be simplified to one object with a value of `3`.

4.2.3   What object names are allowed?

You write code with variable names that make the code readable by other people. Many programming languages, Python included, have restrictions on the names you can use for variables:

- Must begin with a letter (`a` to `z` or `A` to `Z`) or an underscore (`_`).
- Other characters in the variable name can be letters, numbers, or an underscore.
- Names are case-sensitive.
- Names can be any length.

> **Thinking like a programmer**
>
> If you want, you can have a variable name that is 1,000,000,000,000,000 characters long. But don't! It makes your code unreadable. Limit lines of code to at most 80 characters and try to make your names as concise as possible while maintaining readability.

Quick check 4.3   Are the following variable names allowed?

```
1  A
2  a-number
3  1
4  %score
5  num_people
6  num_people_who_have_visited_boston_in_2016
```

Programming languages have a few reserved words that you can't use as variable names. For Python, Spyder has *syntax highlighting,* which changes the color of words that are special reserved Python *keywords.*

> **DEFINITION**   A keyword is a special word. It's reserved because it has special meaning in a programming language.

Figure 4.2 shows an example of syntax highlighting. A good general rule is that if the variable you want to use turns a different color, you shouldn't use it as a variable name.

I. These turned a different color because they're special words in Python (colors may vary if you tinkered with the Spyder settings).

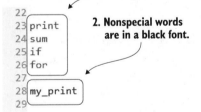

2. Nonspecial words are in a black font.

Figure 4.2   Special words that have a meaning in Python change color in the code editor. As a general rule, you shouldn't name your variables using any words that turn a color other than black.

In addition to the preceding rules for naming variables, here are some guidelines to help you write programs that are more readable:

- Choose descriptive and meaningful names instead of short, single-character names.
- Use underscores to add a pretend space between variable words.
- Don't use variable names that are too long.
- Be consistent throughout your code.

4.2.4 Creating a variable

Before you can work with a variable, you have to set it to a value. You *initialize* the variable by assigning it to an object, using the equal sign. The initialization binds the object to the variable name.

> **DEFINITION** A variable initialization binds a variable name to an object.

After you initialize a variable, you can refer to a particular object by using its variable name. In Spyder, type the following lines in the console to initialize three variables:

```
a = 1
b = 2
c = a + b
```

You can use the variable explorer to see the names of variables, their type, and size (you'll see what this means in following lessons), and their value. Figure 4.3 shows how your screen should look.

You should see that the variable explorer is populated with the variables you create and their values. If you type in the name of a variable in the console and hit Enter, this allows you to *peek* into its value. The variable explorer also tells you an additional bit of information in the second column: the type of the variable. The next section goes into more detail on what this means.

4.2.5 Updating a variable

After you create a variable name, you can update the name to be any object. You saw that these lines initialize three variables:

```
a = 1
b = 2
c = a + b
```

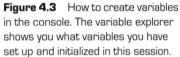

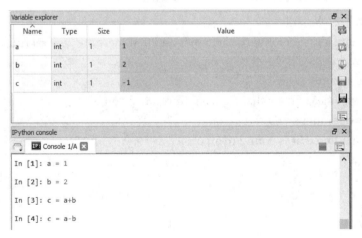

Figure 4.3 How to create variables in the console. The variable explorer shows you what variables you have set up and initialized in this session.

You can update the value of c to be something else. Now you can type c = a - b to reassign the variable c to have a new value. In the variable explorer, you should see that the variable c now has a different value. Figure 4.4 shows how Spyder looks now.

Figure 4.4 The variable explorer has the same variable c, except with a new value.

Variable names merely bind names to objects. The same name can be reassigned to a different object. A Python operation, named `id`, shows the identity of an object in the form of a sequence of digits. The identity is unique for every object and won't change while the object exists. Type the following lines in the console:

```
c = 1
id(c)
c = 2
id(c)
```

After the first `id(c)` command, my console printed out 1426714384. After the second `id(c)` command, I got 1426714416. These are two numbers for the same variable name because the numbers 1 and 2 are different objects.

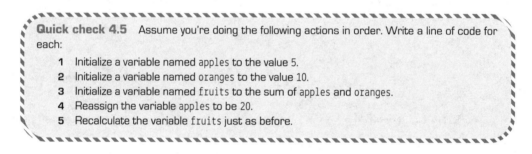

Quick check 4.5   Assume you're doing the following actions in order. Write a line of code for each:

1   Initialize a variable named `apples` to the value 5.
2   Initialize a variable named `oranges` to the value 10.
3   Initialize a variable named `fruits` to the sum of `apples` and `oranges`.
4   Reassign the variable `apples` to be 20.
5   Recalculate the variable `fruits` just as before.

 **Summary**

In this lesson, my objective was to teach you

- To create and initialize variables
- That not all names are allowed for variable names and that there are general rules for naming your variables
- That an object has a value
- That expressions are lines of code that can be reduced to a value
- That an object has operations you can do on it
- That a variable is a name that is bound to an object

Let's see if you got this …

Q4.1   You're given the following problem. Solve the equation for x. Write x in terms of an expression and then find its value.

```
a = 2
b = 2
a + x = b
```

Q4.2   Type a + x = b in the Spyder console and hit Enter. You get an error. Maybe the error happened because you didn't tell the computer what a and b were. Type the following lines in the console, each followed by pressing Enter. Do you still get an error?

```
a = 2
b = 2
a + x = b
```

OBJECT TYPES AND STATEMENTS OF CODE

After reading lesson 5, you'll be able to

- Write code that creates various types of objects
- Write simple lines of code to manipulate Python variables

Suppose you have a family as follows:

- *Four people*—Alice, Bob, Charlotte, and David
- *Three cats*—Priss, Mint, and Jinx
- *Two dogs*—Rover and Zap

Every person, cat, and dog is a separate object. You named each object something different so you can easily refer to them and so that everyone else knows which object you're talking about. In this family, you have three types of objects: people, cats, and dogs.

Each type of object has characteristics that are different from another type. People have hands and feet, whereas cats and dogs have only feet. Cats and dogs have whiskers, but people don't. The characteristics of a type of object uniquely identify all individual objects in that type. In programming, characteristics are called data *attributes*, or *values*, for the type.

Each type of object also has actions or behavior. People can drive a car, but dogs and cats can't. Cats can climb trees, but dogs can't. The actions that a type of object can do are specific to that object only. In programming, actions are called *operations* on the type.

Consider this You have a sphere and a cube. Write some characteristics of each (choose characteristics that uniquely identify them) and some actions you can do with each.

Answer:

Sphere—Round, has a radius/diameter, rolls, bounces
Cube—All sides equal length, stays flat, has points, can stand on it

 ## 5.1   Types of things

So far, you've created variables to store objects. Variables are names given to individual objects. In reality, you can classify objects into groups. All objects in the same group are going to be of the same type; they'll all have the same basic properties, and they'll all have the same basic operations for interacting with them.

5.2   Basic type of objects in programming

Objects have

- A type, which dictates the values they can have
- Operations you can do with them

   DEFINITION   An object type tells you what kinds of values the object can have.

In most programming languages, a few types of objects are the basic building blocks for each language. These types of objects might be called *primitives*, or *scalars*. These basic types are built in to the language, and every other type of object can be made up of combinations of these primitives. This is similar to how the 26 letters in the alphabet are the building blocks of the English language; from the 26 letters, you can make words, sentences, paragraphs, and novels.

Python has five basic *types* of objects: integers, floating point, Booleans, strings, and a special type that represents the absence of a value. In Python, these five types are called *primitives*, and every other type of object in the language can be constructed with these five types.

5.2.1   Integers as whole numbers

An object of type *integer* (in Python, the `int` type) is an object whose values are real whole numbers. For example, 0, 1, 2, 5, 1234, -4, -1000 are all integers.

The kinds of operations you can do on these numbers are, as you might expect, operations that you would do on numbers in math class.

You can add, subtract, multiply, and divide two or more numbers. You may have to surround a negative number with parentheses to avoid confusing the negative number with the subtraction operation. For example,

- `a = 1 + 2` adds an integer object with value 1 and an integer object with value 2 together and binds the resulting object with a value of 3 to the variable named a.
- `b = a + 2` adds the value of the integer object named a and the integer object with value 2 together and binds the resulting object's value to the variable named b.

You can increment a number by a certain value. For example,

- `x = x + 1` means that you add 1 to the value of x and rebind that value to the variable named x. Notice that this is different than in math, where you would solve this equation by moving x from the right to the left of the equal sign (or subtracting x from both sides of the equation) and simplify the expression to 0 = 1.
- `x += 1` is programming shorthand notation for `x = x + 1`. It's alternate, valid syntax. You can replace the `+=` with `*=`, `-=`, or `/=` to stand for `x = x * 1`, `x = x - 1`, or `x = x / 1`, respectively. The 1 on the right-hand side of the equal sign can also be replaced with any other value.

> **Quick check 5.1**   Write a line of code that achieves each of the following:
> 1   Add 2 and 2 and 2 and store the result in a variable named six.
> 2   Multiply the variable six with -6 and store the result in a variable named neg.
> 3   Use shorthand notation to divide the variable neg by 10 and store the result in the same variable, neg.

5.2.2   Floating point as decimal numbers

An object of type *floating point* (in Python, the `float` type) is an object whose values are decimal numbers. For example, 0.0, 2.0, 3.1415927, and -22.7 are all floats. If you've played around with integers, you may have noticed that when you divided two numbers, the result was a float type. The kinds of operations you can do on these numbers are the same as those for integers.

It's important to understand that the following two lines lead to two variables representing objects of two types. The variable a is an integer, but the variable b is a float:

```
a = 1
b = 1.0
```

Quick check 5.2   Write a line of code that achieves each of the following:
1   Multiply 0.25 by 2 and store the result in a variable named half.
2   Subtract the variable half from 1.0 and store the result in a variable named other_half.

5.2.3   Booleans as true/false data

In programming, you often work with more than just numbers. A type of object that's even simpler than a number is the *Boolean* (in Python, the bool type); it has only two possible values, True or False. They replace expressions with one of these two values; for example, the expression 4 < 5 is replaced by False. The kinds of operations you can do on Booleans involve the logic operations and and or and were briefly introduced in lesson 1.

Quick check 5.3   Write a line of code that achieves each of the following:
1   Store the value True in a variable named cold.
2   Store the value False in a variable named rain.
3   Store the result of the expression cold and rain in a variable named day.

5.2.4   Strings as sequences of characters

A useful data type is the string (in Python, the str type), which is covered in a lot more detail in lessons 7 and 8. Briefly, a *string* is a sequence of characters surrounded by quotation marks.

One character is anything you can enter by hitting one key on the keyboard. The quotations surrounding characters can either be single or double quotation marks (' or ") as long as you're consistent. For example, 'hello', "we're # 1!", "m.ss.ng c.ns.n.nts??", and "'" (the single quote inside two double quotes) are possible values for a string.

You can do many operations on strings, and they are detailed in lesson 7.

Quick check 5.4   Write a line of code that achieves each of the following:

1 Create a variable named one with the value "one".
2 Create a variable named another_one with the value "1.0".
3 Create a variable named last_one with the value "one 1".

5.2.5   The absence of a value

You might want to designate the absence of a value in a program. For example, if you get a new pet and haven't named it yet, the pet doesn't have a value for its name. Programming languages allow you to designate a special value in this situation. In many programming languages, this is referred to as null. In Python, the value is None. Because in Python everything is an object, this None also has a type, NoneType.

Quick check 5.5   What is the type of each object?

1 2.7
2 27
3 False
4 "False"
5 "0.0"
6 -21
7 99999999
8 "None"
9 None

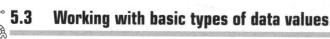 ## 5.3   Working with basic types of data values

Now that you understand a little bit about the types of objects you'll be working with, you can start to write code consisting of more than one line of code. When you're writing a program, each line of code is called a *statement*. A statement may or may not contain an *expression*.

> **DEFINITION**   A statement is any line of code.

5.3.1   Building blocks of expressions

An *expression* is an operation between objects that can be reduced to a single value. The following are examples of expressions (and statements):

- `3 + 2`
- `b - c` (if you know the values of `b` and `c`)
- `1 / x`

A line of code that prints something is a statement but not an expression, because the act of printing can't be reduced to a value. Similarly, a variable assignment is an example of a Python statement but not an expression, because the act of doing the assignment doesn't have a value.

Quick check 5.6   Write down whether each of the following is a statement, expression, or both:

1   `2.7 - 1`
2   `0 * 5`
3   `a = 5 + 6`
4   `print(21)`

5.3.2   Converting between different types

If you're not sure of the type of an object, you can use Spyder to check for yourself. In the console, you can use a special command, `type()`, to get the data type of an object. For example,

- Type in the console `type(3)` and hit Enter to see that the type of `3` is an integer.
- Type in the console `type("wicked")` and hit Enter to see that the type of `"wicked"` is a string.

You can also convert objects from one type to another. To do this in Python, you surround the object you want to convert with parentheses and the name of the type that you want to convert to. For example,

- `float(4)` gives `4.0` by converting the int `4` to the float `4.0`.
- `int("4")` gives `4` by converting the string `"4"` to the int `4`. Notice that you can't convert a string that isn't a number to an int or a float. If you try to convert `int("a")`, you'll get an error.
- `str(3.5)` gives `"3.5"` by converting the float `3.5` to the string `"3.5"`.
- `int(3.94)` gives `3` by converting the float `3.94` to the int `3`. Notice this truncates the number to keep only the whole number before the decimal point.
- `int(False)` gives `0` by converting the bool `False` to the int `0`. Notice that `int(True)` gives `1`.

Quick check 5.7   Write an expression that converts the following objects to the desired types and then predict the converted value. Remember that you can check by typing the expressions in the Python console:

1. `True` to a `str`
2. `3` to a `float`
3. `3.8` to a `str`
4. `0.5` to an `int`
5. `"4"` to an `int`

5.3.3   How arithmetic impacts object types

Mathematical operations are one example of Python expressions. When you do an operation between numbers in Python, you get a value, so all mathematical operations are expressions in Python.

Many of the operators between numbers in math work between numbers (ints or floats) in Python. You're allowed to mix and match integers and floats when you do the mathematical operations. Table 5.1 shows what happens when you do mathematical operations on all possible combinations of ints and floats. The first row of the table says that when you add an int to another int, you get an int result. One example of this is adding 3 and 2 to get 5. When at least one of the operands is a float, the result will be a float. Adding 3.0 + 2, or 3 + 2.0, or 3.0 + 2.0 all result in the float 5.0. The exception to this is division. When you divide two numbers, you always get a float, no matter what the operand types are.

Table 5.1 shows two operations you haven't seen before—the power and the remainder:

- The *power* (**) is a base raised to the power of an exponent. For example, 3^2 is written as `3 ** 2` in Python.
- The *remainder* (%) gives you the remainder when the first object is divided by the second object. For example, `3 % 2` finds out how many times 2 goes into 3 (only one time) and then tells you how much is left (1, because you have to add 1 more to `1 * 2` to get 3).

Table 5.1   Mathematical operations on ints and floats and the resulting types

Type of first object	Operation(s)	Type of second object	Type of result	Example	
int	+ - * ** %	int	int	3 + 2 3 - 2 3 * 2 3 ** 2 3 % 2	gives 5 gives 1 gives 6 gives 9 gives 1
int	/	int	float	3 / 2	gives 1.5
int	+ - * / ** %	float	float	3 + 2.0 3 - 2.0 3 * 2.0 3 / 2.0 3 ** 2.0 3 % 2.0	gives 5.0 gives 1.0 gives 6.0 gives 1.5 gives 9.0 gives 1.0
float	+ - * / ** %	int	float	3.0 + 2 3.0 - 2 3.0 * 2 3.0 / 2 3.0 ** 2 3.0 % 2	gives 5.0 gives 1.0 gives 6.0 gives 1.5 gives 9.0 gives 1.0
float	+ - * / ** %	float	float	3.0 + 2.0 3.0 - 2.0 3.0 * 2.0 3.0 / 2.0 3.0 ** 2.0 3.0 % 2.0	gives 5.0 gives 1.0 gives 6.0 gives 1.5 gives 9.0 gives 1.0

Another operation you can do on numbers is to round them by using the round() command; for example, round(3.1) gives you the int 3, and round(3.6) gives you the int 4.

Quick check 5.8   What is the value and type of the resulting value of each expression? Recall that you can use the type() command to check yourself. You can even put an expression inside the parentheses of type; for example, type(3 + 2).

1   2.25 - 1
2   3.0 * 3
3   2 * 4
4   round(2.01 * 100)
5   2.0 ** 4
6   2 / 2.0
7   6 / 4
8   6 % 4
9   4 % 2

 **Summary**

In this lesson, my objective was to teach you about variables with a few basic types in Python: integers, floats, Booleans, strings, and a special NoneType. You wrote code to work with object types, and to do specific operations on ints and floats. You also wrote statements and expressions. Here are the major takeaways:

- An object has a value and operations you can do on it.
- All expressions are statements, but not all statements are expressions.
- Basic data types are ints, floats, bools, strings, and a special type to represent the absence of a value.

CAPSTONE PROJECT: YOUR FIRST PYTHON PROGRAM—CONVERT HOURS TO MINUTES

After reading lesson 6, you'll be able to

- Read your first programming problem
- Walk through two possible solutions
- Write your first Python program

Here are some of the main ideas you should be familiar with so far:

- Programs are made up of a sequence of statements.
- Some statements initialize variables.
- Some statements can be expressions to do calculations.
- Variables should be given descriptive and meaningful names, especially to help future programmers who might be looking at the code.
- Some calculations you've seen so far are addition, subtraction, multiplication, division, remainder, and power.
- You can convert an object to a different type.
- The `print` command can be used to show output to the console.
- You should write comments in the code to document what the code is doing.

THE PROBLEM   The first programming task you'll see is to write a program in Python that converts minutes to hours. You'll start with a variable that contains the number of minutes. Your program will take that number, do some calculations, and print out the conversion to hours and minutes.

Your program should print the result in the following way. If the number of minutes is 121, the program should print this:

```
Hours
2
Minutes
1
```

6.1   Think-code-test-debug-repeat

Recall that before you begin to code, you should make sure to understand the problem. You can get the big picture by drawing your program as a black box. Figure 6.1 shows your program as a black box, any inputs, and any outputs you must generate.

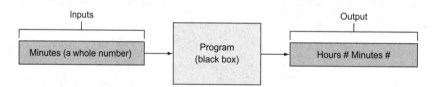

Figure 6.1   The input to the program is any whole number representing minutes. The program does some calculations and prints out how many hours that is and any leftover minutes.

After you understand the inputs and outputs, come up with a few inputs and write down what you expect the outputs to be for each. Here are some other possible inputs for the number of minutes and their conversions to hours:

- "60 minutes" is converted to "1 hour and 0 minutes".
- "30 minutes" is converted to "0 hours and 30 minutes".
- "123 minutes" is converted to "2 hours and 3 minutes".

These input-output pairs are called *sample test cases*. You'll be able to use these inputs and expected outputs to test your program after you write it.

Quick check 6.1 What's the expected output given the following input for the number of minutes?

1 456
2 0
3 9999

 ## 6.2 Divide your task

Now that you understand what the problem is asking, you have to figure out whether you can break it into smaller tasks.

You need to have input to convert, so this can be one task. You're showing the user a result, and this can be another task. These two tasks are going to be easy to implement with at most a couple of lines of code.

Code to set up the input

To set up the input, you need to initialize a variable with a value. Your variable name should be descriptive, and the number of minutes should be an integer. For example,

```
minutes_to_convert = 123
```

Code to set up the output

To show the output to the user, the format required is as follows, where <some number> is calculated by your program:

```
Hours
<some number>
Minutes
<some number>
```

You show the user output by using the print command. Here's the code:

```
print("Hours")
print(hours_part)
print("Minutes")
print(minutes_part)
```

Here, hours_part and minutes_part are variables you'll calculate in your program.

Now the only thing left to do is to come up with a way to do the conversion from minutes to hours and minutes. This is going to be the most involved part of the overall task.

6.3   Implement the conversion formula

When you're dealing with time units, you know that 1 hour has 60 minutes. Your first instinct may be to divide the number of minutes you're given by 60. But the division gives you a decimal number: at a first pass, given 123 minutes, your result will be 2.05, not 2 hours and 3 minutes.

To do the conversion properly, you must divide the problem into two parts: find out the number of hours and then find out the number of minutes.

6.3.1   How many hours?

Recall that given 123 minutes, dividing 123/60 gives 2.05. Notice that the whole number part, 2, represents the number of hours.

> **Quick check 6.2**   Divide the following numbers by 60 and determine the whole number part of the result. You can do the division in Spyder to check yourself:
> 1   800
> 2   0
> 3   777

Recall that in Python, you can convert one type to another type. For example, you can covert the integer 3 to a float by using float(3) to give you 3.0. When you convert a float to an int, you remove the decimal point and everything after it. To get the whole number part of a division, you can convert the float result to an int.

> **Quick check 6.3**   Write a line of code for each of the following points and then answer the questions at the end:
> 1   Initialize a variable named stars with the value 50.
> 2   Initialize another variable named stripes with the value 13.
> 3   Initialize another variable named ratio with the value stars divided by stripes. Question: what is the type of ratio?
> 4   Convert ratio to an int and save the result in a variable named ratio_truncated. Question: what is the type of ratio_truncated?

In the given task, you'll divide the minutes by 60 and convert the result to an integer to give you the number of whole hours, like so:

```
minutes_to_convert = 123
hours_decimal = minutes_to_convert/60
hours_part = int(hours_decimal)
```

At this point, your hours_part variable holds the number of hours converted from the input.

6.3.2   How many minutes?

Finding out the number of minutes is a little bit trickier. In this section, you'll see two ways of doing this:

- *Method 1*—Use the decimal portion of the result from the division. If you use the 123 minutes example, how can you convert the decimal part 0.05 into minutes? You should multiply 0.05 by 60 to give you 3.
- *Method 2*—Use the remainder operator, %. Again, use the 123 minutes example. The remainder when 123 is divided by 60 is 3.

 ## 6.4   Your first Python program: one solution

The code for the final program using method 1 is shown in listing 6.1. The code is separated into four parts. The first part initializes the variable to hold the given number of minutes to convert. The second converts the given input into a whole number of hours. The third converts the given input into the whole number of minutes. The last part prints the results.

Listing 6.1 Convert minutes to hours and minutes using the decimal part

```
minutes_to_convert = 123
hours_decimal = minutes_to_convert/60          Finds the decimal version of the number
hours_part = int(hours_decimal)                of hours and gets the whole number of
                                               hours by converting to an int type

minutes_decimal = hours_decimal-hours_part
minutes_part = round(minutes_decimal*60)       Gets the part after the
                                               decimal point and converts
                                               it to whole minutes
print("Hours")
print(hours_part)
print("Minutes")          Prints the results
print(minutes_part)
```

The part where you calculate the number of minutes from the decimal number may look a bit intimidating, but you can break it down to understand what's going on. The following line gets the part after the decimal point from the division:

```
minutes_decimal = hours_decimal-hours_part
```

For the example, if `minutes_to_convert` is 123, this calculates as `minutes_decimal = hours_decimal -hours_part = 2.05 - 2 = 0.05`. You now have to convert the 0.05 into minutes.

The following line is made up of two separate operations, as shown in figure 6.2:

```
minutes_part = round(minutes_decimal * 60)
```

First it multiplies `minutes_decimal * 60`:

Then it rounds that result with `round(minutes_decimal * 60)`.

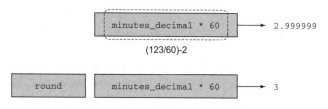

(123/60)-2

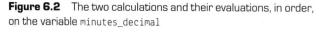

Figure 6.2 The two calculations and their evaluations, in order, on the variable `minutes_decimal`

Why do you need to do all these operations? If you run the program with the line

```
minutes_part = minutes_decimal * 60
```

instead of

```
minutes_part = round(minutes_decimal * 60)
```

you'll notice something interesting. The output is

```
Hours
2
Minutes
2.9999999999999893
```

You expected to see 3 but see 2.999999999893. What's going on? This behavior occurs because of the way that Python stores floats. Computers can't store decimal numbers precisely because they can't represent fractions exactly. When they represent 0.05 in memory, they approximate this number. When you multiply floats, the small differences between their exact value and how they're represented in memory are amplified.

When you multiply 0.05 by 60, the result is off by 0.0000000000000107. You can solve this by rounding your final answer to an integer with `round(minutes_decimal * 60)`.

Quick check 6.4   Change the program in listing 6.1 to find the hours and minutes when starting with 789 minutes. What's the output?

6.5   Your first Python program: another solution

The code for the final program using method 2 is shown in the next listing. The code is separated into the same four parts as the previous solution: initializing, getting the whole number of hours, getting the whole number of minutes, and printing the result.

Listing 6.2 Convert minutes to hours and minutes using the remainder

```
minutes_to_convert = 123          ◄─────────  The given number of minutes

hours_decimal = minutes_to_convert/60   ◄
hours_part = int(hours_decimal)    ◄           Finds the decimal version
                                               of the number of hours
minutes_part = minutes_to_convert%60  ◄
                                               Gets the whole number of hours
print("Hours")                                 by converting to an int type
print(hours_part)
print("Minutes")          Uses the remainder when you
print(minutes_part)       divide the number of minutes by
                          60 to get the whole minutes
```

The output of this program is as follows:

```
Hours
2
Minutes
3
```

This version of the program uses the remainder idea to give a more concise program in which you don't need to do any "post-processing" to round or convert to integers, as you had to do with the previous method. But good style would be to leave a comment right above the line `minutes_part = minutes_to_convert % 60` to remind yourself that the remainder when divided by 60 gives you the whole number of minutes. An appropriate comment is shown here:

```
# the remainder gives the number of minutes remaining
```

 **Summary**

In this lesson, my objective was to teach you how to put together many ideas to write your first Python program. The program incorporated the following main ideas:

- Thinking about the given task and dividing it into a few smaller tasks
- Creating variables and initializing them to a value
- Performing operations on variables
- Converting variable types to other types
- Printing output to the user

Let's see if you got this ...

Q6.1   Write a program that initializes a variable with the value 75 to represent the temperature in Fahrenheit. Then convert that value into Celsius by using the formula c = (f - 32) / 1.8. Print the Celsius value.

Q6.2   Write a program that initializes a variable with the value 5 to represent a number of miles. Then convert this value into kilometers and then meters by using km = miles / 0.62137 and meters = 1000 * km. Print the result in the following form:

```
miles
5
km
8.04672
meters
8046.72
```

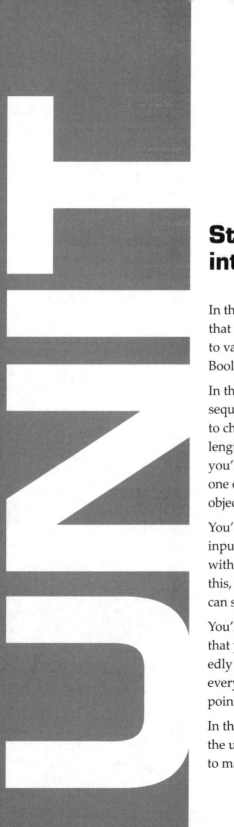

Strings, tuples, and interacting with the user

In the previous unit, you wrote simple lines of code that created variable names and bound your names to various types of objects: integers, floating point, Booleans, and briefly, strings.

In this unit, you'll write code that manipulates sequences of characters, called *strings*. You'll be able to change case, replace substrings, and find the length of words with single lines of code. Then you'll see how to create objects that store more than one object in a sequence and how to access each object stored.

You'll begin writing interactive code. You'll get user input, do some computations or manipulations with it, and then show the user some output. With this, your programs become a lot more fun, and you can start showing off.

You'll learn about a few common error messages that you've been encountering (and will undoubtedly continue to encounter). I want to stress that everyone writes code that doesn't work at some point. And this is the best learning experience!

In the capstone project, you'll get two names from the user and then mash them together in some way to make up a "couple name."

INTRODUCING STRING OBJECTS: SEQUENCES OF CHARACTERS

After reading lesson 7, you'll be able to

- Understand what string objects are
- See what values a string object can have
- Do some basic operations using string objects

Working with sequences of characters is common. These sequences are known as *strings*, and you can store any sequence of characters inside a string object: your name, your phone number, your address including the new lines, and so on. Storing information in a string format is useful. You can do many operations after you have data represented in a string. For example, if you and a friend are both doing research for a project, you can take notes on separate concepts and then combine your findings. If you're writing an essay and discover that you overused a word, you can remove all instances of that word or replace some instances with another word. If you discover that you accidentally had Caps Lock on, you can convert the entire text to lowercase instead of rewriting.

> **Consider this**   Look at your keyboard. Pick out 10 characters and write them down. String them together in any order. Now try to string them in some combination to form words.
>
> Answer:
>
> ```
> hjklasdfqw
> shawl or hi or flaw
> ```

7.1   Strings as sequences of characters

In lesson 4, you learned that a string is a sequence of characters and that all characters in that string are denoted inside quotation marks. You can use either " or ' as long as you're consistent for one string. The type of a string in Python is str. The following are examples of string objects:

- `"simple"`
- `'also a string'`
- `"a long string with Spaces and special sym&@L5_!"`
- `"525600"`
- `""` (Nothing between double quotes is an empty string.)
- `''` (Nothing between single quotes is an empty string.)

The sequence of characters can contain numbers, uppercase and lowercase letters, spaces, special characters representing a newline, and symbols in any order. You know that an object is a string because it starts with a quotation mark and ends with a quotation mark. Again, the kind of quotation mark used to end a string must be the same as the kind you used to start it.

> **Quick check 7.1**   Are each of the following valid string objects?
>
> 1   `"444"`
> 2   `"finish line"`
> 3   `'combo'`
> 4   `checkered_flag`
> 5   `"99 bbaalloonnss"`

7.2 Basic operations on strings

Before working with strings, you must create a string object and add content to it. Then you can start using the string by performing operations on it.

7.2.1 Creating a string object

You can create a string object by initializing a variable to be bound to the object. For example:

- In the statement num_one = "one", the variable num_one is bound to an object of type str whose value is "one".
- In the statement num_two = "2", the variable num_two is bound to an object of type str whose value is "2". It's important to understand that "2" is a string and not the integer 2.

7.2.2 Understanding indexing into a string

Because strings are made up of a sequence of characters, you can determine the value of a character at a certain position in the string. Called *indexing* into a string, this is the most basic operation you can do with a string object.

In computer science, you start counting from 0. This is used when you manipulate string objects. Take a look at figure 7.1, which shows a string object whose value is "Python rules!" Each character is located at an index. The first character in a string is always at index 0. For the string "Python rules!", the last character is at index 12.

You can also count backward. The last character in any string is always at index -1 when you're counting backward. For the string "Python rules!", the first character, P, is at index -13. Notice that the space is also a character.

P	y	t	h	o	n		r	u	l	e	s	!

Index	0	1	2	3	4	5	6	7	8	9	10	11	12
	−13	−12	−11	−10	−9	−8	−7	−6	−5	−4	−3	−2	−1

Figure 7.1 The string "Python rules!" and the index of each character. The first row shows indexing with positive integers, and the second row shows indexing with negative integers.

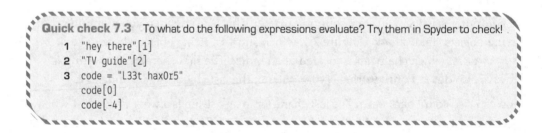

> **Quick check 7.2**   For the string, `"fall 4 leaves"`, what's the index number of the following characters? Give the forward and backward index values:
>
> **1** 4
> **2** f
> **3** s

There's a special way to index into a string to give you the value of the character at a particular index. You use square brackets, [], and inside the square brackets you put any index value that you want, provided that it's an integer value. Here are two examples using the string `"Python rules!"`:

- `"Python rules!"[0]` evaluates to `'P'`.
- `"Python rules!"[7]` evaluates to `'r'`.

The number for the index is allowed to be any integer. What happens if it's a negative number? The last character in the string is considered to be at index -1. You're essentially counting through the strings backward.

If you assign the string to a variable, you can index into it as well, in a more concise way. For example, if `cheer = "Python rules!"`, then `cheer[2]` gives you the value `'t'`.

> **Quick check 7.3**   To what do the following expressions evaluate? Try them in Spyder to check!
>
> **1** `"hey there"[1]`
> **2** `"TV guide"[2]`
> **3** `code = "L33t hax0r5"`
>   `code[0]`
>   `code[-4]`

7.2.3   Understanding slicing a string

So far, you know how to get the character at one index in the string. But sometimes you may want to know the value of a group of characters, starting from one index and ending with another. Let's say you're a teacher and have information on all students in your class in the form "##### FirstName LastName". You're only interested in the names and notice that the first six characters are always the same: five digits and then a space. You can extract the data you want by looking at the part of the string that starts from the seventh character until the end of the string.

Extracting data in this way is called getting a *substring* of the string. For example, the characters `snap` in the string `s = "snap crackle pop"` are a substring of s.

The square brackets can be used in a more sophisticated way. You can use them to *slice* the string between two indices and get a substring, according to certain rules. To slice a string, you can put up to three integers, separated by colons, in square brackets:

`[start_index:stop_index:step]`

where

- `start_index` represents the index of the first character to take.
- `stop_index` represents the index up to which you take the characters, but not including the one at `stop_index`.
- `step` represents how many characters to skip (for example, take every second character or every fourth character). A positive step means that you're going left to right through the string, and vice versa for a negative step. It's not necessary to explicitly give the step value. If omitted, the step is 1, meaning you take every character (you don't skip any characters).

The following examples are depicted in figure 7.2, showing the order in which the characters are selected and put together to give a final value. If `cheer = "Python rules!"`, then

- `cheer[2:7:1]` evaluates to `'thon '` because you're stepping left to right, taking every character in order, starting with the one at index 2 and not including the one at index 7.
- `cheer[2:11:3]` evaluates to `'tnu'` because you're stepping left to right, taking every third character, starting with the one at index 2 and not including the one at index 11.
- `cheer[-2:-11:-3]` evaluates to `'sun'` because you're stepping right to left, taking every third character, starting with the one at index -2 and not including the one at index -11.

Figure 7.2 Three examples of slicing into the string "Python rules!". The numbered circles on each row indicate the order in which Python retrieves the characters from the string to form a new substring from the slice.

> **Quick check 7.4**   To what do the following expressions evaluate? Try them in Spyder to check yourself!
>
> 1 `"it's not impossible"[1:2:1]`
> 2 `"Keeping Up With Python"[-1:-20:-2]`
> 3 `secret = "mai p455w_zero_rD"`
>   `secret[-1:-8]`

7.3   Other operations on string objects

A string is an interesting object type because you can do quite a few complex operations with strings.

7.3.1   Getting the number of characters in a string with len()

Suppose you're reading student essays and you've imposed a 2,000-character limit. How can you determine the number of characters a student used? You can set up the entire essay inside a string and then use command, `len()`, to get the number of characters in the string. This includes all characters between the quotation marks, including spaces and symbols. The empty string has a length of 0. For example,

- `len("")` evaluates to 0.
- `len("Boston 4 ever")` evaluates to 13.
- If `a = "eh?"`, then `len(a)` evaluates to 3.

The command `len()` is special in that you can use it on other types of objects, not just on a string object.

The next few operations that you can do on strings will take on a different look. You'll use *dot notation* to make commands to the string objects. You have to use dot notation when the command you want was created to work on only a specific type of object. For example, a command to convert all letters in a string to uppercase was created to work with only a string object. It doesn't make sense to use this command on a number, so this command uses dot notation on a string object.

The dot notation commands look a little different from `len()`. Instead of putting the string object name in the parentheses, you put the name before the command and place a dot between them; for example, `a.lower()` instead of `lower(a)`. You can think of the dot as indicating a command that will work with only a given object—in this case, a string.

This touches upon a much deeper idea called *object-oriented programming*, something that you'll see in greater detail in lesson 30.

7.3.2 Converting between letter cases with upper() and lower()

Suppose you're reading student essays, and one student wrote everything in capital letters. You can set up the essay inside a string and then change the case of letters in the string.

A few commands are available to manipulate the case of a string. These commands affect only the letter characters in the string. Numbers and special characters aren't affected:

- `lower()` converts all letters in the string to lowercase. For example, `"Ups AND Downs".lower()` evaluates to `'ups and downs'`.
- `upper()` converts all the letters in the string to uppercase. For example, `"Ups AND Downs".upper()` evaluates to `'UPS AND DOWNS'`.
- `swapcase()` converts lowercase letters in the string to uppercase, and vice versa. For example, `"Ups AND Downs".swapcase()` evaluates to `'uPS and dOWNS'`.
- `capitalize()` converts the first character in the string to a capital letter and makes the rest of the letters lowercase. For example,
  `"a long Time Ago...".capitalize()` evaluates to `'A long time ago... '`.

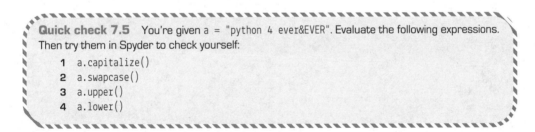

Quick check 7.5 You're given a = `"python 4 ever&EVER"`. Evaluate the following expressions. Then try them in Spyder to check yourself:

1. `a.capitalize()`
2. `a.swapcase()`
3. `a.upper()`
4. `a.lower()`

 **Summary**

In this lesson, my objective was to teach you about string objects. You saw how to get elements at each position by indexing a string and how to slice a string to get substrings. You saw how to get the length of a string, and how to convert all letters to lowercase or uppercase. Here are the major takeaways:

- Strings are sequences of single-character strings.

- String objects are denoted by quotation marks.
- You can do many operations on strings to manipulate them.

Let's see if you got this...

Q7.1   Write one or more commands that uses the string `"Guten Morgen"` to get `TEN`. There is more than one way to do this.

Q7.2   Write one or more commands that uses the string `"RaceTrack"` to get `Ace`.

ADVANCED STRING OPERATIONS

After reading lesson 8, you'll be able to

- Manipulate substrings
- Do mathematical operations with strings

If you're given a long file, it's typical to read the entire file as one large string. But working with such a large string can be cumbersome. One useful thing you might do is break it into smaller substrings—most often, by new lines, so that every paragraph or every data entry could be looked at separately. Another beneficial thing is to find multiple instances of the same word. You could decide that using the word *very* more than 10 times is annoying. Or if you're reading the transcript of someone's award acceptance speech, you may want to find all instances of the word *like* and remove those before posting it.

> **Consider this**   While researching the way that teens text, you gather some data. You're given a long string with many lines, in the following format:
>
> #0001: gr8 lets meet up 2day
> #0002: hey did u get my txt?
> #0003: ty, pls check for me
>
> ...
>
> Given that this is originally one large string, what are some steps that you could take to make the data more approachable by analyzing it?
>
> Answer:
>
> 1 Separate the big data string into a substring for each line.
> 2 Replace common acronyms with proper words (for example, pls with please).
> 3 Count the number of times certain words occur in order to report on the most popular acronyms.

8.1   Operations related to substrings

In lesson 7, you learned to retrieve a substring from a string when you knew what indices you wanted to use. You can do more-advanced operations that can give you more information regarding the composition of a string.

8.1.1   Find a specific substring in a string with find()

Suppose you have a long list of filenames on your computer and want to find out whether a specific file exists, or you want to search for a word in a text document. You can find a particular case-sensitive substring inside a larger string by using the `find()` command.

As with the commands to manipulate case, you write the string you want to do the operation on, then a dot, then the command name, and then the parentheses. For example: `"some_string".find()`. Note that the empty string, `''`, is in every string.

But this isn't all. In addition, you tell the command what substring you want to find by putting it in the parentheses—for example, `"some_string".find("ing")`.

The substring you want to find must be a string object. The result you get back is the index (starting from 0), in the string, where the substring starts. If more than one substring matches, you get the index of the first one found. If the substring isn't in the string, you get -1. For example, `"some_string".find("ing")` evaluates to 8 because `"ing"` starts at index 8 in `"some_string"`.

If you want to start looking for a substring from the end of the string instead of the beginning, you can use a different command, `rfind()`. The r in `rfind` stands for *reverse find*. It looks for the substring nearest to the end of the string and reports the index (starting from 0) at which the substring starts.

If you have `who = "me myself and I"`, then figure 8.1 shows how to evaluate the following:

- `who.find("and")` evaluates to 10 because the substring starts at index 10.
- `who.find("you")` evaluates to -1 because the substring isn't in the string.
- `who.find("e")` evaluates to 1 because the first occurrence of the substring is at index 1.
- `who.rfind("el")` evaluates to 6 because the first occurrence of the substring nearest to the end of the string is at index 6.

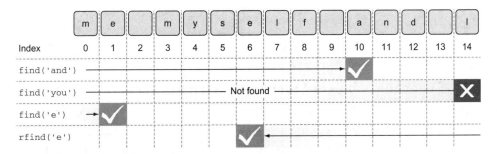

Figure 8.1 Four examples of substrings to find in the string `"me myself and I"`. The arrows indicate the direction in which you're finding the substring. The check mark tells you the index in which you found the substring. An x tells you that the substring wasn't found.

> **Quick check 8.1** You're given `a = "python 4 ever&EVER"`. Evaluate the following expressions. Then try them in Spyder to check yourself:
>
> 1 `a.find("E")`
> 2 `a.find("eve")`
> 3 `a.rfind("rev")`
> 4 `a.rfind("VER")`
> 5 `a.find(" ")`
> 6 `a.rfind(" ")`

8.1.2   Find out whether a substring is in the string with "in"

The find and rfind operations tell you where to find a substring. Sometimes you only want to know whether the substring is in the string. This is a small variation on find and rfind. You can use the yes or no answer to this question more efficiently when you don't need to know the exact location of the substring. Because there are only two values, the answer to this question is an object of type Boolean, and the value you get back will be either True or False. The operation to find the answer to this question uses the keyword in. For example, "a" in "abc" is an expression that evaluates to True because the string "a" is in the string "abc". The keyword in is used frequently in Python because it makes a lot of the code you write look very much like English.

> **Quick check 8.2**   You're given a = "python 4 ever&EVER". Evaluate the following expressions. Then try them in Spyder to check yourself:
>   1 "on" in a
>   2 "" in a
>   3 "2 * 2" in a

8.1.3   Count the number of times a substring occurs with count()

Especially when editing a document, you'll find it useful to make sure you aren't over-using words. Suppose you're editing an essay and find that within the first paragraph, you used the word *so* five times already. Instead of manually counting the number of times that word occurs in the whole essay, you can take the text you've written and automatically find the number of times the substring "so" occurs by using an operation on strings.

You can count the number of times a substring occurs in a string by using count(), which will give you back an integer. For example, if you have fruit = "banana", then fruit.count("an") evaluates to 2. One important point about count() is that it doesn't count overlapping substrings. fruit.count("ana") evaluates to 1 because the "a" overlaps between the two occurrences of "ana", as shown in figure 8.2.

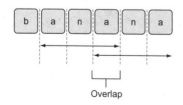

Figure 8.2   Counting the number of occurrences of "ana" in the string "banana". The answer is 1 because "a" overlaps between the two occurrences, and the Python count() command doesn't take this into account.

Quick check 8.3 You're given a = "python 4 ever&EVER". Evaluate the following expressions. Then try them in Spyder to check yourself:

1 `a.count("ev")`
2 `a.count(" ")`
3 `a.count(" 4 ")`
4 `a.count("eVer")`

8.1.4 Replace substrings with replace()

Suppose your son wrote a short report on his favorite fruit: apples. The morning of the day it's due, he changes his mind, hates apples, and now loves pears. You can take his entire report as a string and easily replace all instances of the word *apple* with *pear*.

A final useful string operation is to replace one substring in the string with another substring. This command operates on a string, as the previous ones do, but you have to put in two items in the parentheses, separated by a comma. The first item is the substring to find, and the second is the substring replacement. This command replaces all occurrences. For example, `"variables have no spaces".replace(" ", "_")` replaces all occurrences of the space string with the underscore string in the string `"variables have no spaces"`, and evaluates to `"variables_have_no_spaces"`.

Quick check 8.4 You're given a = "Raining in the spring time." Evaluate the following expressions. Then try them in Spyder to check yourself:

1 `a.replace("R", "r")`
2 `a.replace("ing", "")`
3 `a.replace("!", ".")`
4 `b = a.replace("time","tiempo")`

 ## 8.2 Mathematical operations

You can do only two mathematical operations on string objects: addition and multiplication.

Addition, which is allowed only between two string objects, is called *concatenation*. For example, `"one" + "two"` evaluates to `'onetwo'`. When you add two strings, you put the values of each string together, in the order of the addition, to make a new string object. You may want to add one string to another if, for example, you have three people who worked on a report and wrote individual sections; all that remains is to combine the first, then the second, and lastly, the third.

Multiplication, which is allowed only between a string object and an integer, is called *repetition*. For example, 3 * "a" evaluates to 'aaa'. When you multiply a string by an integer, the string is repeated that many times. Multiplying a string by a number is often used to save time and for precision. For example, let's say you want to create a string representing all unknown letters when playing hangman. Instead of initializing a string as "----------", you could do "-" * 10 . This is especially useful if you don't know the size of the word to guess in advance, and you can store the size in a variable that you'll then multiply by the "-" character.

> **Quick check 8.5**   Evaluate the following expressions. Then try them in Spyder to check yourself:
>
> **1** "la" + "la" + "Land"
> **2** "USA" + " vs " + "Canada"
> **3** b = "NYc"
>   c = 5
>   b * c
> **4** color = "red"
>   shape = "circle"
>   number = 3
>   number * (color + "-" + shape)

Summary

In this lesson, my objective was to teach you about more operations you can do with string objects, specifically related to substrings. You learned how to find whether a substring is in a string, get its index location, count the number of times it occurred, and replace all occurrences of the substring. You also saw how to add two strings and what it means to multiply a string with a number. Here are the major takeaways:

- You can manipulate a string with just a few operations to make it look the way you'd like.
- Concatenating two strings means you're adding them together.
- Repeating a string means you're multiplying the string by a number.

Let's see if you got this...

Q8.1   Write a program that initializes a string with the value "Eat Work Play Sleep repeat". Then, use the string manipulation commands you've learned so far to get the string "working playing".

SIMPLE ERROR MESSAGES

After reading lesson 9, you'll be able to

- Understand where error messages appear
- Develop your intuition for reading error messages

One important thing to remember as you're starting to program is that you can't write a program that will break your computer. If anything goes wrong, you can always close Spyder and restart it without affecting how anything else on your computer runs.

It's fine to make mistakes as you're writing and testing your programs. Any mistakes left in the production environment may mean that your program crashes while being used by customers, leading to poor reviews.

9.1 Typing up statements and trying things out

You shouldn't be afraid of trying commands in Spyder (the console or the file editor) to see what happens. This is the best way to develop your intuition for working with objects that you've seen so far. If you ever find yourself asking, "What happens if …?", most likely you can test it out for yourself and get an answer immediately.

9.2   Understanding string error messages

So far, you've seen some simple operations that you can do on Python strings. I hope that you've been trying things out in Spyder. If you have, you may have tried to do something that's not allowed, in which case you got an error message.

For example, you may have asked yourself what happens when you index into a string too far, using an integer that's bigger than the length of the string. Figure 9.1 shows what happens when you try to do this in two ways: in the console or in the editor. In the console, you get the error message as soon as you hit Enter for the line that tries to index too far into the list. The error name is shown first (IndexError) and then a brief explanation of the error (string index out of range).

In the file editor, you can write lines of code that lead to an error, but the errors don't manifest until you run the code (by clicking the green arrow in the toolbar at the top). In figure 9.1, when you execute line 9 in the editor, you're trying to index too far into the list. Because you're running a Python file, a lot more information shows up on the console, but the important part is at the end of all that text. It shows you the line that caused the error and the same error name and description as the console case.

You'll encounter many errors as you write more and more complicated programs. Don't be afraid of getting them, because they offer great learning opportunities.

Summary

In this lesson, my objective was to teach you that error messages are useful and can guide you to lines that led to the error. Don't be afraid to try commands to figure out what various commands or combinations of commands do.

Let's see if you got this...

Q9.1   Type the following commands in either the console or the editor. Then see if you can understand what the error means based on the string commands in lessons 7 and 8:

1   `"hello"[-6]`
2   `"hello".upper("h")`
3   `"hello".replace("a")`
4   `"hello".count(3)`
5   `"hello".count(h)`
6   `"hello" * "2"`

1. Type the lines in the console directly. The text in the console after that is what happens when you run the file on the left with the erroneous line.

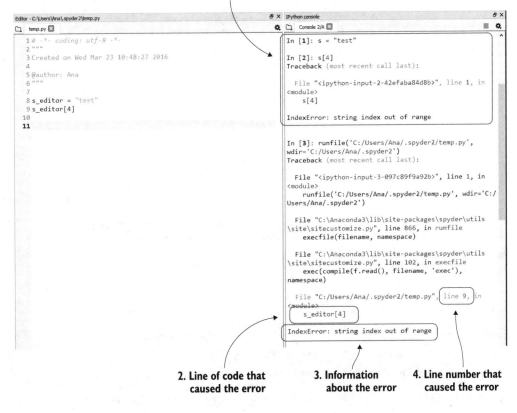

2. Line of code that caused the error

3. Information about the error

4. Line number that caused the error

Figure 9.1 Error message when you try to index into a string using a number that's too big

TUPLE OBJECTS: SEQUENCES OF ANY KIND OF OBJECT

After reading lesson 10, you'll be able to

- Create a sequence of any kind of object by using a tuple
- Do a few operations on tuple objects
- Swap variable values by using tuples

Suppose I give you the simple task of keeping track of your favorite superhero characters. Let's say you have three: Spiderman, Batman, and Superman.

Using what you know so far, you could try to create a string containing every one of these names, separated by a space, like so: `"Spiderman Batman Superman"`. Using the commands you learned in lessons 7 and 8, you'd be able, with a little effort and care, to keep track of indices in the string and extract each name as needed.

But what if you kept full names in the string, like so: `"Peter Parker Bruce Wayne Clark Kent"`. It now becomes considerably harder to extract each person's name because the first and last names are also separated by spaces. You could use other special characters, such as a comma, to separate full names, but this doesn't solve the most annoying problem with using strings to store this data: it's tedious to extract items of interest because you have to keep track of starting and ending indices.

Consider this Look in your fridge. Write down all the objects you can see in there, separated by commas. Now look in your clothes hamper. Write down all the objects you can see in there, separated by commas.

In each set of items:

- How many items did you put down?
- What is the first item? What is the middle item (if you have an even number of items, round down)?

Answer:

Fridge: Milk, cheese, cauliflower, carrots, eggs

- Five items
- First: milk; middle: cauliflower

Hamper: T-shirt, socks

- Two items
- First: T-shirt; middle: T-shirt

10.1 Tuples as sequences of data

Strings store sequences of characters. It'd be a lot more convenient if there were a way to store individual objects in a sequence, as opposed to only string characters. As you write more-complicated code, it becomes useful to be able to represent sequences of any kind of objects.

10.1.1 Creating tuple objects

Python has a data type that represents a sequence of any objects, not just single-character strings. This data type is a *tuple*. In the same way that a string is represented within quotation marks, a tuple is represented in parentheses, (). Individual objects within the tuple are separated by a comma. An example of a tuple is (1, "a", 9.9). Other examples of tuples are as follows:

- () — An empty tuple.
- (1, 2, 3) — A tuple containing three integer objects.
- ("a", "b", "cde", "fg", "h") — A tuple containing five string objects.
- (1, "2", False) — A tuple containing an integer, a string, and a Boolean object.

- (5, (6, 7))—A tuple containing an integer and another tuple made up of two integers.
- (5,)—A tuple containing a single object. Notice the extra comma, which tells Python that the parentheses are used to hold a singleton tuple and not to denote precedence in a mathematical operation.

Quick check 10.1   Are each of the following valid tuple objects?

1 ("carnival",)
2 ("ferris wheel", "rollercoaster")
3 ("tickets")
4 ((), ())

10.2 Understanding operations on tuples

Tuples are a more general version of strings, because every item in the tuple is a separate object. Many operations on tuples are the same as on strings.

10.2.1 Getting the tuple length with len()

Recall that the command len() can be used on other objects, not just on strings. When you use len() on a tuple, you get a value that represents the number of objects inside the tuple. For example, the expression len((3, 5, "7", "9")) means that you're finding the length (the number of objects) of the tuple (3, 5, "7", "9"). The expression evaluates to 4 because this tuple has four elements.

Quick check 10.2   Evaluate the following expressions. Then try them in Spyder to check yourself:

1 len(("hi", "hello", "hey", "hi"))
2 len(("abc", (1, 2, 3)))
3 len(((1, 2),))
4 len(())

10.2.2 Indexing into and slicing a tuple with []

Because tuples are a sequence of objects, indexing into a tuple is the same as indexing into a string. You use the [] operator, and the first object is at index 0, the second object is at index 1, and so on. For example,

- (3, 5, "7", "9")[1] evaluates to 5.
- (3, (3, 5), "7", "9")[1] evaluates to (3, 5).

One difference from strings is in the special case when one of the objects in the tuple is another tuple. For example, (3, (3, ("5", 7), 9), "a") is a tuple whose object at index 1 is another tuple, (3, ("5", 7), 9). In turn, that object can also be indexed.

You can access an element deep down in a sequence of nested tuples by doing a series of indexing operations. For example, (3, (3, ("5", 7), 9), "a")[1][1][1] evaluates to 7. This is a bit tricky because you can have tuples inside tuples inside tuples. Figure 10.1 shows how you can visualize the expression.

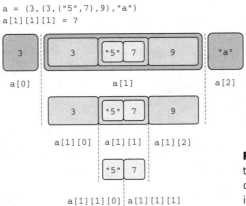

Figure 10.1 The structure of the tuple (3, (3, ("5", 7), 9), "a"). The dashed lines indicate separate objects in the tuple.

Going step-by-step, you evaluate the tuple as follows:

- (3, (3, ("5", 7), 9), "a")[1] evaluates to the tuple (3, ("5", 7), 9).
- (3, ("5", 7), 9)[1] evaluates to the tuple ("5", 7).
- ("5", 7)[1] evaluates to 7.

Slicing a tuple is the same as slicing a string, with the same rules. But you have to be careful to recognize that you might have other tuples as elements at a certain position.

Quick check 10.3 Evaluate the following expressions. Then try them in Spyder to check yourself:

1 ("abc", (1, 2, 3))[1]
2 ("abc", (1, 2, "3"))[1][2]
3 ("abc", (1, 2), "3", 4, ("5", "6"))[1:3]
4 a = 0
   t = (True, "True")
   t[a]

10.2.3 Performing mathematical operations

The same operations you're allowed to do on strings, you're allowed to do on tuples: addition and multiplication.

You can add two tuples to *concatenate* them. For example, (1, 2) + (-1, -2) evaluates to (1, 2, -1, -2).

You can multiply a tuple by an integer to get a tuple that contains the original tuple repeated that many times. For example, (1, 2) * 3 evaluates to (1, 2, 1, 2, 1, 2).

Quick check 10.4   Evaluate the following expressions. Then try them in Spyder to check yourself:

1 len("abc") * ("no",)
2 2 * ("no", "no", "no")
3 (0, 0, 0) + (1,)
4 (1, 1) + (1, 1)

10.2.4 Swapping objects inside tuples

In this section, you'll see one more interesting way to use tuples. You can use tuples to swap the object values associated with variable names, if the variables are elements of the tuple. For example, say you start with these two variables:

```
long = "hello"
short = "hi"
```

You want to write a line that yields the equivalent of the following swap:

```
long = "hi"
short = "hello"
```

Figure 10.2 shows the visualization you should have in mind for the following code, which accomplishes the swap:

```
long = "hello"
short = "hi"
(short, long) = (long, short)
```

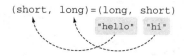

(short, long)=(long, short)

You start with "hello" bound to the variable long, and "hi" bound to the variable short. After the line (short, long) = (long, short) is executed, the value of short is "hello", and the value of long is "hi".

Figure 10.2 Using tuples to swap the values of the two objects between the variable names

You might think that having two variables on the left side of the equal sign isn't allowed. But recall that the variables are in the context of a tuple object, and surrounded by parentheses, so the item to the left of the equal sign is only one object, a tuple. This tuple has variables that are bound to other objects at each of its indices. You'll see why using tuples in this way is useful in lesson 19.

Quick check 10.5   Write a line to swap the values of the following:

```
1  s = "strong"
   w = "weak"
2  yes = "affirmative"
   no = "negative"
```

 ## Summary

In this lesson, my objective was to teach you about tuples and how they behave in a similar way to strings. You learned how to get elements at each position by indexing into a tuple and how to slice a tuple to get at elements inside it; these elements can be primitive objects or might even be tuples themselves. Unlike strings, an object inside a tuple can be another tuple, effectively nesting tuples inside tuples. Lastly, you can use tuples to swap the values of two variables. Here are the major takeaways:

- Tuples are sequences of any kind of object, even other tuples.
- You can index into multiple levels of tuples.
- You can use tuples to swap the values of variables.

Let's see if you got this...

Q10.1   Write a program that initializes the string `word = "echo"`, the empty tuple `t = ()`, and the integer `count = 3`. Then, write a sequence of commands by using the commands you learned in this lesson to make `t = ("echo", "echo", "echo", "cho", "cho", "cho", "ho", "ho", "ho", "o", "o", "o")` and print it. The original word is added to the end of the tuple, and then the original word without the first letter is added to the tuple, and so on. Each substring of the original word gets repeated `count` number of times.

INTERACTING WITH THE USER

After reading lesson 11, you'll be able to

- Print values for the user
- Ask the user for input
- Store user input in variables and do operations with it

Many programs are written to do computations behind the scenes, but few of them are useful without some sort of input from a user. One main reason you'd want to write a program is to provide users with a certain experience; that experience relies on a back-and-forth between the user and the program.

Consider this Find another person and have a conversation. What kinds of questions can you ask? What responses do you get? Can you build upon a specific response you get?

Answer:

How are you?
Good, looking forward to the weekend.
Me too! Any weekend plans?
Yes, we're going camping, then checking out the science museum. If we have time, maybe hit the beach and then going out for a nice dinner. You?
Watching TV.

11.1 Showing output

To get started with this lesson, recall that you can use the print() command to show the user values on the console in Python. You'll use print a lot from now on.

11.1.1 Printing expressions

You can put any expression inside the parentheses of print(), because all expressions evaluate to a value. For example, the float 3.1 has a value 3.1, and the expression 3 * "a" has a value "aaa".

Listing 11.1 shows how to print the values of a few expressions to the user. You can have fairly complex expressions in the parentheses. The code in this listing prints out the following:

```
hello!
89.4
abcdef
ant
```

Listing 11.1 Printing expressions

```
print("hello!")          ←──────── A string
print(3*2*(17-2.1))      ←──────── A mathematical expression
print("abc"+"def")       ←──────── Concatenating two strings
word = "art"             ←──────── Creates a variable
print(word.replace("r", "n"))  ←──────── Replaces "r" with "n"
```

Notice that in every example in this listing, what you put in the parentheses isn't necessarily an object of type str. For example, print(3*2* 17-2.1)) evaluates to an object of type float. The print command works with any type of object in the parentheses.

> **Quick check 11.1** Write each statement in a file in the editor and run the file. What do the following statements print, if anything? Type them in Spyder to check yourself:
>
> 1 print(13 - 1)
> 2 "nice"
> 3 a = "nice"
> 4 b = " is the new cool"
>   print(a.capitalize() + b)

11.1.2 Printing multiple objects

It's possible to place multiple objects in the parentheses after `print` and mix and match their types. If you want to put in different objects, separate each object by a comma. The Python interpreter automatically inserts a space between the values of your printed objects. If you don't want the extra space, you'll have to convert every one of your objects to strings, concatenate them together, and use this in the parentheses of `print`. Listing 11.2 shows an example. In the program, you want to divide one number by another and print the result. The code in this listing prints the following:

```
1 / 2 = 0.5
1/2=0.5
```

Notice that the first line that is printed has a space between every object, but the second line doesn't.

Listing 11.2 Printing multiple objects

```
a = 1
b = 2                        Initializes variables
c = a/b          ◄──────── Calculates the division
print(a,"/",b,"=",c)                     ◄──────────── Uses commas to separate the
                                                        integers (variables a, b, and c)
add = str(a)+"/"+str(b)+"="+str(c)  ◄                  and the strings ("/" and "=")
print(add)  ◄

        Prints the string        Converts the integers to strings
                                 with (str) and then uses the +
                                 operator to concatenate them
                                 with the strings "/" and "="
```

Quick check 11.2   Convert each of the following points into a Python statement to create a program. After you're finished, run the program to see what's printed:

1 Make a variable named `sweet` with the string value `"cookies"`.
2 Make a variable named `savory` with the string value `"pickles"`.
3 Make a variable named `num` with the int value `100`.
4 Write a `print` statement that uses as many of the variables as you can to print `100 pickles and 100 cookies`.
5 Write a `print` statement that uses as many of the variables as you can to print `I choose the COOKIES!`

11.2 Getting user input

The fun in creating programs comes when you can interact with the user. You want to use input from the user to guide calculations, computations, and operations.

11.2.1 Prompting the user

You can use the `input()` command to get input from the user. Suppose you want to ask the user to input their name. In the parentheses of `input()`, you put in a string object that represents the prompt for the user. For example, the line

```
input("What's your name? ")
```

will show the following text on the console and then wait for the user to type something:

```
What's your name?
```

Notice the extra space at the end of the prompt string. Figure 11.1 shows the difference between a string prompt with a space and without. You can see that whatever text the user will type in starts immediately after the end of the prompt string. A good rule is to leave a space as the last character in your prompt string so that the user can distinguish the prompt from their input.

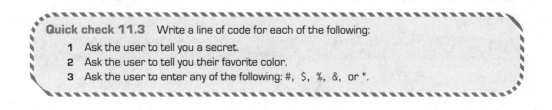

Figure 11.1   How to prompt the user for input

Quick check 11.3   Write a line of code for each of the following:

1   Ask the user to tell you a secret.
2   Ask the user to tell you their favorite color.
3   Ask the user to enter any of the following: #, $, %, &, or *.

11.2.2 Reading the input

After prompting the user for input, you wait for the user to type something. If you're testing your program, you can take the role of the user and type in different things yourself. The user indicates that they're finished by hitting Enter. At that point, your program continues executing the line right after the one asking for input.

The code in the following listing shows a program that asks the user to input the city they live in. No matter what the user inputs, the program then always prints I live in Boston.

Listing 11.3 Where does the user live?

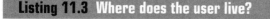

```
input("Where do you live? ")
print("I live in Boston.")
```

After the user hits
Enter, this executes,
and the program ends.

Prompts for user input, at which
point the program stops and waits
for the user to input something

Notice that the program isn't doing anything with the user input. This is an interactive program, but it's not particularly interesting or useful. More-complicated programs store the input from the user into a variable and then do operations on it.

11.2.3 Storing the input in a variable

Most programs act on user input. Anything a user types is converted into a string object. Because it's an object, you can bind it to a variable by assigning the input from the user to a variable. For example, word_in = input("What is your fav word? ") takes whatever the user inputs and stores it in the variable named word_in.

The following listing shows how to use the user input to print a more customized message. No matter what the user inputs, you make the first letter of their input capitalized, add an exclamation mark to the end of it, and then print the result along with a final message.

Listing 11.4 Storing the user input

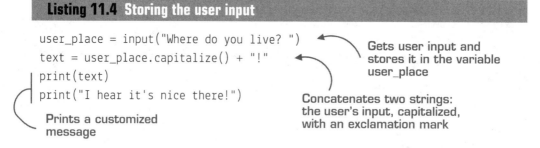

```
user_place = input("Where do you live? ")
text = user_place.capitalize() + "!"
print(text)
print("I hear it's nice there!")
```

Gets user input and
stores it in the variable
user_place

Concatenates two strings:
the user's input, capitalized,
with an exclamation mark

Prints a customized
message

After you get the user's input as a string, you can do any operations on it that you're allowed to do on strings. For example, you can convert it to lowercase or uppercase, find indices of substrings, and check whether certain substrings are in the user's input.

11.2.4 Converting the user input to a different type

Anything that the user types in is converted to a string object. This isn't convenient when you want to write programs that manipulate numbers.

Listing 11.5 shows a program that asks the user for a number and prints the square of that number. For example, if the user enters 5, the program prints 25.

You need to understand a few things about this program. If the user inputs something that's not an integer, the program will end immediately with an error, because Python doesn't know how to convert anything that's not a string whole number to an integer object. Run the program in listing 11.5 by typing in a or 2.1 for the user input; both will cause the program to crash and show an error.

When the user gives a valid number (any integer), recall that even though it looks like a number, everything the user inputs is a string. If the user types in 5, Python see this as the string "5". To work with the number, you must first convert the string into an integer by *casting* it—surround the string with parentheses and the type int before the string object.

Listing **11.5** Calculations with user input

```
user_input = input("Enter a number to find the square of: ")
num = int(user_input)
print(num*num)
```

Gets user input and stores it

Converts the user's input to an integer

Prints the square of the number. The first two lines can be merged into num = int(input("Enter a number to find the square of: ")).

> **Quick check 11.5**   Modify the program in listing 11.5 so that the output printed to the console is a decimal number.

11.2.5 Asking for more input

You can write programs that ask for more than one input from the user. Listing 11.6 shows a program that asks the user for one number, then another, and prints the result of multiplying those numbers. But instead of only printing out the result, you're also printing helpful additional text that tells the user which operation you're doing and on which numbers. For example, if the user enters 4.1 and 2.2, the program shows 4.1 * 2.2 = 9.02.

Listing 11.6 Calculations with more than one user input

```
num1 = float(input("Enter a number: "))
num2 = float(input("Enter another number: "))
print(num1, "*", num2, "=", num1*num2)
```

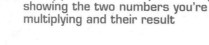 Gets one number and converts it to a float

Gets another number and converts it to a float

Pretty-prints the multiplication by showing the two numbers you're multiplying and their result

 ## Summary

In this lesson, my objective was to teach you how to show output and how to get input from the user. You learned that you can print multiple objects by using only one print statement and that Python automatically adds a space between each object.

You learned about using the input() command to wait for user input. The command converts anything that the user enters into a string object. If you want to work with numbers, you have to convert the input to an appropriate type yourself in the program code. Here are the major takeaways:

- print can be used on multiple objects in one go.
- You can ask the user for input as many times as you want. Each time, the program halts and waits for the user to enter something, and users indicate that they're done by pressing the Enter key.
- You can convert the user input into other types to do appropriate operations on it.

Let's see if you got this…

Q11.1 Write a program that asks the user for two numbers. Store these numbers in variables b and e. The program calculates and prints the power b^e with an appropriate message.

Q11.2 Write a program that asks the user's name and then age. Use appropriate variable names to store these variables. Calculate how old the user will be in 25 years. For example, if the user enters Bob and 10, the program should print Hi Bob! In 25 years you will be 35!

CAPSTONE PROJECT: NAME MASHUP

After reading lesson 12, you'll be able to

- Write code to solve a programming task
- Read requirements for a program
- Get input from the user for two first and last names, mash them up (combine them in some way), and show the user the result
- Systematically build up code to write program solutions

THE PROBLEM   This is your first interactive programming task, so let's have some fun with the user! You want to write a program that automatically combines two names given by the user. That's an open-ended problem statement, so let's add a few more details and restrictions:

- Tell the user to give you two names in the format FIRST LAST.
- Show the user two possible new names in the format FIRST LAST.
- The new first name is a combination of the first names given by the user, and the new last name is a combination of the last names given by the user. For example, if the user gives you Alice Cat and Bob Dog, a possible mashup is Bolice Dot.

12.1 Understanding the problem statement

The checkpoint exercises you've seen so far have been simple. This is your first complicated program, and you'll have to think about how you'll accomplish the task rather than starting to code right away.

When you encounter a problem statement, you should look for the following:

- A general description of what the program should accomplish
- The inputs you should get from the user, if any
- What the program should output
- The behavior of the program in various situations

You should first organize your thoughts on the task you're given by using a method that works for you. Ideally, you'll do all three of the following:

- Draw sketches to understand what's being asked
- Come up with a couple of examples that you can use to test your code
- Abstract your drawing and examples into pseudocode

12.1.1 Drawing a sketch of the problem

In this problem, you're asked to get input from the user. The user will give you two names. You'll separate the names into first and last names. Then you'll take the two first names and mash them up. Similarly, you'll take the two last names and mash them up. Finally, you'll present the user with your new first- and last-name mashups. Figure 12.1 shows these three parts of the problem.

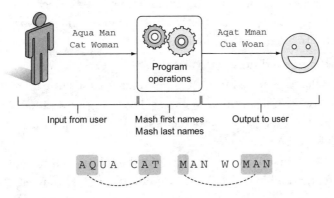

Figure 12.1 Drawing the inputs to the program, a sample mashup of the input names, and the output shown to the user

12.1.2 Coming up with a few examples

After you have an idea of the main parts of the program, you should come up with a few examples that you'll be able to use to test your program.

This is an important step. You, as a programmer, get to simulate what the user might input into the program. Users are unpredictable, and one of their favorite pastimes is to try to crash your program.

In this step, you should try to come up with as many different inputs as possible. Think about short names, long names, and combinations of different lengths of first and last names. Are there any unique names? Here are a few sample types of names for testing:

- A first/last name that has two letters (CJ Cool and AJ Bool)
- A first/last name that has many letters (Moonandstarsandspace Knight)
- A first/last name that has an even number of letters (Lego Hurt)
- A first/last name that has an odd number of letters (Sting Bling)
- A first/last name with the same letters (Aaa)
- Two names that are the same (Meg Peg and Meg Peg)

You should stick to examples that don't deviate from what you told the user to input. In this case, you ask the user for a first and last name. You don't make any guarantees about how your program works when the user puts in anything that doesn't match this. For example, a user who inputs `Ari L Mermaid` shouldn't expect the program to work as advertised.

12.1.3 Abstracting the problem into pseudocode

Now you're ready to divide your program into *blocks* of code. In this step, you start writing pseudocode: a mix of English and programming syntax. Each block will tackle a separate step in your program. Each step aims to gather data in a variable for use in a later step. Here are the main steps in this program:

1 Get user input and store it in variables.
2 Split up the full names into first and last names and store them in variables.
3 Decide how you'll split up the names. For example, find halfway points in each first name and last name. Store the first half of each in variables, and the last half of each in variables.
4 Combine the first half of one name with the second half of another name. Repeat for as many combinations as you want of first and last names.

The next few sections discuss each of these steps in detail.

12.2 Splitting up first and last names

You'll notice that the purpose of everything you've done so far has been to try to understand what's being asked in the problem. Coding should be the last step, to reduce the number of errors you might run into.

At this point, you can start to code up the individual blocks of statements. When writing interactive programs, you almost always start with getting input from the user. The following listing shows the lines of code that achieve this.

Listing 12.1 Getting user input

```
print("Welcome to the Mashup Game!")
name1 = input("Enter one full name (FIRST LAST): ")        Asks the user
name2 = input("Enter another full name (FIRST LAST): ")    for input in the
                                                            desired format
```

The user input is now stored in two variables, with appropriate names.

12.2.1 Finding the space between the first and last name

After getting user input, you should split it into first and last names. You'll have to mash up first names together and mash up last names together, so full names stored in one variable aren't helpful. The first step to splitting up the full name is to find the space between the first and last name.

In lesson 7, you learned about various operations you can do with strings. One operation, find, can tell you the index location of a particular character. In this case, you're interested in the index of the space character, " ".

12.2.2 Using variables to save calculated values

Now you'll save the first and last names into variables to use later. Figure 12.2 shows how to split the full name.

You first find the index location of the space. Everything from the start of the full name to the location of the space is the first name. Everything from one letter past the space is the last name.

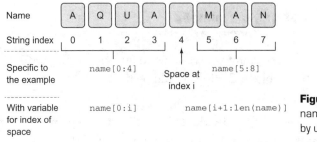

Name

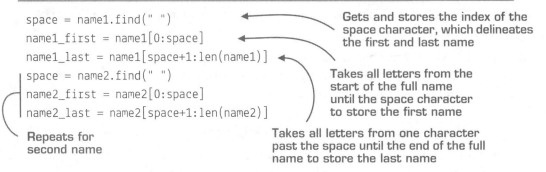

Specific to
the example   name[0:4]

                          Space at
                          index i

With variable   name[0:i]   name[i+1:len(name)]
for index of
space

Figure 12.2   Splitting the full
name into first and last names
by using the index of the space

You should store the first and last names so that you can work with them later. Listing 12.2 shows how to do this. You use the find operation on strings to get the index location of the space character.

Knowing this location, you can take all letters from the start of the full name (starting from index 0) until the space character index and store that substring as the first name. Recall that indexing into a string with some_string[a:b] means that you take all letters from index a to index b - 1. To get the last name, you start at one character past the space character index and take all letters until the end of the full name (up to and including the index of the last character in the string).

Listing 12.2 Storing the first and last names in variables

```
space = name1.find(" ")
name1_first = name1[0:space]
name1_last = name1[space+1:len(name1)]
space = name2.find(" ")
name2_first = name2[0:space]
name2_last = name2[space+1:len(name2)]
```

Gets and stores the index of the
space character, which delineates
the first and last name

Takes all letters from the
start of the full name
until the space character
to store the first name

Repeats for
second name

Takes all letters from one character
past the space until the end of the full
name to store the last name

At this point, you have the two first names and the two last names stored in variables.

12.2.3 Testing what you have so far

With the code in listing 12.2 written up, now is a good time to run the program on a couple of test cases. Testing the code so far means printing the values of the variables you created. You should check to make sure the output is what you expect. If you put in Aqua Man and Cat Woman, the print statements

```
print(name1_first)
print(name1_last)
print(name2_first)
print(name2_last)
```

will print this:

```
Aqua
Man
Cat
Woman
```

This checks out, so you can move on to the next part of the code.

12.3 Storing the halves of all names

With what you know so far, you can't do any fancy letter detection to make the resulting mashup look and sound just right. Instead, you can do something simpler that works well most of the time. Given two first names, take the first half of one name and the second half of the other name and combine them, as shown in figure 12.3.

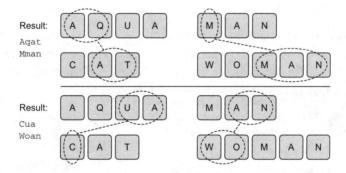

Figure 12.3 Two ways to mash up Aqua Man and Cat Woman. You take half of each of the first names and combine them. Then you take half of each of the last names and combine them.

12.3.1 Finding the midpoint of names

You want to find the index in the string that's halfway in a name. The user can enter names of any length, and names that have an even or an odd number of characters.

Names with an even number of characters

With names that have an even number of characters, dividing the name in half is easy. You take the length of the word and divide by 2 to give you a whole number for the half-way index point in the string. In figure 12.3, the name *Aqua* is an example of this.

Names with an odd number of characters

What should you do when a name has an odd number of characters? In figure 12.3, Cat and Woman are examples. Dividing an odd number by 2 in Python gives you a floating-point number, such as 3.5 or 5.5. A floating-point number can't be used as an index into the string.

Recall that you can cast a floating-point number to an integer. For example, int(3.5) gives you 3. Now, names that have an odd number of letters will have indices that are rounded down for the first half of the name; *Man* in the top part of figure 12.3 is an example. Therefore, names with an odd number of letters will start one index early for the second half of the name: *Woman* in the top part of figure 12.3 is an example.

The code to save halves into variables

Listing 12.3 shows how to store halves of each name. The user entered two full names. You have to find halves of each name, but the same basic process is repeated for each name.

You first find the halfway point in the name. You use the casting function in Python to deal with names that have an odd number of letters. If a name has five letters, the first half will have two letters, and the second half will have three letters. Casting to an int doesn't affect names with an even number of letters because, for example, int(3.0) is 3.

Listing 12.3 Storing halves of each name

```
len_name1_first = len(name1_first)
len_name2_first = len(name2_first)
len_name1_last = len(name1_last)
len_name2_last = len(name2_last)
```
Stores lengths of the first and last names extracted from the input

```
index_name1_first = int(len_name1_first/2)
index_name2_first = int(len_name2_first/2)
index_name1_last = int(len_name1_last/2)
index_name2_last = int(len_name2_last/2)
```
Stores halfway indices of each name by casting the halfway point to an integer to round down to get a whole-number index

```
lefthalf_name1_first = name1_first[0:index_name1_first]
righthalf_name1_first = name1_first[index_name1_first:len_name1_first]
lefthalf_name2_first = name2_first[0:index_name2_first]
righthalf_name2_first = name2_first[index_name2_first:len_name2_first]
```

Name from start to halfway   Name from halfway to the end

```
lefthalf_name1_last = name1_last[0:index_name1_last]
righthalf_name1_last = name1_last[index_name1_last:len_name1_last]
lefthalf_name2_last = name2_last[0:index_name2_last]
righthalf_name2_last = name2_last[index_name2_last:len_name2_last]
```

Now you have all the halves of names stored. The final thing left to do is to combine them.

12.4 Combining the halves

To combine the halves, you can concatenate the relevant variables. Recall that concatenation uses the + operator between two strings. Notice that this step is now simple because you already computed and stored everything necessary.

The code for this is in listing 12.4. In addition to combining the halves, you should also make sure to capitalize the relevant half so that it looks like a name—for example, Blah and not blah. You can use the capitalize operation on the first half to capitalize the first letter only. You use the lower operation on the second half to make all of its letters lowercase.

A final thing to note about the code in listing 12.4 is the use of the backslash on some lines. The backslash is used to break up statements in your code over more than one line. If you insert a line break in a line of code, the backslash tells Python to keep reading the next line to find the rest of the statement; without the backslash, you'll get an error when you run the program.

> **Listing 12.4 Combining the names**

```
newname1_first = lefthalf_name1_first.capitalize() + \
righthalf_name2_first.lower()
newname1_last = lefthalf_name1_last.capitalize() + \
righthalf_name2_last.lower()

newname2_first = lefthalf_name2_first.capitalize() + \
righthalf_name1_first.lower()
newname2_last = lefthalf_name2_last.capitalize() + \
righthalf_name1_last.lower()

print("All done! Here are two possibilities, pick the one you like best!")
print(newname1_first, newname1_last)
print(newname2_first, newname2_last)
```

Capitalizes the first half string

Ensures that the second half string is all lowercase

Shows the user two possible names

This code repeats the same thing four times: to get two new first-name combinations and then to get two new last-name combinations. First, you take the left half of the first name from the first user input and use the `capitalize` operation to ensure that the first letter is capitalized and all others are lowercase. Then you take the second half of the first name from the second user input and ensure that all letters are lowercase. The backslash tells Python that the statement spans two lines.

After you combine the halves, the final remaining step is to show the user the results. Use the `print` operation and display the new names. Try playing around with the program and different input names!

Summary

In this lesson, my objective was for you to write a program that asks the user for two names in a specific format. You manipulated the names so that you created variables to hold halves of each first name and each last name. You combined the halves to mash up the input names and then showed the user the results. Here are the main takeaways:

- The user can provide input more than once in your program.
- You can use the `find` operation to find the location of substrings in the user input.
- You saved manipulated strings as variables, and you used the + operator to concatenate strings together.
- You used the `print` operation to show output to the user.

Making decisions in your programs

In the previous unit, you learned about strings as sequences of characters and about tuples as objects that can contain other objects. You also saw how to interact with users by prompting them for input, getting their input, manipulating their input, and showing them output in the console.

In this unit, you'll write code that makes decisions. This is the first step to writing a cool artificially intelligent being. You'll insert *branches* that will execute different statements in the code, depending on the user input or on the values of certain variables.

In this unit's capstone project, you'll write your own Choose Your Own Adventure game. You'll strand users on a deserted island, present them with an allowed set of words they can pick from, and see whether they can survive.

INTRODUCING DECISIONS IN PROGRAMS

After reading lesson 13, you'll be able to

- Understand how the Python interpreter makes decisions
- Understand which lines of code get executed when a decision is made
- Write code that automatically decides which lines to execute depending on user input

When you write a program, you write lines of code. Each line of code is called a *statement*. You've been writing linear code, which means that when you run your program, every line of code is executed in the order that you wrote it; none of the lines are executed more than once, and none of the lines are skipped. This is equivalent to going through life without being allowed to make any decisions; this would be a constraining way to experience the world. You react to different stimuli in the world to make decisions, which leads to much more interesting experiences.

Consider this   It's Monday morning. Your first meeting is at 8:30 A.M., and your commute takes 45 minutes. Your alarm clock wakes you up promptly at 7:30 A.M. Use the following decision-maker to figure out whether you have time to eat breakfast.

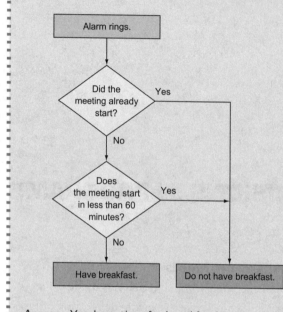

A flowchart to decide whether you have time to eat breakfast after your alarm clock rings and you have a meeting that morning

Answer: You have time for breakfast!

13.1 Making decisions with conditionals

You want programs to behave differently when given different stimuli. Stimuli come in the form of inputs to the program. The inputs can be given by a user interacting with the program or could be the result of an internal computation. Regardless, programs become more interesting, interactive, and useful when they're reactive.

13.1.1 Yes/no questions and true/false statements

In your day-to-day life, you're often faced with making decisions: which shoes to wear, what to have for lunch, which game you should play on your phone during a break, and many others. A computer is great at doing what it's told, and you can program it to make these decisions for you.

When you make a decision, you ask a question. Questions such as "Is it sunny today?" can be answered with yes or no. All yes/no questions can be converted to statements that are either true or false. The Python interpreter doesn't understand yes/no, but it does understand true/false (Boolean logic). The question "Is it sunny today?" can be converted to the statement "It is sunny today." If you answered yes to the question, the statement is true. If you answered no, the statement is false. All decisions can be simplified to one (or more) yes/no questions, or equivalently, a series of true/false statements.

Quick check 13.1   Answer yes or no to the following questions:
1   Are you afraid of the dark?
2   Does your phone fit in your pocket?
3   Are you going to the movies tonight?
4   Does 5 times 5 equal 10?
5   Is the word *nibble* longer than the word *googol*?

Recall that every line of code in Python is a statement. Also recall that an expression is a specific kind of statement or part of a statement; an expression can be reduced to a value. The value is an object in Python; for example, an integer, float, or Boolean. Just as you make decisions in your day-to-day life, you can write programs that get the computer to make decisions. The true/false decision is a Python expression that evaluates to a Boolean, called a *Boolean expression*. Statements that contain a Boolean expression are called *conditional statements*.

Quick check 13.2   If possible, convert the following questions to Boolean expressions. Are there any that can't be converted?
1   Do you live in a treehouse?
2   What are you eating for dinner?
3   What color is your car?
4   Is the word youniverse in the dictionary?
5   Is the number 7 even?
6   Are variables a and b equal?

Thinking like a programmer
A computer works in terms of true and false, as opposed to yes and no. You should start to think about expressions that contain decisions as Boolean expressions, which evaluate to true or false.

13.1.2 Adding a condition to a statement

The same thought process can be applied to the code that you write. You can have special statements that contain an expression whose value is either true or false. We say that these statements are conditional statements and that they contain an expression that evaluates to the Python values of True or False. The part of the statement that evaluates to True or False is the conditional Boolean expression. This part drives the program to make a decision.

13.2 Writing the code to make the decision

Python has a set of reserved keywords. They have a special meaning and therefore can't be used as variable names. One word, if, is reserved because it's used to write the simplest of all conditional statements, the if *conditional statement*.

13.2.1 Coding up a decision—an example

Listing 13.1 shows a simple conditional statement in code. You get an input number from the user. Then you check whether the user input is greater than 0. If that's true, you print an additional message. Lastly, you print a final message to the user that doesn't depend on the result of the conditional check.

Listing 13.1 Example of a simple conditional statement

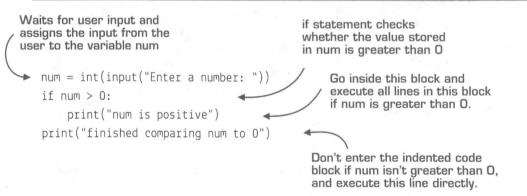

Waits for user input and assigns the input from the user to the variable num

if statement checks whether the value stored in num is greater than 0

```
num = int(input("Enter a number: "))
if num > 0:
    print("num is positive")
print("finished comparing num to 0")
```

Go inside this block and execute all lines in this block if num is greater than 0.

Don't enter the indented code block if num isn't greater than 0, and execute this line directly.

This is a simple way of writing an if statement. The code execution stops when it encounters a conditional statement, and performs the requested Boolean check. Depending on the result of the check, it'll either execute statements inside the condition's code block or not. Listing 13.1 can be rewritten as a flowchart, as shown in figure 13.1.

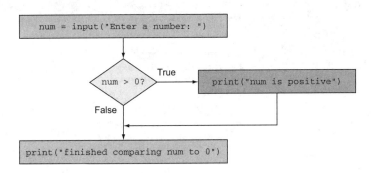

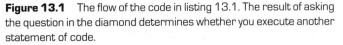

Figure 13.1 The flow of the code in listing 13.1. The result of asking the question in the diamond determines whether you execute another statement of code.

Figure 13.1 is a visual representation of listing 13.1. You can think of the conditional statement as a question you ask to decide whether to bypass executing statements inside its code block. In the visual representation, if the result of the conditional check is false, you take the "false" route and bypass the conditional's code block. If the result of the conditional check is true, you must enter the code block, visually represented by taking a small detour to execute the statements inside the conditional's code block.

Quick check 13.3 Take a look at this code snippet:

```python
if num < 10:
    print("num is less than 10")
print("Finished")
```

1 What will the user see on the screen if num has a value of 5?
2 What will the user see on the screen if num has a value of 10?
3 What will the user see on the screen if num has a value of 100?

13.2.2 Coding up a decision—a general way

Conditional statements have a certain look to them, and you must write them in this exact way so Python knows what you want to do (see the following listing). This is part of the *syntax* of the Python language.

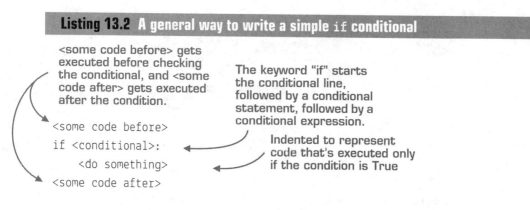

Listing 13.2 A general way to write a simple `if` conditional

<some code before> gets executed before checking the conditional, and <some code after> gets executed after the condition.

The keyword "if" starts the conditional line, followed by a conditional statement, followed by a conditional expression.

```
<some code before>
if <conditional>:
    <do something>
<some code after>
```

Indented to represent code that's executed only if the condition is True

In listing 13.2, you see that the structure of the programs you're writing starts to change. Some lines of code are indented four spaces.

The conditional breaks up the flow of the program. Before, you were executing every line of code. Now, you're choosing whether to execute a line of code depending on whether a certain condition is met.

Quick check 13.4   Write simple conditional statements to do these tasks:

1 Ask the user for a word. Print the word that the user gave you. If the user gives you input that contains a space, also print that the user didn't follow the directions.
2 Ask the user for two numbers. Print their sum. If the sum is less than zero, also print "Wow, negative sum!"

13.3 Structuring your programs

At this point, you can see that the structure of the programs you're writing is starting to change as you design them to make decisions:

- The conditional breaks up the flow of the program, which allows your program to make a decision.
- Some lines of code are indented, which tells Python how they relate to the statements above and below them.
- Before, you were executing every line of code. Now, you're choosing whether to execute a line of code depending on whether a certain condition is met.

13.3.1 Making many decisions

You can combine conditionals one after another to have a series of if statements. Every time you encounter the if statement, you decide whether to execute the code within that if statement's code block. In the following listing, you can see three conditional statements in a series. Each one checks for a different condition: a number is greater than 0, a number is less than 0, and a number is equal to 0.

Listing 13.3 Code with many conditional statements in a series

```
num_a = int(input("Pick a number: "))  ←——— Input from user
if num_a > 0:                          ←——————————— Check whether the number is greater than 0.
    print("Your number is positive")   ←——— Do only if the preceding is true
if num_a < 0:                          ←——————————— Check whether the number is less than 0.
    print("Your number is negative ")  ←——— Do only if the preceding is true
if num_a == 0:                         ←——————————— Check whether the number equals 0.
    print("Your number is zero")       ←——— Do only if the preceding is true
print("Finished!")                     ←——————————— Executes no matter what
```

Notice that you check for equality by using a double equal sign. This differentiates between equality (==) and variable assignment (=). Also, notice that the conditional print statements are all indented by the same amount.

> **Quick check 13.5**   Draw a flowchart for the code in listing 13.3 to make sure you understand that decisions are made sequentially. Flowcharts are a great way to organize all the possible paths through the code in a visual way. This is like figuring out all the possible ways to carry out a recipe.

13.3.2 Making decisions based on another decision's outcomes

Sometimes you want to consider a second decision based on the result of a previous decision. For example, you decide which cereal to buy only after you determine that you don't have any more cereal.

One way to do this in a Python program is using *nested conditionals*: a second conditional executes only if the result of the first conditional is True. Everything inside a conditional code block is a part of that code block—even a nested conditional. Further, the nested conditional will have its own code block.

Listing 13.4 compares two pieces of code; one code example nests a conditional inside the other, and the other code example leaves the conditionals in a series. In the nested code, the nested conditional statement (if num_b < 0) is executed only when the outer conditional (if num_a < 0) is True. Further, the code block inside the nested conditional (print("num_b is negative")) is executed only when both conditionals are True. In the unnested code, the nested conditional statement (if num_b < 0) is executed every time the program runs. The code block inside the nested conditional (print("num_b is negative")) is executed only when num_b is less than 0.

Listing 13.4 Combining conditionals by nesting or by putting them in series

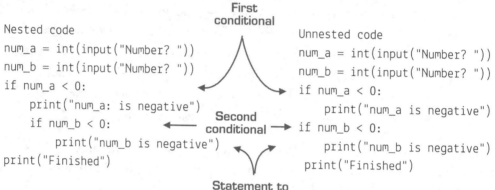

```
Nested code
num_a = int(input("Number? "))
num_b = int(input("Number? "))
if num_a < 0:
    print("num_a: is negative")
    if num_b < 0:
        print("num_b is negative")
print("Finished")
```

First
conditional

Second
conditional

Statement to
be executed

```
Unnested code
num_a = int(input("Number? "))
num_b = int(input("Number? "))
if num_a < 0:
    print("num_a is negative")
if num_b < 0:
    print("num_b is negative")
print("Finished")
```

Quick check 13.6   What result will you get from the nested and unnested code in listing 13.4 if you input these values for num_a and num_b? Type up the code to check yourself!

num_a	num_b	Nested	Unnested
-9	5		
9	5		
-9	-5		
9	-5		

If you're not sure what happens or why you get a certain result from the code, try to trace through with the same values in the following flowchart.

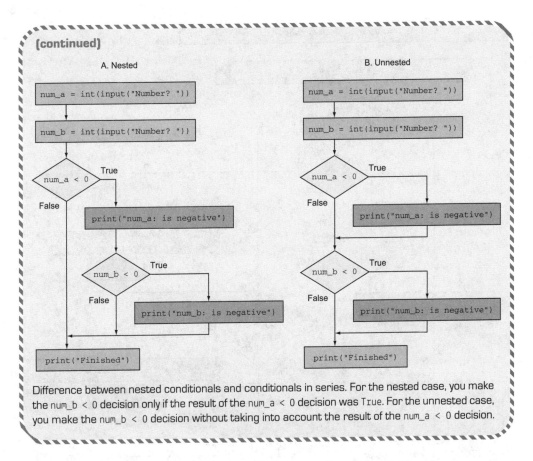

(continued)

Difference between nested conditionals and conditionals in series. For the nested case, you make the `num_b < 0` decision only if the result of the `num_a < 0` decision was `True`. For the unnested case, you make the `num_b < 0` decision without taking into account the result of the `num_a < 0` decision.

13.3.3 A more complicated example with nested conditionals

As a last exercise, look at this more complicated task. You're going to the grocery store to buy groceries for the week. You notice chocolate bars as you enter the store. The program will help you decide the number of chocolate bars to buy. Start by looking at the flowchart in figure 13.2 for a program with these steps, to help you with this decision:

- It asks whether you're hungry.
- It asks how much a chocolate bar costs.
- If you're hungry and a chocolate bar costs less than a dollar, buy all of them.
- If you're hungry and a chocolate bar costs between 1 and 5 dollars, buy 10.
- If you're hungry and a chocolate bar costs more than 5 dollars, buy only 1.
- If you're not hungry, don't buy any.
- Then, depending on the number of bars you bought, the cashier will make a remark.

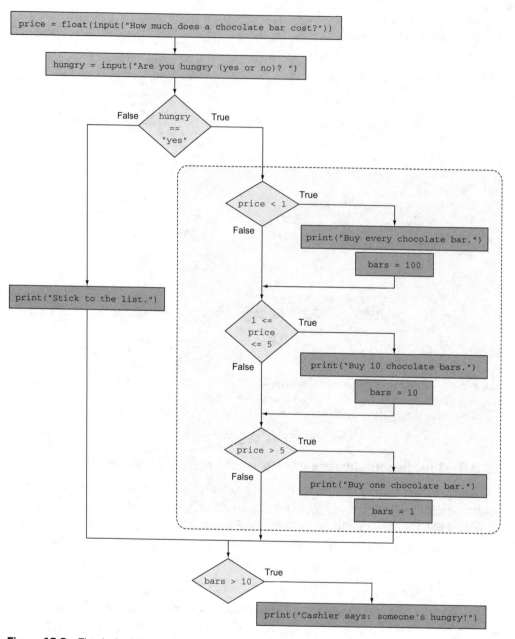

Figure 13.2　The dashed-line box represents the code block for when the `hungry == "yes"` conditional is true. Inside the dashed line is another conditional to determine the number of chocolate bars to buy, depending on the price.

You can see that the main flow of the program follows a vertical path from top to bottom. Every decision offers the possibility to deviate from the main path. The program contains three conditionals: one to determine whether you're hungry, one to determine the number of chocolate bars to buy, and one to determine the cashier's reply.

A code block for one conditional can contain other conditionals. The conditional to determine the number of chocolate bars to buy is nested inside the one that determines whether you're hungry.

Quick check 13.7 Using the flowchart in figure 13.2 as a guide, try to write a Python program that performs this more complicated task. From the think-write-test-debug-repeat programming cycle, you're given the recipe, so you need to focus on the write-test-debug part. Specifically, the test step tells you how your program behaves. Your program should give the same output for the same input. When you're finished, compare your code to listing 13.5 and keep the following points in mind:

- Variable names can differ.
- Comments should be used to help you understand which parts are where.
- You can reorder some of the conditionals to get the same behavior; the same inputs should produce the same outputs.
- Most important, there's always more than one correct implementation.

Listing 13.5 Conditionals to decide how much chocolate to buy

Conditional check to decide if you're hungry

Input from user

```python
price = float(input("How much does a chocolate bar cost? "))
hungry = input("Are you hungry (yes or no)? ")
bars = 0

if hungry == "yes":
    if price < 1:
        print("Buy every chocolate bar they have.")
        bars = 100
    if 1 <= price <= 5:
        print("Buy 10 chocolate bars.")
        bars = 10
```

Conditional check to see whether the price of a bar is less than $1

Actions to do when the price of a bar is less than $1

Conditional check and actions to do when the price of a bar is between $1 and $5

```
if price > 5:
    print("Buy only one chocolate bar.")
    bars = 1
```
Conditional check and actions to do when the price is greater than $5

```
if hungry == "no":
    print("Stick to the shopping list.")
```
Conditional check and actions to do when you say "no" when prompted if you're hungry

```
if bars > 10:
    print("Cashier says: someone's hungry!")
```
Prints a message only when the number of bars is greater than 10

 ## Summary

In this lesson, my objective was to teach you how to implement decisions in code by using the if conditional statement. Conditional statements add a layer of complexity to your programs. They give programs the capability to deviate from the main program flow and to follow detours through other parts of the code. Here are the major takeaways:

- The if statement starts a conditional code block.
- A program can have more than one conditional, in a series or nested.
- A nested conditional is one within the code block of another conditional.
- You can visualize a program that includes conditional statements by using flowcharts.

As you're starting to write programs that involve a few concepts, it's important to actively engage in solving them. Take out a pen and paper and draw out your solution or write out your thought process. Then open up Spyder, type up your code, and run, test, and debug your program. Don't forget to comment out your code.

Let's see if you got this…

Q13.1 You're given the following two statements: "*x* is an odd number" and "*x* + 1 is an even number." Write a conditional statement and outcome using these two statements in the form: if <condition> then <outcome>.

Q13.2 Write a program that creates one variable, which can be an integer or a string. If the variable is an integer, print I'm a numbers person. If the variable is a string, print I'm a words person.

Q13.3 Write a program that reads in a string from the user. If the string contains at least one space, print This string has spaces.

Q13.4 Write a program that prints Guess my number! and assign a secret number to a variable. Read in an integer from the user. If the user's guess is lower than the secret number, print Too low. If the user's guess is higher than the secret number, print Too high. Finally, if the user's guess is the same as the secret number, print You got it!

Q13.5 Write a program that reads in an integer from the user and prints the absolute value of that number.

14

MAKING MORE-COMPLICATED DECISIONS

After reading lesson 14, you'll be able to

- Combine many decisions in one conditional statement
- Make a choice when presented with various options
- Write code that gets the computer to decide between a few choices

It's limiting and time-consuming if every decision you make is the result of asking only one question at a time. Say you want to buy a new phone. There are only three phones that you're considering, but you're not sure how much money you have in your bank account. Additionally, one other criteria is that the phone is available in green. Using yes or no questions, you could ask the following:

- Do I have between $400 and $600?
- Do I have between $200 and $400?
- Do I have between $0 and $100?
- Does Phone 1 come in green?
- Does Phone 2 come in green?
- Does Phone 3 come in green?

Because you have more than one condition you want to check, you can combine two (or more) together. For example, you could ask, "Do I have between $400 and $600, and does Phone 1 come in green?"

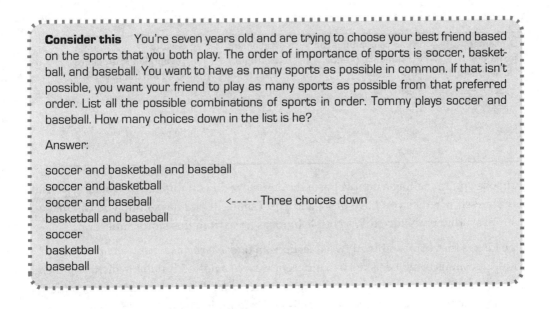

Consider this   You're seven years old and are trying to choose your best friend based on the sports that you both play. The order of importance of sports is soccer, basketball, and baseball. You want to have as many sports as possible in common. If that isn't possible, you want your friend to play as many sports as possible from that preferred order. List all the possible combinations of sports in order. Tommy plays soccer and baseball. How many choices down in the list is he?

Answer:

soccer and basketball and baseball
soccer and basketball
soccer and baseball   <----- Three choices down
basketball and baseball
soccer
basketball
baseball

14.1 Combining multiple conditions

You know how to write code that depends on whether one condition is true. This means deciding "this or not this." Sometimes, the decision you want to make might be "this or that or that or some other thing."

For example, if "It is raining" is true and "I am hungry" is false, then "It is raining and I am hungry" is false. Table 14.1 shows the truth values of statements made up of two statements.

Table 14.1   Truth values for combinations of two statements with "and" and "or"

Statement 1 (example: "It is raining")	Word to combine the statements (<and>, <or>, <not>)	Statement 2 (example: "I am hungry")	Result (example: "It is raining <_> I am hungry")
True	<and>	True	True
True	<and>	False	False
False	<and>	True	False
False	<and>	False	False
True	<or>	True	True
True	<or>	False	True

Table 14.1   Truth values for combinations of two statements with "and" and "or" (continued)

Statement 1 (example: "It is raining")	Word to combine the statements (<and>, <or>, <not>)	Statement 2 (example: "I am hungry")	Result (example: "It is raining <_> I am hungry")
False	<or>	True	True
False	<or>	False	False
N/A	<not>	True	False
N/A	<not>	False	True

Suppose you're making a simple pasta dinner. How do you think about making it? You ask yourself whether you have pasta and pasta sauce. If you have both, you can make your pasta dinner. Notice that a couple of ideas arise from this simple question.

One idea is that you combined two questions in one: *Do you have pasta and pasta sauce?* These questions could be asked in a different way, in a nested fashion, which would end up giving you the same final answer: *Do you have pasta? If yes, do you have pasta sauce?* But combining the two questions in one is easier to understand.

The other idea is that you used an important word, *and*, to link two questions that have yes/no answers. The word *and* and the word *or* are both Boolean operators, which are used to link two questions that have yes/no answers.

> **Quick check 14.1**   Combine the following questions by using the Boolean operators and/or:
> 1   Do you need milk? If yes, do you have a car? If yes, drive to the store and buy milk.
> 2   Is variable a zero? If yes, is variable b zero? If yes, is variable c zero? If yes, then all variables are zero.
> 3   Do you have a jacket? Do you have a sweater? Take one of these; it's cold outside.

The code examples so far have only one expression that evaluates to true or false inside the conditional statement. In reality, you can make decisions based on more than one condition. In programming, you can combine multiple conditional expressions in one if statement. This way, you don't have to write separate if statements for every separate conditional. This leads to cleaner code that's easier to read and understand.

14.1.1   Conditionals are made up of true/false expressions

You've seen conditionals in which only one expression evaluates to true/false; for example, num_a < 0. An if statement can check multiple conditionals and act accordingly, depending on whether the entire expression, made up of multiple conditionals, is true/false. This is where the truth table you saw in table 14.1 is useful. You use it to combine more than one expression by using the Boolean operators and and or. In Python, the words and and or are keywords.

You can have an if statement made up of more than one expression, as shown in the following listing.

Listing 14.1 Multiple conditional expressions in one if statement

```
if num_a < 0 and num_b < 0:
    print("both negative")
```

Here, two decisions must be made before entering inside the code block of the if statement: one decision is if num_a < 0, and the other decision is if num_b < 0.

14.1.2 Operator precedence rules

Recall that expressions are evaluated to a value that's a Python object—for example, an integer value. After you start to combine multiple expressions, you need to be careful about the order in which expressions and parts of each expression are evaluated.

In math, you learned about the operator precedence of addition, subtraction, multiplication, and division. In programming, the same precedence exists as in math, but additional operations must be taken into account—things like comparison operators and logical operators to combine Boolean expressions.

Table 14.2 shows a complete set of operator precedence rules, which tells you which operations are done before others in Python. These precedence rules are used, among other things, for evaluating the result of a larger conditional made up of smaller conditional expressions.

Table 14.2 Order of operations, with those at the top being executed first. Operations at the same precedence level within one cell are left-associative; they're executed left to right as encountered in an expression.

Operator	Meaning
()	Parentheses
**	Exponent
*	Multiplication
/	Division
//	Floor division
%	Modulus

Table 14.2 Order of operations, with those at the top being executed first. Operations at the same precedence level within one cell are left-associative; they're executed left to right as encountered in an expression. (continued)

Operator	Meaning
+	Addition
-	Subtraction
==	Is equal to
!=	Is not equal to
>	Greater than
>=	Greater than or equal to
<	Less than
<=	Less than or equal to
is	Identity (object is another object)
is not	Identity (object is not another object)
in	Membership (object is in another object)
not in	Membership (object isn't in another object)
not	Logical NOT
and	Logical AND
or	Logical OR

Quick check 14.2 Evaluate the following expressions by using the operator precedence in table 14.2:

```
1  3 < 2 ** 3 and 3 == 3
2  0 != 4 or (3/3 == 1 and (5 + 1) / 3 == 2)
3  "a" in "code" or "b" in "Python" and len("program") == 7
```

Take a look at the following (incorrect) code. It's similar to the code in listing 14.1, except that the line num_a < 0 and num_b < 0 is written as num_a and num_b < 0.

Listing 14.2 Code that doesn't do what you think it does

```
if num_a and num_b < 0:
    print("both negative")
```

If you run the code with the following different values for num_a and num_b, you'll get the output in table 14.3. An empty entry means no output. Notice that one of the pairs of values gives a misleading printout.

When num_a = 1 and num_b = -1, the output printed to the console is both negative, which is incorrect. Use the precedence rules to see what's going on. Add parentheses to denote expressions that are evaluated first in listing 14.2.

By the precedence rules in table 14.2, the and logical operator has lower precedence than the "less than" comparison. The expression num_a and num_b < 0 can be rewritten as (num_a and (num_b < 0)).

Table 14.3 Result in the console output after running the code in listing 14.2 with different values for num_a and num_b

num_a	num_b	Console output
-1	-1	both negative
-1	1	
0	-1	
0	1	
1	-1	both negative
1	1	

In Python, all integer values except 0 are considered True, and the integer value 0 is considered False. if -1 evaluates to if True, and if 0 evaluates to if False. Because of the precedence rules, whenever num_a is anything except 0, the expression evaluates to True. When num_a = 1 and num_b = -1, the code incorrectly prints both negative because (num_a and (num_b < 0)) evaluates to (1 and (-1 < 0)), which evaluates to (True and True), which is True.

> **Quick check 14.3**   Go back to the code in listing 14.1. The conditional there can be rewritten, using the precedence rules and parentheses, as ((num_a < 0) and (num_b < 0)). Draw a table for a few combinations of num_a and num_b to convince yourself that all possible pairs of values give the expected printout.

14.2 Choosing which lines to execute

Now you understand the purpose of a conditional statement and how to write one in Python. Conditionals don't have to be used as only single "detours" in code. They can also be used to make a decision as to which blocks of code to execute.

14.2.1 Do this or that

Sometimes you want to perform one task but not another. For example, you might say something like "If it is sunny, then I will walk to work; otherwise, if it is cloudy, then I will take an umbrella and walk to work; but otherwise, I will drive." For this, the elif and else keywords will be used in combination with an if statement.

Listing 14.3 shows a simple if-elif-else conditional statement in code. You get an input number from the user. If the number is greater than 0, you print positive. Otherwise, if the number is less than zero, you print negative. Otherwise, you print that the number is zero. Only one of the messages will be printed.

Listing 14.3 Example of a simple if-elif-else conditional statement

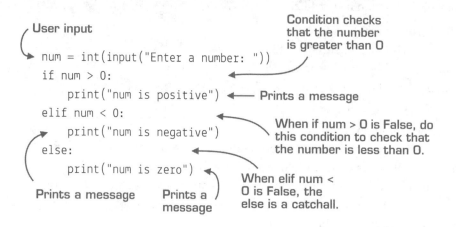

User input

Condition checks that the number is greater than 0

```
num = int(input("Enter a number: "))
if num > 0:
    print("num is positive")
elif num < 0:
    print("num is negative")
else:
    print("num is zero")
```

Prints a message

When if num > 0 is False, do this condition to check that the number is less than 0.

Prints a message　　Prints a message

When elif num < 0 is False, the else is a catchall.

Here, you start a conditional with the if statement. Any elif or else statements that come after it are associated with that if statement. This kind of structure means that you'll execute the code block that belongs to the first decision that's true.

Quick check 14.4　What's printed when you run listing 14.3 with the following values for num: -3, 0, 2, 1?

Figure 14.1 shows how to visualize multiple decisions. Each decision is a conditional statement; a group of decisions are part of an if-elif-else code block. Follow any path in figure 14.1 by tracing the paths denoted by arrows. The main program decisions are shown by the diamonds. The first decision starts with an if statement and indicates the start of a decision block. If you trace any path from the if statement to the box labeled <rest of program>, you'll notice that you can deviate from the main path of the program at most only once. The path you'll deviate to is the first path whose condition evaluates to True.

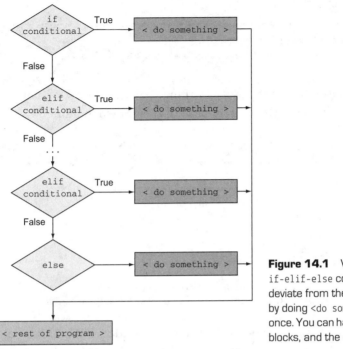

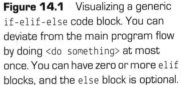

Figure 14.1 Visualizing a generic if-elif-else code block. You can deviate from the main program flow by doing <do something> at most once. You can have zero or more elif blocks, and the else block is optional.

The if-elif-else code block in figure 14.1 is a generic block. You can have the following variations:

- Only one if statement (you saw this in the previous lesson)
- One if statement and one elif statement
- One if statement and many elif statements
- One if statement and one else statement
- One if statement, one or more elif statements, and one else statement

For all of these variations, the detour executed is the first one whose condition evaluates to True. If none evaluate to True, the else detour is executed. If the preceding variations don't include an else statement, it's possible that none of the detours to <do something> are executed.

The following listing shows the generic way of writing code that does one thing or another, depending on whether certain conditions hold, as shown in figure 14.1.

Listing 14.4 A General way to write a simple `if-elif-else` conditional

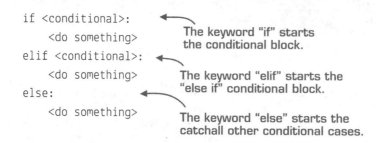

```
if <conditional>:
    <do something>
elif <conditional>:
    <do something>
else:
    <do something>
```

The keyword "if" starts
the conditional block.

The keyword "elif" starts the
"else if" conditional block.

The keyword "else" starts the
catchall other conditional cases.

The keyword `if` starts the conditional block, as before, followed by a conditional expression and then the colon character. When the `if` statement conditional is `True`, the code block for that `if` statement is executed, and then all remaining code blocks that are part of the `if-elif-else` group are skipped. When the `if` statement conditional is `False`, you check the conditional in the `elif` statement.

If the conditional in the `elif` statement is `True`, the code block for that `elif` statement is executed, and all remaining code blocks that are part of the `if-elif-else` group are skipped. You can have as many `elif` statements as you want (zero or more). Python looks at conditionals one after another and will execute the first code block that evaluates to `True`.

When none of the conditionals from the `if` or any of the `elif` statements are `True`, the code block inside the `else` is executed. You can think of the `else` as a catchall conditional for when nothing else is `True`.

When there's no `else` statement, and none of the conditionals evaluate to `True`, the conditional block won't do anything.

Quick check 14.6   Take a look at these code snippets:

```
With if-elif-else statements          With if statements
if num < 6:                           if num < 6:
    print("num is less than 6")           print("num is less than 6")
elif num < 10:                        if num < 10:
    print("num is less than 10")          print("num is less than 10")
elif num > 3:                         if num > 3:
    print("num is greater than 3")        print("num is greater than 3")
else:                                 print("Finished.")
    print("No relation found.")
print("Finished.")
```

What will the user see on the screen if num has the following values?

num	With if-elif-else	With if
20		
9		
5		
0		

14.2.2 Putting it all together

At this point, you can see that the structure of the programs is changing yet again:

- You can decide to do one of many things by checking different conditions.
- The if-elif structure is used to enter the first code block that's True.
- The else is used to do something when nothing else is True.

Listing 14.5 shows a simple program that checks the user input. When the user enters a noninteger value for either input, the program prints a message to the user and then moves on to the next group, at the same indentation level, of if-elif-else statements. It doesn't enter the else code block associated with the first if statement because it already executed the block within the if.

When the user enters two valid integers, you enter the else code block and print a message depending on the sign of the numbers inputted. Only the message associated with the first time a condition evaluates to True within the nested if-elif-else statement will be printed. After that code block finishes, you move on to check the next `if-elif-else` group, seeing whether the user guessed the lucky number.

Listing 14.5 Example of how to use `if-elif-else` statements

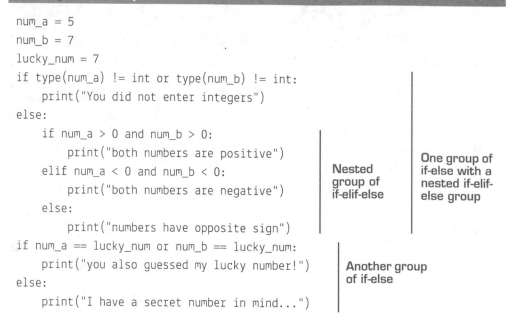

```
num_a = 5
num_b = 7
lucky_num = 7
if type(num_a) != int or type(num_b) != int:
    print("You did not enter integers")
else:
    if num_a > 0 and num_b > 0:
        print("both numbers are positive")
    elif num_a < 0 and num_b < 0:
        print("both numbers are negative")
    else:
        print("numbers have opposite sign")
if num_a == lucky_num or num_b == lucky_num:
    print("you also guessed my lucky number!")
else:
    print("I have a secret number in mind...")
```

Nested group of if-elif-else

One group of if-else with a nested if-elif-else group

Another group of if-else

Thinking like a programmer

Programmers write readable code, both for others to be able to read and for themselves to look back on later. It's a good idea to create variables to store complex computations and give them descriptive names rather than including them in conditionals directly. For example, don't do `if (x ** 2 - x + 1 == 0) or (x + y ** 3 + x ** 2 == 0)`. Instead, create variables `x_eq = x ** 2 - x + 1` and `xy_eq = x + y ** 3 + x ** 2` and then check `if x_eq == 0 or xy_eq == 0`.

Python makes it easy to visualize which lines should be executed because the code blocks are indented. You can take listing 14.5 and visualize the code in terms of blocks. In figure 14.2, you see that the conditionals have a cascading look.

Within the conditional group, you'll execute only the first branch that evaluates to `True`. Whenever you have another `if` statement at the same level as another `if` statement, you're starting another conditional group.

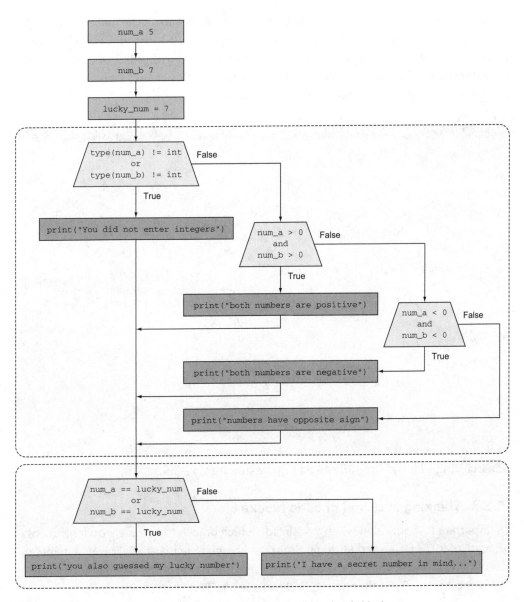

Figure 14.2 Visualization of listing 14.5, showing the conditional code blocks

You can see in figure 14.2 that two major conditional blocks are at the main level: the one that checks the user input and the one that checks for the lucky number. Using this visualization, you can even propose a rewrite of the code in listing 14.5 to eliminate the else statement for the first code block that checks the user input, and convert that to an elif statement. The code rewrite is in the next listing.

Listing 14.6 Rewrite of listing 14.5 to convert an else to a series of elifs

```
num_a = 5
num_b = 7
lucky_num = 7
if type(num_a) != int or type(num_b) != int:
    print("You did not enter integers")
elif num_a > 0 and num_b > 0:
    print("both numbers are positive")
elif num_a < 0 and num_b < 0:
    print("both numbers are negative")
else:
    print("numbers have opposite sign")
if num_a == lucky_num or num_b == lucky_num:
    print("you also guessed my lucky number!")
else:
    print("I have a secret number in mind...")
```

The else block from listing 14.5 converted to a series of elif blocks

As an exercise, you can check all combinations of inputs and compare the outputs of the code in listing 14.5 and in listing 14.6 to make sure it's the same.

14.2.3 Thinking in terms of code blocks

It's important to realize that when you decide which branch to execute, you look at only the particular if-elif-else conditional group, as shown in listing 14.7. The if statement has one check, to see whether the input from the user is one of the strings in the tuple greet_en or greet_sp. The other two elifs each have a nested if-elif code block.

Listing 14.7 Example with multiple if-elif-else code blocks

```
greeting = input("Say hi in English or Spanish! ")
greet_en = ("hi", "Hi", "hello", "Hello")
greet_sp = ("hola", "Hola")
```

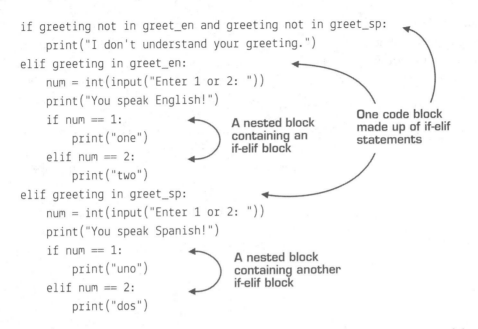

```
if greeting not in greet_en and greeting not in greet_sp:
    print("I don't understand your greeting.")
elif greeting in greet_en:
    num = int(input("Enter 1 or 2: "))
    print("You speak English!")
    if num == 1:
        print("one")
    elif num == 2:
        print("two")
elif greeting in greet_sp:
    num = int(input("Enter 1 or 2: "))
    print("You speak Spanish!")
    if num == 1:
        print("uno")
    elif num == 2:
        print("dos")
```

A nested block containing an if-elif block

One code block made up of if-elif statements

A nested block containing another if-elif block

The program will enter only one path through the if-elif-elif, through one of the following:

- The if when the user enters a greeting that isn't in greet_en and not in greet_sp
- Through the elif when greeting in greet_en
- Through the elif when greeting in greet_sp

Summary

In this lesson, my objective was to teach you how to make decisions by using the if-elif-else conditional statements, and to teach you how various combinations of their parts affect the program flow. The decisions you can make are now even more complex, because you can choose which code to execute. These are the major takeaways:

- Operator precedence is important when evaluating many expressions inside one conditional.
- The if statement indicates whether to take a detour. The if-elif-else statements indicate which detour to take.
- Visualize more-complicated programs, which include conditional statements, by using flowcharts.

As you're starting to write programs that involve a few concepts, it's important to actively engage in solving them. Take out a pen and paper and draw out your solution or write out your thought process. Then open your preferred IDE, type your code, and then run, test, and debug your program. Don't forget to comment your code.

Let's see if you got this...

Q14.1   Write a program that reads in two numbers from the user. The program should print the relation between the two numbers, which will be one of the following: `numbers are equal`, `first number is less than the second number`, `first number is greater than the second number`.

Q14.2   Write a program that reads in a string from the user. If the string contains at least one of every vowel (a, e, i, o, u), print `You have all the vowels!` Additionally, if the string starts with the letter *a* and ends with the letter *z*, print `And it's sort of alphabetical!`

15

CAPSTONE PROJECT: CHOOSE YOUR OWN ADVENTURE

After reading lesson 15, you'll be able to

- Write code for a choose-your-own-adventure program
- Use branches to set up paths through the program

This capstone project is somewhat open-ended.

> **THE PROBLEM** You'll use conditionals and branching to create a story. At each scene, the user will enter a word. The word will tell the program which path to continue following. Your program should handle all possible paths that the user might choose, but doesn't need to handle any unexpected input from the user.

The walk-through you'll see is one of many possible others; be as creative as you want with your storyline!

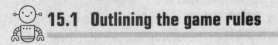

15.1 Outlining the game rules

Anytime you're getting input from users, you should be aware that they might not play by the rules. In your program, specify what you expect from them and warn them that anything else might make the program end.

A simple `print` statement will suffice, as in the following listing.

Listing 15.1 Getting user input

```
print("You are on a deserted island in a 2D world.")
print("Try to survive until rescue arrives!")
print("Available commands are in CAPITAL letters.")
print("Any other command exits the program")
print("First LOOK around...")
```

How to play

Unexpected behavior
closes the program.

According to the program rules, you'll have to handle branches for any input in capital letters. There's only one option at the start of the program, to help the user get accustomed to this input format.

15.2 Creating different paths

The general flow of the program is as follows:

- Tell users the choices they have.
- Get user input.
- If the user puts in choice 1, print a message. For this path, if the user now has more choices, indicate the choices, get input, and so on.
- Otherwise, if the user puts in choice 2, print another message. For this path, if the user now has more choices, indicate the choices, get input, and so on.
- And so on, for however many choices there are. For each path, if the user now has more choices, indicate the choices, get input, and so on.

You'll use nested conditionals to create subpaths within paths. One simple program is shown in listing 15.2. It goes only two conditionals deep; one nested conditional is inside another. The user can make at most two choices when running the program once.

The code listing begins by asking for user input. Then it makes sure the user understands the rules of the game with a conditional for the keyword LOOK. If the user types anything else, it shows a message indicating what commands are allowed and what the user will see. The first conditional checks whether the user typed LOOK. If the user did, the code gets user input again, and handles one of two possibilities from that input: that the user typed either LEFT or RIGHT. The code prints a different message for these choices.

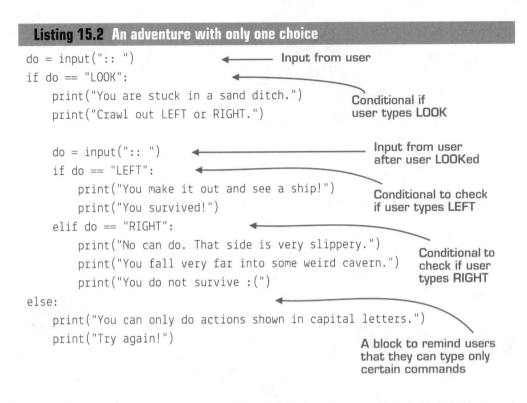

Listing 15.2 An adventure with only one choice

```
do = input(":: ")                        ← Input from user
if do == "LOOK":                          ←
    print("You are stuck in a sand ditch.")   Conditional if
    print("Crawl out LEFT or RIGHT.")         user types LOOK

    do = input(":: ")              ←      Input from user
    if do == "LEFT":               ←      after user LOOKed
        print("You make it out and see a ship!")
        print("You survived!")            Conditional to check
    elif do == "RIGHT":            ←      if user types LEFT
        print("No can do. That side is very slippery.")
        print("You fall very far into some weird cavern.")   Conditional to
        print("You do not survive :(")    check if user
                                          types RIGHT
else:                              ←
    print("You can only do actions shown in capital letters.")
    print("Try again!")
                                          A block to remind users
                                          that they can type only
                                          certain commands
```

Two choices in a program don't sound fun. You can add more choices for different scenarios.

15.3 More choices? Yes, please!

A choose-your-own-adventure game should have more than one or two choices. Use many nested conditionals to create many subpaths through the code. You can make the adventure as easy or as hard as you want; for example, out of 20 possible paths through the code, maybe only one leads to survival.

Figure 15.1 shows one possible code structure. A decision is marked by the user entering a word. Depending on the chosen word, the user will see a new situation for that chosen path. The user will continue making choices until the final outcome is reached.

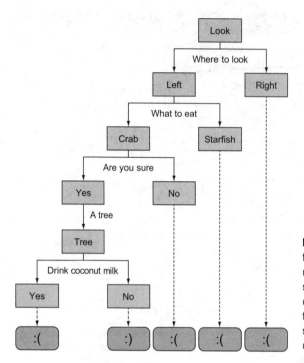

Figure 15.1 The boxes represent choices for the user. The text below the boxes represents the situation. The gray arrows show the path with the choice made. The dotted black lines to a smiley face or a sad face represent the end of the program, with survival or not. Out of five possible outcomes, only one leads to survival.

The following listing provides the code associated with figure 15.1. Only one path leads to survival. The user must enter LEFT, then CRAB, then YES, then TREE, and then NO. Any other choice leads to text indicating that the user has perished on the island.

Listing 15.3 One possible choose-your-own-adventure code

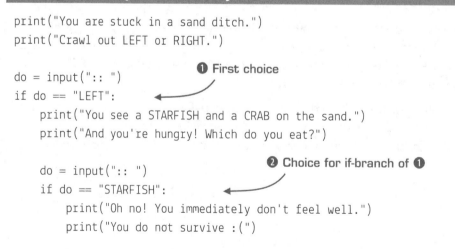

```
print("You are stuck in a sand ditch.")
print("Crawl out LEFT or RIGHT.")

do = input(":: ")                    ① First choice
if do == "LEFT":
    print("You see a STARFISH and a CRAB on the sand.")
    print("And you're hungry! Which do you eat?")

    do = input(":: ")                ② Choice for if-branch of ①
    if do == "STARFISH":
        print("Oh no! You immediately don't feel well.")
        print("You do not survive :(")
```

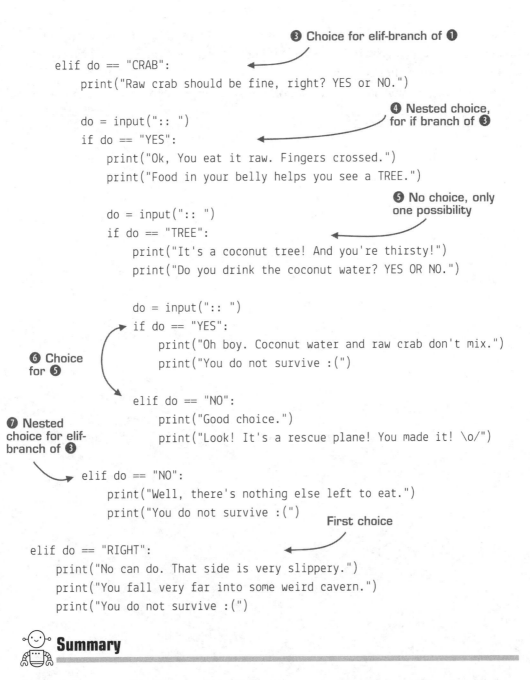

❸ Choice for elif-branch of ❶

```
elif do == "CRAB":
    print("Raw crab should be fine, right? YES or NO.")

    do = input(":: ")
    if do == "YES":
        print("Ok, You eat it raw. Fingers crossed.")
        print("Food in your belly helps you see a TREE.")

    do = input(":: ")
    if do == "TREE":
        print("It's a coconut tree! And you're thirsty!")
        print("Do you drink the coconut water? YES OR NO.")

    do = input(":: ")
    if do == "YES":
        print("Oh boy. Coconut water and raw crab don't mix.")
        print("You do not survive :(")

    elif do == "NO":
        print("Good choice.")
        print("Look! It's a rescue plane! You made it! \o/")

elif do == "NO":
    print("Well, there's nothing else left to eat.")
    print("You do not survive :(")

elif do == "RIGHT":
    print("No can do. That side is very slippery.")
    print("You fall very far into some weird cavern.")
    print("You do not survive :(")
```

❹ Nested choice, for if branch of ❸

❺ No choice, only one possibility

❻ Choice for ❺

❼ Nested choice for elif-branch of ❸

First choice

Summary

In this lesson, my objective was to teach you to use conditionals to write a program in which the user makes choices to try to survive the scenario outlined at the beginning of the program. To create paths for different choices that the user can make after having already made a choice, you used nested conditionals. Here are the major takeaways:

- Conditionals offer choices to the user.
- Nested conditionals are useful for offering a different set of choices after making one choice.

4

Repeating tasks

In the previous unit, you learned to write code that automatically makes decisions based on input from users or computations done within the program. In this unit, you'll write code that can automatically execute one or more statements.

Often you'll find yourself wanting to do the same task over and over again in code. Computers don't mind being told what to do and are especially great at doing the same task quickly. You'll see how to use this to your advantage and write code that will get computers to help you repeat tasks.

In the capstone project, you'll write a program that will tell you all the words you can make, given a set of letters. You can use this program when you play Scrabble to help you make the best words with tiles from your hand!

16

REPEATING TASKS WITH LOOPS

After reading lesson 16, you'll be able to

- Understand what it means for a line of code to repeat execution
- Write a loop in a program
- Repeat actions a certain number of times

The programs you've seen so far have statements that are executed once, at most. In the preceding unit, you learned to add decision points in your programs, which can break up the flow by making the program react to input. The decision points are governed by conditional statements that may cause your program to take a detour to execute other lines of code if a certain condition holds.

These kinds of programs still have a type of linearity to them; statements are executed top to bottom, and a statement can be executed either zero times or at most one time. Therefore, the maximum number of statements that can be executed in your program is the maximum number of lines in the program.

Consider this   It's a new year, and your resolution is to do 10 push-ups and 20 sit-ups every day. Look at the following flowchart to determine the number of sit-ups and push-ups you'll do in one year.

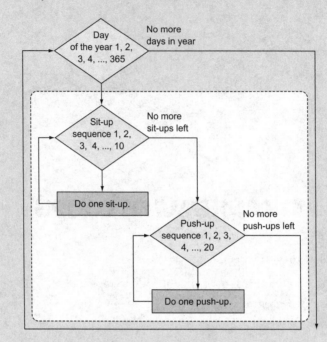

A flowchart illustrating how you can repeat certain tasks. Sit-ups are repeated 10 times, and push-ups are repeated 20 times. Both sit-ups and push-up sequences are done every day of the year

Answer: 3,650 sit-ups and 7,300 push-ups

16.1 Repeating a task

The power of computers comes from their capability to do computations quickly. Using what you've learned so far, if you wanted to execute a statement or a slight variation on a statement more than once, you'd have to type it in your program again so that the interpreter sees it as a separate command. Doing this defeats the purpose of having a computer do the work for you. In this lesson, you'll construct loops, which tell the interpreter to repeat a certain task (represented by a set of statements) many times.

16.1.1 Adding nonlinearity to programs

In your everyday life, you often repeat a certain task while changing a small part of it. For example, when you arrive at work or school, you might greet people with "Hi Joe" and then "Hi Beth" and then "Hi Alice." This task has something in common among all the repetitions (the word *Hi*), but a small part is changed with every repetition (a person's name). As another example, your shampoo bottle might indicate "lather, rinse, repeat." To *lather* and to *rinse* can be thought of as smaller subtasks that are both done, in the same order, with every repetition.

One of the many uses of computers is their capability to perform many computations in a short time. Doing repetitive tasks is what computers are best at, and programming a task such as playing every song in a playlist is easy. Every programming language has a way to tell the computer how to repeat a certain set of commands.

16.1.2 Infinite repetitions

Computers do only what you tell them to do, so you must be careful and explicit in your instructions. They can't guess your intentions. Suppose you write a program to implement the "lather, rinse, repeat" procedure. Pretend you've never used shampoo before and you're following the instructions without applying any other logic or reasoning. Notice anything wrong with the instructions? It's unclear when to stop the "lather, rinse" steps. How many times should you "lather and rinse"? If there's no set number of repetitions, when do you stop? These particular instructions are so vague that if you told a computer to do them, it would perform the "lather, rinse" procedure infinitely. A better instruction would be "lather, rinse, repeat as needed." The flowchart in figure 16.1 shows what happens when you tell a computer to "lather-rinse-repeat" and when you add an "as needed" clause to stop it from infinitely repeating.

Because computers do only what they're told, they can't make the decision of whether to repeat a set of commands on their own. You have to be careful to be specific when telling the computer to repeat commands: are there a certain number of times you want the commands to be repeated, or is there a condition that determines whether to repeat again? In the lather-rinse example, "as needed" was a condition that determined whether you were going to repeat lather-rinse. Alternatively, you might say that you want to lather-rinse three times and then stop.

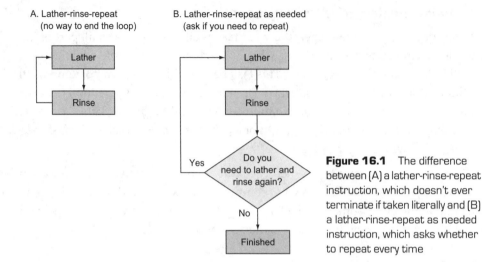

A. Lather-rinse-repeat
(no way to end the loop)

B. Lather-rinse-repeat as needed
(ask if you need to repeat)

Figure 16.1   The difference between (A) a lather-rinse-repeat instruction, which doesn't ever terminate if taken literally and (B) a lather-rinse-repeat as needed instruction, which asks whether to repeat every time

---

Thinking like a programmer

Humans can fill in knowledge gaps and infer certain ideas in different situations. Computers do only what they're told. When writing code, the computer will execute everything you write according to the rules of the programming language. A bug doesn't spontaneously appear in your code. If a bug exists, it's because you put it there. Lesson 36 discusses formal ways to debug your programs.

16.2   Looping a certain number of times

In programming, you achieve repetition by constructing loops. One way to stop a program from infinitely repeating a set of instructions is to tell it the number of times to repeat the instructions. The name for this type of loop is a for *loop*.

16.2.1   for loops

In Python, the keyword that tells you how to loop a certain number of times is for. To start, here's one way to use the keyword to repeat a command many times:

Without using loops

```
print("echo")
print("echo")
print("echo")
print("echo")
```

Using loops

```
for i in range(4):
    print("echo")
```

Without using loops, you have to repeat the same command as many times as you need to. In this case, the command is printing the word *echo* four times. But using loops, you can condense the code into only two lines. The first line tells the Python interpreter the number of times to repeat a certain command. The second line tells the interpreter the command to repeat.

Quick check 16.1

1 Write a piece of code that prints the word *crazy* eight times on separate lines.
2 Write a piece of code that prints the word *centipede* 100 times on separate lines.

Now suppose you're playing a board game; on your turn, you have to roll the dice three times. After each roll, you move your game piece that many steps. Suppose the player rolls a 4, then a 2, and then a 6.

Figure 16.2 shows a flowchart of every step. With only three rolls, it's easy to model the game by writing commands to do the dice roll and move the piece, repeating those two actions three times. But this would get messy quickly if you allowed the player to do 100 rolls on their turn. Instead, it's better to model the player's turn by using a for loop.

The player rolls the dice three times to get a sequence of values. Represent the number on the dice as a variable n. The loop goes through the sequence representing the dice rolls, starting with the first number—in this case n = 4. Using this variable for the number of steps to take, you move the piece n steps. Then you go to the next number in the sequence, n = 2, and move the piece 2 steps. Lastly, you go to the final number in the sequence, n = 6, and move the piece 6 steps. Because there are no more numbers in the sequence, you can stop moving your piece, and your turn ends.

Listing 16.1 shows the general structure of a for loop. The same structure can be visualized using the flowchart in figure 16.3. The idea is that you're given a sequence of values. The body of the loop repeats execution as many times as there are values. With each repetition, you're changing a loop variable to be an item in the sequence of values. The loop stops repeating when you've gone through all the values in the sequence.

Listing 16.1 A general way to write a for loop

```
for <loop_variable> in <values>:        ← Indicates beginning of loop.
    <do something>      ←                  <loop_variable> systematically
                                           takes on the value of each
                   Code block to execute for   item in <values>.
                   each item in <values>
```

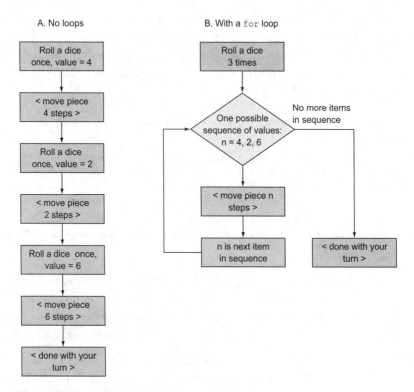

A. No loops

Roll a dice
once, value = 4

< move piece
4 steps >

Roll a dice
once, value = 2

< move piece
2 steps >

Roll a dice once,
value = 6

< move piece
6 steps >

B. With a `for` loop

Roll a dice
3 times

One possible
sequence of values:
n = 4, 2, 6

No more items
in sequence

< move piece n
steps >

n is next item
in sequence

Figure 16.2   In both (A) and (B), you roll a dice three times to give you values 4, 2, 6. (A) represents how you can move a game piece by explicitly writing out commands step-by-step. (B) shows how you can represent doing the same thing, except that you're using a `for` loop that iterates over the values representing each dice roll and you're generalizing the values by using a variable n.

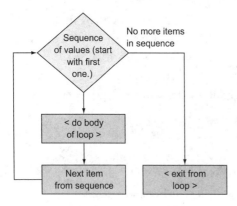

Sequence
of values (start
with first
one.)

No more items
in sequence

< do body
of loop >

Next item
from sequence

< exit from
loop >

Figure 16.3   A general way of writing a `for` loop. You start with the first item in the sequence of values and then execute the body of the loop by using that item. You get the next item in the sequence of values and execute the body of the loop using that item. The loop ends when you've gone through and executed the body of the loop by using every item in the sequence.

A `for` loop consists of two parts: the `for` loop line definition, and the code block that gets executed a certain number of times.

The keyword `for` tells Python you're introducing a block that will be repeated a certain number of times. After the keyword, you name a loop variable. This can be any valid variable name you want. This loop variable automatically changes its value for every repetition, with subsequent values taken from the values determined by what comes after the keyword `in`.

As with conditionals, indentation matters with loops. The indented code block tells Python that everything in that code block is part of the loop.

 16.3 Looping N times

In the previous section, you didn't impose any constraints on the sequence of values. It's often useful to have loops whose sequence of values follows a pattern. For example, a common and useful pattern is to have the items in a sequence of values be sequentially increasing 1, 2, 3... until some value N. Because in computer science counting starts from 0, an even more common sequence of numbers is 0, 1, 2... until some value $N - 1$, to give a total of N items in a sequence.

16.3.1 Loops over the common sequence 0 to N – 1

If you want to loop N times, you replace the `<values>` in listing 16.1 with the expression `range(N)`, where N is an integer number. `range` is a special procedure in Python. The expression `range(N)` yields the sequence 0, 1, 2, 3, ... $N - 1$.

> **Quick check 16.2**   What sequence of values does the following evaluate to?
> 1 `range(1)`
> 2 `range(5)`
> 3 `range(100)`

Listing 16.2 shows a simple `for` loop that repeatedly prints the value of the loop variable `v`. In listing 16.2, the loop variable is `v`, the sequence of values that the loop variable takes on is given by `range(3)`, and the body of the loop is one `print` statement.

When the program in listing 16.2 runs, and it first encounters the `for` loop with `range(3)`, it first assigns `0` to the loop variable `v` and then executes the `print` statement. Then it assigns 1 to the loop variable v and executes the print statement. Then it assigns 2 to the loop variable v and executes the print statement. In this example, this process is repeated three times, effectively assigning the loop variable the numbers 0, 1, 2.

Listing 16.2 A for loop that prints the loop variable value

```
for v in range(3):      ⟵——— v is the loop variable.
    print("var v is", v)  ⟵——— Prints the loop variable
```

You can generalize the behavior in listing 16.2 by using a different variable, say n_times, instead of 3, to give a sequence of numbers denoted by range(n_times). Then the loop will repeat n_times times. Every time the loop variable takes on a different value, the statements inside the code block are executed.

16.3.2 Unrolling loops

You can also think of loops in a different way. Listing 16.3 shows how to unroll a loop (write the repeated steps) to see exactly how Python executes the code in listing 16.2. In listing 16.3, you see that the variable v is assigned a different value. The lines that print the variable are the same for every different value of v. This code is inefficient, boring, and error-prone to write because the line to print the value of the variable v is repeated. Using loops instead of this code is much more efficient to write and easier to read.

Listing 16.3 Unrolled for loop from listing 16.2

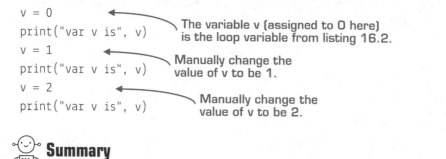

```
v = 0
print("var v is", v)
v = 1
print("var v is", v)
v = 2
print("var v is", v)
```

The variable v (assigned to 0 here) is the loop variable from listing 16.2.

Manually change the value of v to be 1.

Manually change the value of v to be 2.

Summary

In this lesson, my objective was to teach you why loops are useful. You saw what a for loop does and how to set up a for loop in code. At a high level, a for loop repeats statements that are part of its code block a certain number of times. A loop variable is a variable whose value changes with every loop repetition going through items in the loop sequence.

Sequences can be a series of integers. You saw a special sequence created by the expression range(N), where N is an integer. This expression creates the sequence 0, 1, 2, … N – 1. Here are the major takeaways:

- Loops are useful for writing concise and easy-to-read code.
- A for loop uses a loop variable that takes on values from a sequence of items; the items can be integers.
- When the items in the sequence are integers, you can use a special range expression to create special sequences.

Let's see if you got this…

Q16.1 Write a piece of code that asks the user for a number. Then write a loop that iterates that number of times and prints Hello every time. Is it possible to write this code without using a for loop?

17

CUSTOMIZING LOOPS

After reading lesson 17, you'll be able to

- Write more-complicated for loops that start and end at custom values
- Write loops that iterate over strings

You write programs so you can make the user's life easier in some way, but that doesn't mean that the programmer's experience with writing a program should be tedious. Many programming languages have added customizations to certain language constructs so that a programmer can take advantage of them and write code more efficiently.

Consider this You give your spouse a list of movies you want to watch over the course of one year. Every odd-numbered movie is action, and every even-numbered movie is comedy:

- What pattern can you follow to reliably make sure you watch every comedy movie in the list?
- What pattern can you follow to reliably make sure you watch every action movie in the list?

Answer:

- Go through the list and watch every other movie, starting with the second in the list.
- Go through the list and watch every other movie, starting with the first in the list.

 **17.1 Customizing loops**

You can specify starting values, ending values, and step sizes when using the range keyword. range(start,end,step) takes at least one number and can take up to three numbers in its parentheses. The numbering rules are similar to indexing into strings:

- The first number represents the index value at which to start.
- The middle number represents the index value at which to stop, but for which the code won't be executed.
- The last number represents a step (every "how many numbers to skip").

You can remember the following rules of thumb:

- When you give only one number in the parentheses, this corresponds to the end in range(start,end,step). The start is by default 0, and the step is by default 1.
- When you give only two numbers in the parentheses, this corresponds to the start and end (in that order) in range(start,end,step). The step is 1 by default.
- When you give all three numbers in the parentheses, this corresponds to start, end, and step (in that order) in range(start,end,step).

Here are examples of using range and the sequence of values to which each corresponds:

- range(5) is equivalent to range(0, 5) and range(0,5,1) —0, 1, 2, 3, 4
- range(2,6) —2, 3, 4, 5
- range(6,2) —No values
- range(2,8,2) —2, 4, 6
- range(2,9,2) —2, 4, 6, 8
- range(6,2,-1) —6, 5, 4, 3

Quick check 17.1 To what sequence of values do the following expressions evaluate? If you want to check yourself in Spyder, write a loop that iterates over the ranges and prints the value of the loop variable:

1 range(0,9)
2 range(3,8)
3 range(-2,3,2)
4 range(5,-5,-3)
5 range(4,1,2)

A for loop can iterate over any sequence of values, not just numbers. For example, a string is a sequence of character strings.

17.2 Looping over strings

Recall that a loop variable successively takes on the value of each item in a sequence with each iteration. A loop variable iterating over the numbers 0, 1, 2 takes on the value 0 the first time through the loop, then the value 1 the second time through the loop, and then the value 2 the third time through the loop. If you iterate over a sequence of characters in a string, then instead of a sequence 0, 1, 2, you may have a sequence a, b, c. A loop variable iterating over the sequence of characters will take on the value a the first time through the loop, the value b the second time through the loop, and the value c the third time through the loop.

In section 16.2, you saw the `in` keyword used in the context of `for` loops. There, the `in` keyword was used when you wanted to iterate over a sequence of values; in section 16.2, the values were numbers from 0 to N. The `in` keyword can also be used to iterate over characters in a string, as in the following listing. Given a string, say `"abcde"`, you can think of it as made up of a sequence of string characters a, b, c, d, e.

Listing 17.1 A `for` loop that iterates over each character in a string

```
for ch in "Python is fun so far!":     ◀——  ch is the loop variable.
    print("the character is", ch)      ◀——  Prints the loop variable
```

Any string you create has a set length, so a `for` loop that iterates over every character in a string will repeat however many times the length of the string is. In listing 17.1, `ch` is the loop variable, and this can be named any legal Python variable name. The length of the string you're iterating over is 21, because spaces and punctuation also count as characters. The `for` loop in listing 17.1 repeats 21 times; each time, the variable `ch` will take on the value of every different character in the string `"Python is fun so far!"`. Inside the code block, you're printing the value of the loop variable to the Python console.

> **Quick check 17.2**   Write a piece of code that asks the user for input. Then write a loop that iterates over every character. The code prints `vowel` every time it encounters a vowel character.

The method depicted in listing 17.1 is an intuitive way to iterate over every character in a string and should always be your go-to method when dealing with characters in a string.

If Python didn't allow you to iterate over the characters in a string directly, you'd have to use a loop variable that iterates over a sequence of integers representing the position of every character, 0, 1, 2, … to the length of the string minus 1. Listing 17.2 shows a rewrite of listing 17.1 using this technique. In listing 17.2, you must create a variable for the string so you can later access it inside the loop code block. The loop still repeats 21 times, except now the loop variable takes on values 0, 1, 2,…20 to represent every index location in the string. Inside the code block, you must index into your string variable to find the value of the character at each index. This code is cumbersome and not nearly as intuitive as listing 17.1.

Listing 17.2 A `for` loop that iterates over each index in a string

```
my_string = "Python is fun so far!"        Stores string and its
len_s = len(my_string)                      length in a variable
for i in range(len_s):        ←———————————  Iterates between 0 to len_s - 1
    print("the character is", my_string[i])  ←———  Indexes into the string
```

Figure 17.1 shows a flowchart of listing 17.1 (on the left) and listing 17.2 (on the right). When you iterate over the characters directly, the loop variable gets the value of each character in the string. When you iterate over the indices, the loop variable gets the value of integers 0 to the length of the string minus 1. Because the loop variable contains integers, you have to use the integer to index into the string to retrieve the value of the character at that position. This is an extra step calculated using my_string[i]. Notice that you have to keep track of a lot more things in listing 17.2, whereas in listing 17.1 the loop variable already knows the value of the character directly.

Thinking like a programmer

Writing more lines of code or code that looks complicated doesn't make you a better programmer. Python is a great language to start with because it's easy to read, so write your code to follow this idea. If you find yourself writing convoluted logic to achieve a simple task or repeating yourself several times, take a step back and use a piece of paper to draw out what you want to achieve. Use the internet to see whether Python has an easy way to do what you want to do.

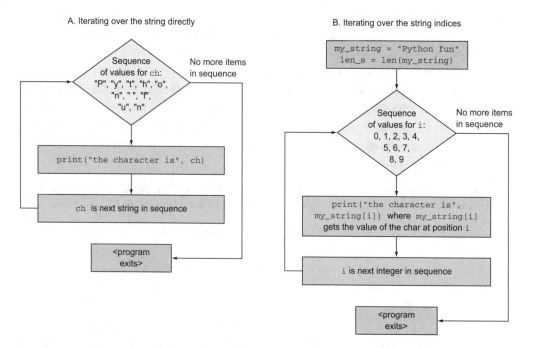

Figure 17.1 Comparison of the flowcharts for (A) listing 17.1 and (B) listing 17.2. In (A), the loop variable ch takes on the values of each character. In (B), the loop variable takes on integer values representing the indices in a string 0 to the length of the string minus 1. In (B) there's an extra step inside the body of the loop to convert the loop index into the character at that loop index.

Summary

In this lesson, my objective was to introduce you to sequences that can be a series of integers. You saw that the expression range can be customized by changing the sequence start value or end value, or even skipping over numbers. Sequences can also be a series of string characters. You saw how to write code that takes advantage of the capability to iterate over string characters directly. Here are the major takeaways:

- A for loop uses a loop variable that takes on values from a sequence of items; the items can be integers or character strings.
- When the items in the sequence are integers, you can use a special range expression to create special sequences.

- When the items in the sequence are string characters, the loop variable iterates over the characters in a string directly as opposed to using the index of the string as a middleman.

Let's see if you got this...

Q17.1 Write a program that iterates over all even numbers between 1 and 100. If the number is also divisible by 6, increment a counter. At the end of your program, print how many numbers are even and also divisible by 6.

Q17.2 Write a program that asks the user for a number, n. Then use loops to repeatedly print a message. For example, if the user inputs 99, your program should print this:

```
99 books on Python on the shelf 99 books on Python
Take one down, pass it around, 98 books left.
98 books on Python on the shelf 98 books on Python
Take one down, pass it around, 97 books left.
```

... < and so on >

```
1 book on Python on the shelf 1 book on Python
Take one down, pass it around, no more books!
```

Q17.3 Write a program that asks the user to input names separated by a single space. Your program should print a greeting for every name entered, separated by a newline. For example, if the user enters Zoe Xander Young, your program prints out Hi Zoe and then on the next line Hi Xander and then on the next line Hi Young. This problem is a bit more involved. Think back to what you learned about strings; you'll have to use a loop to look at every character in the input and save what you see up to a space in a variable representing the name. Don't forget to reset your name variable when you see the space!

18

REPEATING TASKS WHILE CONDITIONS HOLD

After reading lesson 18, you'll be able to

- Understand the syntax of another way to write a loop in a program
- Repeat actions while a certain condition is true
- Exit out of loops early
- Skip statements in a loop

In the previous lessons, you assumed that you knew the number of times you wanted to repeat a block of code. But suppose, for example, that you're playing a game with your friend. Your friend is trying to guess a number that you have in mind. Do you know in advance how many times your friend will guess? Not really. You want to keep asking them to try again until they get it right. In this game, you don't know how many times you want to repeat the task. Because you don't know, you can't use a for loop. Python has another type of loop that's useful in these kinds of situations: a while loop.

Consider this   Using only the information given in the following scenarios, do you know the maximum number of times you want to repeat the task?

- You have five TV channels and you cycle though using the Up button until you've checked out what's on every channel.
- Eat a cookie until there are no more cookies in the box.
- Say "punch buggy" every time you see a VW Beetle.
- Click Next on your jogging song playlist until you've sampled 20 songs.

Answer:

- Yes
- Yes
- No
- Yes

18.1   Looping while a condition is true

If you have a task that must be repeated an uncertain number of times, a for loop won't be appropriate because it won't work.

18.1.1   Looping to make a guess

Start with a guessing game. You think of a secret word and ask a player to guess your word. Every time the player makes a guess, tell them whether they're right. If they're wrong, ask again. Keep track of the number of guesses a player makes until they get it right. Figure 18.1 shows a flowchart of this game.

Listing 18.1 shows an implementation of the game in code. The user is trying to guess a secret word chosen by the programmer. The user is first prompted to enter a word. The first time you reach the while loop, you compare the user guess with the secret word. If the guess isn't correct, you enter the while loop code block, consisting of three lines. You first print the number of times the user guessed so far. Then you ask the user for another guess; notice that the user's guess is assigned to the variable guess, which is used in the while loop's condition to check the guess against the secret word. Lastly, you increment the number of tries to keep an accurate count of the number of times the user tried to guess the word.

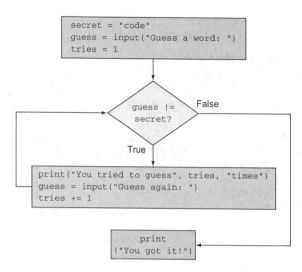

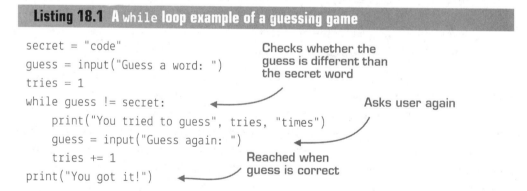

Figure 18.1 Flowchart of the guessing game. A user guesses a word. The guessing loop is represented by the gray diamond, which checks whether the user guess is equal to the secret word. If it is, the game finishes. If it isn't equal, you tell the player that they're wrong, ask them to guess again, and add 1 to the number of times that they made a guess.

After these three lines are executed, you check the condition of the while loop again, this time with the updated guess. If the user continues to guess the secret word incorrectly, the program doesn't go past the while loop and its code block. When the user gets the secret word correct, the while loop condition becomes false, and the while loop code block isn't executed. Instead, you skip the while code block, move to the statement immediately following the while loop and its code block, and print a congratulatory message. In this game, you must use a while loop because you don't know the number of wrong guesses the user will give.

Listing 18.1 A while loop example of a guessing game

```
secret = "code"
guess = input("Guess a word: ")          Checks whether the
tries = 1                                 guess is different than
                                          the secret word
while guess != secret:
    print("You tried to guess", tries, "times")     Asks user again
    guess = input("Guess again: ")
    tries += 1                    Reached when
print("You got it!")             guess is correct
```

At this point, you should notice that the code block has to include a statement to change something about the condition itself. If the code block is independent of the condition, you enter an infinite loop. In listing 18.1, the guess was updated by asking the user to enter another word.

18.1.2 while loops

In Python, the keyword that begins a while loop is, not surprisingly, while. The following listing shows a general way of writing a while loop.

Listing 18.2 A general way to write a while loop

```
while <condition>:          ←——— Indicates beginning of loop
    <do something>
```

When Python first encounters the while loop, it checks whether the condition is true. If it is, it enters the while loop code block and executes the statements as part of that block. After it finishes with the code block, it checks the condition again. It executes the code block inside the while loop as long as the condition is true.

> **Quick check 18.1**   Write a piece of code that asks the user for a number between 1 and 14. If the user guesses right, print You guessed right, my number was and then print the number. Otherwise, keep asking for another guess.

18.1.3 Infinite loop

With while loops, it's possible to write code that will never finish. For example, this piece of code infinitely prints when will it end?!

```
while True:
    print("when will it end?!")
```

Letting a program like this run for a long time will slow your computer. But if this happens, don't panic! There are a few ways to manually stop a program that entered an infinite loop, as shown in figure 18.2. You can do one of the following:

- Click the red square at the top of the console.
- Click into the console and then hit Ctrl-C (press and hold the Ctrl key and then press the C key).
- Click the menu in the console (beside the red square) and choose Restart Kernel.

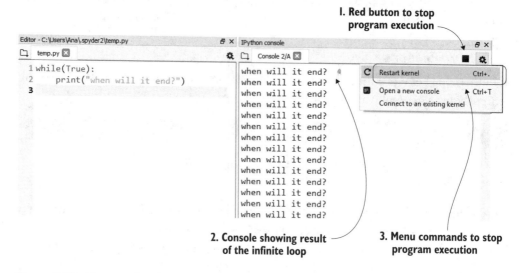

I. Red button to stop program execution

2. Console showing result of the infinite loop

3. Menu commands to stop program execution

Figure 18.2   To manually exit out of an infinite loop, you can click the red square, or press Ctrl-C, or choose Restart Kernel from the console menu beside the red square.

18.2 Using for loops vs. while loops

Any for loop can be converted into a while loop. A for loop iterates a set number of times. To convert this to a while loop, you need to add a variable whose value is checked in the while condition. The variable is changed every time through the while loop. The following listing shows a for loop and while loop side by side. The while loop case is more verbose. You must initialize a loop variable yourself; otherwise, Python doesn't know to what variable x you're referring inside the loop. You must also increment the loop variable. In the for loop case, Python does these two steps automatically for you.

Listing 18.3 A for loop rewritten as a while loop

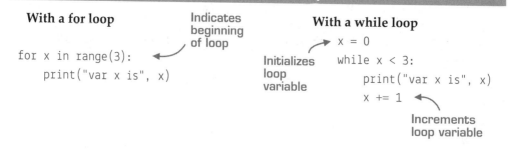

With a for loop

Indicates beginning of loop

```
for x in range(3):
    print("var x is", x)
```

With a while loop

Initializes loop variable

Increments loop variable

```
x = 0
while x < 3:
    print("var x is", x)
    x += 1
```

In listing 18.3, you have to create another variable. You must manually increment its value inside the while loop; remember that the for loop increments the value of the loop variable automatically. Figure 18.3 shows how to visualize the code in listing 18.3.

A. Code executed with a for loop

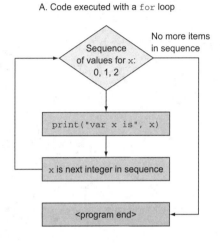

B. Code executed with a while loop

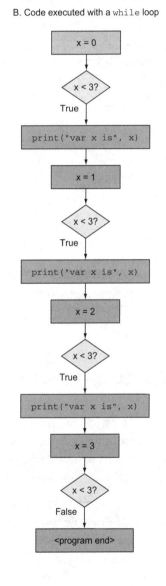

Figure 18.3 [A] shows the for loop code that prints the value of the loop variable with each iteration of the loop. [B] shows the while loop code and how the variables in change values when the for loop is converted into a while loop. You have to create your own variable and increment it yourself inside the body of the while loop. Additionally, you have to write a conditional as a function of your variable that will cause the body of the while loop to repeat three times.

Any for loop can be converted into a while loop. But not all while loops can be converted into for loops, because some while loops don't have a set number of times to iterate. For example, when you ask the user to guess a number, you don't know how many tries the user will take to guess the number, so you don't know what sequence of items to use with a for loop.

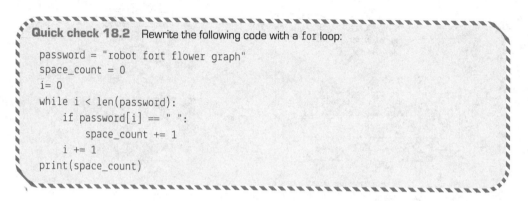

Quick check 18.2   Rewrite the following code with a for loop:

```
password = "robot fort flower graph"
space_count = 0
i= 0
while i < len(password):
    if password[i] == " ":
        space_count += 1
    i += 1
print(space_count)
```

Thinking like a programmer

In programming, there's usually more than one way to do something. Some ways are terse, and some are verbose. A good Python programmer should find a way to write code that's as simple and short as possible, while being easy to understand.

 ## 18.3 Manipulating loops

You've seen the basic structure of for and while loops. Their behavior is straightforward, but they're a bit limiting. When you use a for loop, you go through the loop as many times as you still have items in your sequence of values (either integers or string characters). With a while loop, the only way to stop repeating it is for the while loop condition to become false.

But to write more-flexible code, you may want the option to exit out of a for loop early. Or you may want to exit out of a while loop early if an event happens inside the code block that's independent of the while loop condition.

18.3.1 Exiting early out of a loop

The only way that you know how to exit out of a while loop is for the while condition to become false. But you'll often want to exit out of a loop early (either a for or while loop). A keyword in Python, break, makes it possible to exit out of a loop whenever Python executes that keyword, even if the while loop condition is still true. Listing 18.4 shows example code using the break keyword.

In listing 18.4, you see the addition of an extra condition within the loop to check whether the user tried to guess at least 100 times. When that condition is true, you print a message and break out of the loop. When you encounter the break statement, the loop immediately terminates; nothing after the break statement, but within the loop, is executed. Because there's now a possibility of exiting the loop for causes other than the user getting the word right, you have to add a conditional after the loop to check why the loop terminated.

Listing 18.4 Using the break keyword

```python
secret = "code"
max_tries = 100
guess = input("Guess a word: ")
tries = 1
while guess != secret:
    print("You tried to guess", tries, "times")
    if tries == max_tries:                          Breaks out of loop
        print("You ran out of tries.")              when exceed max_tries
        break    ⟵
    guess = input("Guess again: ")
    tries += 1
if tries <= max_tries and guess == secret:          Checks why exited
    print("You got it!")                            out of loop
```

Why does this code have an extra if statement after the while loop? Think about what happens in two cases: the user guesses the secret word, or the user runs out of tries. In either case, you stop executing the while loop and execute any statements right after the while loop block. You want to print a congratulatory message only if the exit from the loop was due to the correct guess. The congratulatory message has to come after the while loop terminates, but you can't just print the message outright. The while loop may have terminated because the user ran out of tries; you just don't know why you exited the while loop.

You need to add a conditional that checks whether the user still has tries left and whether the user's guess matched the secret. The conditional ensures that if the user still has tries left, you exited the while loop because the user guessed the secret word and not because the user ran out of tries.

> **Thinking like a programmer**
>
> It's always a good idea to create variables to store values that you're going to reuse many times in your code. In listing 18.4, you created a variable named max_tries to hold the number of times to ask the user to guess. If you ever decide to change the value, you have to change it in only one place (where it's initialized) instead of trying to remember everywhere you used it.

The break statement works with for and while loops. It can be useful in many situations, but you have to use it with caution. If you have loops within loops, only the loop that the break statement is a part of terminates.

> **Quick check 18.3**   Write a program that uses a while loop to ask the user to guess a secret word of your choosing. The user gets 21 tries. When the user gets it right, end the program. If the user uses up all 21 tries, exit the loop and print an appropriate message.

18.3.2 Going to the beginning of a loop

The break statement in the previous section caused any remaining statements in a loop to be skipped, and the next statement executed was the one right after the loop.

Another situation you might find yourself in is that you want to skip any remaining statements inside a loop and go to the beginning of the loop to check the conditional again. To do this, you use the continue keyword, which is often used to make code look cleaner. Consider listing 18.5. Both versions of the code do the same thing. In the first version, you use nested conditionals to make sure all conditions are satisfied. In the second version, the continue keyword skips all subsequent statements inside the loop and fast-forwards to the beginning of the loop with the next x in the sequence.

Listing 18.5 Comparing code that does and doesn't use the continue **keyword**

```
### Version 1 of some code ###
x = 0
for x in range(100):
    print("x is", x)
    if x > 5:
        print("x is greater than 5")
        if x%10 != 0:
            print("x is not divisible by 10")
            if x==2 or x==4 or x==16 or x==32 or x==64:
                print("x is a power of 2")
                # perhaps more code


### Version 2 of some code ###
x = 0
for x in range(100):
    print("x is", x)
    if x <= 5:
        continue
    print("x is greater than 5")       Get here
    if x%10 == 0:                       when x > 5
        continue
    print("x is not divisible by 10")   Get here when
    if x!=2 and x!=4 and x!=16 and x!=32 and x!=64:   x%10 ! = 0
        continue
    print("x is a power of 2")
    # perhaps more code            Get here when x is
                                   2, 4, 16, 32, or 64
  Skips remaining
  loop statements
```

In listing 18.5, you can write two versions of the same code: with and without the continue keyword. In the version that contains the continue keyword, when the conditionals evaluate to true, all remaining statements in the loop are skipped. You go to the beginning of the loop and assign the next value for x, as if the loop statements are executed. But the code that doesn't use the continue keyword ends up being a lot more convoluted than the one that does. In this situation, it's useful to use the continue keyword when you have a lot of code that you want to execute when a bunch of nested conditions hold.

 **Summary**

In this lesson, my objective was for you to write programs that repeat certain tasks with a while loop. while loops repeat tasks while a certain condition holds.

Whenever you write a for loop, you can convert it into a while loop. The opposite isn't always possible. This is because for loops repeat a certain number of times, but the condition for entering inside a while loop might not have a known, set number of times that it can happen. In the examples, you saw that you can ask the user to enter a value; you don't know how many times the user will enter the wrong value, which is why a while loop is useful in that situation.

You also saw how to use the break and continue statements within loops. The break statement is used to stop executing all remaining statements inside the innermost loop. The continue statement is used to skip all remaining statements inside the innermost loop and continue from the beginning of the innermost loop.

Here are key takeaways from this lesson:

- while loops repeat statements as long as a certain condition holds.
- A for loop can be written as a while loop, but the opposite may not be true.
- A break statement can be used to exit a loop prematurely.
- A continue statement can be used to skip remaining statements in the loop and check the while loop conditional again or go to the next item in the for loop sequence.
- There's no penalty for trying one kind of loop (for or while) and finding it's not working out in your program. Try out a couple of things and think of it as trying to put together a coding puzzle.

Let's see if you got this…

Q18.1 This program has a bug. Change one line to avoid the infinite loop. For a few pairs of inputs, write what the program does and what it's supposed to do.

```
num = 8
guess = int(input("Guess my number: "))
while guess != num:
    guess = input("Guess again: ")
print("Right!")
```

Q18.2 Write a program that asks a user whether they want to play a game. If the user enters y or yes, indicate that you're thinking of a number between 1 and 10 and ask the user to guess the number. Your program should continue asking the user to guess the number until they get it right. If they get it right, print a congratulatory message and then ask if they want to play again. This process should be repeated as long as the user enters y or yes.

19

CAPSTONE PROJECT: SCRABBLE, ART EDITION

After reading lesson 19, you'll be able to

- Apply conditionals and loops to write a more complicated program
- Understand what's being asked of you in a program
- Draw up a plan of how to solve a problem before starting to code
- Break the problem into smaller subproblems
- Write code for the solution

You're playing a simpler version of Scrabble with your kids. The kids have been winning most games so far, and you realize it's because you aren't picking the best word from the given tiles. You decide that you need a bit of help in the form of a computer program.

THE PROBLEM   Write a program that can tell you words that you can form from a set of tiles; the set of all valid words is a subset of all the English words (in this case, only words related to art). When dealing with choosing the best word from the given tiles, here are some details to remember:

- All valid words related to art are given to you as a string, each word separated by a newline. The string organizes the words by length, shortest to longest. All valid words contain only letters in the alphabet (no spaces, hyphens, or special symbols). For example,

```
"""art
hue
ink
oil
pen
wax
clay
draw
film

...

crosshatching
"""
```

- The number of tiles you get can vary; it's not a fixed number.
- Letters on tiles don't have point values; they're all worth the same.
- The tiles you get are given as a string. For example, tiles = "hijklmnop".
- Report all valid words you can form with your tiles in a tuple of strings; for example, ('ink', 'oil', 'kiln').

 ## 19.1 Understanding the problem statement

This programming task sounds involved, so try to break it into a few subtasks. There are two big parts to this problem:

- Represent all the possible valid words in a format that you can work with. Convert the words from a long string of characters into a tuple of string words.
- Decide whether a word in the list of all valid words can be made with the set of tiles you're given.

19.1.1 Change the representation of all valid words

Let's tackle the first part, which will help you create a tuple of all the valid words so you can work with them later. You need to do this step because if you keep the valid words as is, you have a big string of characters that's hard to work with.

The set of all valid words is given to you as a string. To the computer, each "line" that a human sees isn't a line with a word on it, but a long sequence of characters.

Draw out the problem

It's always a good idea to start with a small sketch of what you need to do. To the human eye, the string looks nicely organized, and you can tell the words apart, but the computer doesn't know the concept of words in a string, only single characters. The computer sees something like `"""art\nhue\nink\noil\n...\ncrosshatching"""`.

The line breaks that you can see with your eyes are single characters themselves, each called the *newline* (or *linebreak*) character, represented by `\n`. You'll have to find out the position of every newline character so you can separate each word. Figure 19.1 shows how you might think about this in a more systematic way.

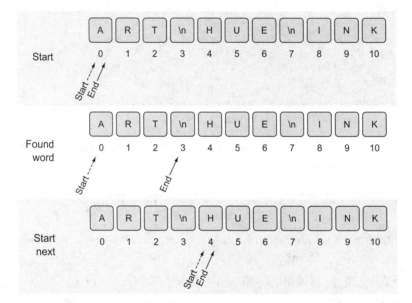

Figure 19.1 Converting a string of characters into words. In the top example named *start*, you can keep track of where you are in the character string by using a *start* and *end* pointer. In the middle example named *found word*, you stop changing *end* when you reach a newline character. In the bottom example named *start next*, you reset the *start* and *end* pointers to the character right after the newline.

With this simple sketch, you can already see how to achieve this task. The *start* and *end* pointers start at the beginning of the big string. As you're looking for a newline character to mark the end of the word, you'll increment the *end* pointer until you find the `\n`. At that point, you can store the word from the *start* pointer to the *end* pointer. Then, move both pointers to one index past the newline character to start looking for the next word.

Come up with some examples

Write some test cases that you may want to think about as you're writing your program. Try to think of simple cases and complex ones. For example, all valid words might be just one word, such as words = """"art"""", or it might be a few words, such as the example given in the problem statement.

Abstract the problem into pseudocode

Now that you have an idea of how to convert characters to words, you can start writing a mixture of code and text to help you put the big picture into place, and to start thinking about the details.

Because you need to look at all letters in the string, you need a loop. In the loop, you decide whether you've found a newline character. If you found the newline character, save the word and reset your pointer indexes. If you didn't find a newline character, keep incrementing only the *end* index until you do. The pseudocode might look like this:

```
word_string = """art
hue
ink
"""

set start and end to 0
set empty tuple to store all valid words
for letter in word_string:
    if letter is a newline:
        save word from start to ends in tuple for all valid words
        reset start and end to 1 past the newline character
    else:
        increment end
```

19.1.2 Making a valid word with the given tiles

Now you can think about the logic for deciding whether you can make a valid word using the given tiles, with the valid word coming from the list of allowed words.

Draw out the problem

As usual, it helps to draw what you need to do. The logic for this part of the problem can be approached in a couple of ways:

- You can start by looking at the tiles in your hand. Find all combinations of them. Then you can look at each combination of letters and see whether they match any of the valid words.

- You can start by looking at the valid words and see whether each can be made using the tiles you have.

Thinking like a programmer

This part is crucial when you're trying to decide which way to approach a problem. The process of drawing helps you think of a few ways before settling on one. If you start to code immediately, you'll feel boxed into one path that may or may not even be appropriate for the problem at hand. The process of sketching will help you see what issues may arise with a few solutions without committing to any yet.

The first option, although possibly more intuitive, is a bit harder to implement with what you know so far because it involves finding all combinations and permutations of all the tiles. The second option is more appropriate at this time. Figure 19.2 illustrates the second option.

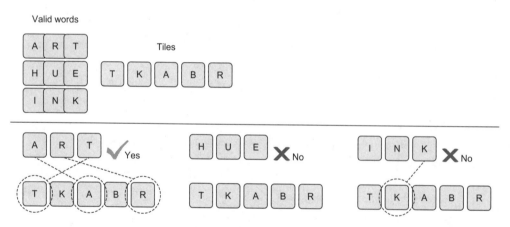

Figure 19.2   Given the valid words and a set of tiles, start with the first valid word and check whether all its letters are in the set of tiles. If so, add it to the set of words you can make. If at least one letter is in a valid word but not in the tiles, you can't make the word.

You'll go through each valid word and then look at each letter in that word, checking whether you can find the letter in your tiles. After you've gone through all the letters of the word and you're able to find them in your tiles, you can make that word with your tiles. As soon as you find that there's one letter not in your tiles, you can immediately stop because you can't make that word.

Come up with some examples

Coming up with examples can help you determine special situations you may have to take care of in your code. Here are some examples of tiles you may want to make sure your code can handle:

- A single tile—in this case, you can't make any valid word.
- All the tiles given make exactly one valid word—with `tiles = "art"`, you can make the word *art*.
- All the tiles given make exactly two valid words—with `tiles = "euhtar"`, you can make *art* and *hue*.
- You can make one valid word but have extra tiles left over—with `tiles = "tkabr"`, you can make *art* and have *k* and *b* left over.
- You have only one tile of a certain letter, but a valid word uses two of that letter—with `tiles = "colr"`, you can't make the word *color* because you have only one *o*.

Abstract the problem into pseudocode

With pseudocode, you can start to think about more of the details that you discovered while coming up with examples. You'll need to go through each valid word to see whether you can make it with your tiles, so you'll need a loop. Then you'll go through each letter in that word; you'll need a nested loop inside the first one. You can immediately exit the inner loop as soon as you find one letter that isn't in your tiles. But if each letter you look at is in your tiles, keep going.

This logic has two tricky parts: (1) how to keep track of words that have multiples of the same letter and (2) how to tell when you found the full word in your tiles. You don't have to outline exactly how to do these in the pseudocode, but you should be able to tell whether they're issues that can be resolved. I can tell you that they can be resolved, and you'll see how in the next section. The pseudocode for this part might be

```
for word in valid_words:
    for letter in word:
        if letter not in tiles:
            stop looking at remaining letters and go to next word
        else:
            remove letter from tiles (in case of duplicates)
    if all letters in valid word found in tiles:
        add word to found_words
```

Notice that there's a lot going on and a few more variables to keep track of in this problem than you're used to! Without thinking about the problem first, you'd quickly get lost. At this point, with an understanding of the major components to this problem, you can start to write the code. An important first step is deciding how to divide your code into smaller, more manageable chunks.

Thinking like a programmer

Dividing code into smaller pieces is a necessary and important skill for a programmer for a few important reasons:

- Large problems look less intimidating after they're broken into smaller pieces.
- Pieces are easier to code when you can focus on only the relevant parts of the problem.
- Pieces are much easier to debug than an entire program, because the number of possible inputs to a module is typically a lot smaller than the number of possible inputs to your entire program.

When you know that each separate piece works as expected, you can put them together to create your final program. The more you program, the more you'll get the hang of what would make a good, coherent piece of code.

19.2 Dividing your code into pieces

You can now start thinking about how to divide the code into small chunks of logic. The first chunk is usually to look at the input given and extract all the useful information you want to use.

- Set up the valid words related to art (as a string) and set up the tiles you're starting out with (as a string).
- Set up initializations for *start* and *end* pointers to find all valid words.
- Set up an empty tuple to add to it all valid words as you find them.
- Set up an empty tuple for the words found in your tiles.

Listing 19.1 provides the code for these initializations. You'll notice something new: a string variable that contains characters within two sets of triple quotes. The triple quotes allow you to create a string object that spans multiple lines. All characters inside the triple quotes are part of the string object, including line breaks!

Listing 19.1 Scrabble: Art Edition code for initializations

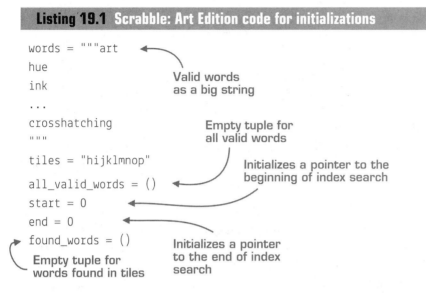

In this program, the second chunk of logic is to convert the big string of all words into a tuple containing string elements as each word. With the pseudocode written previously, all you have to do is convert the English parts to code. The one part you must be careful of is how to add the valid word to your tuple of valid words. Notice that the word you find is a single word that's added to the tuple, so you'll have to use the concatenation operator between your valid words tuple and the singleton tuple of the word that you just found.

Listing 19.2 shows the code. Pointers start and end are initially 0, pointing to the first character. Words are read as one big string, so you iterate through each character. When the character is a newline, you know that you've reached the end of a word. At that point, you save the word by indexing using the start and end pointer positions. Then, reset the pointers to be one position past the newline's position; this is the character that starts the next valid word. If the character isn't a newline, you're still reading what word it is, so move only the end pointer over.

Listing 19.2 Scrabble: Art Edition code to get all valid words

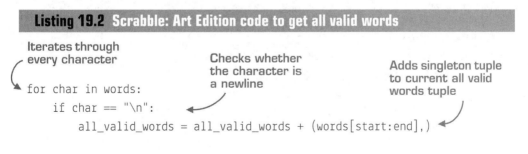

```
        start = end + 1        |  Moves start and end pointers
        end = end +1           |  to start of next word
    else:
        end = end + 1   ◄────  Moves only end pointer
```

The third and last chunk of logic is to check whether each of the valid words can be made using your tiles. As with the previous chunk, you can copy the pseudocode and fill in the blanks. A couple of interesting things to note were left unanswered in the pseudocode: (1) how to keep track of words that have multiples of the same letter and (2) how to tell when you found the full word in your tiles.

To solve (1), you can write code that removes tiles as they're matched from a valid word. With each new valid word, you can use a variable named `tiles_left`, initially all the tiles you have, that keeps track of the tiles you have left. As you iterate through each letter in a valid word and find that it's in your tiles, you can update `tiles_left` to be all the letters except the letter just found.

To solve (2), you know that if you found all the tiles and you've been removing tiles from `tiles_left` as you find them, then the number of tiles removed plus the length of the valid word are going to be equal to the number of tiles you started with.

The following listing shows the code. There's a nested loop in this code. The outer one goes through each valid word, and the inner one goes through each letter for a given valid word. As soon as you see a letter in a word that's not in your tiles, you can stop looking at this word and go on to the next one. Otherwise, keep looking. The variable `tiles_left` stores the tiles you have left after checking whether a letter from a valid word is in your tiles. Every time you find that a letter is in your tiles, you get its position and make a new `tiles_left` with all the remaining letters. The final step is to check whether you made a full, valid word with your tiles by using up all the letters. If so, add the word.

Listing 19.3   Game code to check whether valid words can be made with tiles

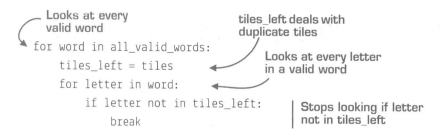

```
  ┌─ Looks at every                 tiles_left deals with
  │  valid word                     duplicate tiles
  ├► for word in all_valid_words:
         tiles_left = tiles   ◄──── Looks at every letter
         for letter in word:  ◄──── in a valid word
             if letter not in tiles_left:    │ Stops looking if letter
                 break                       │ not in tiles_left
```

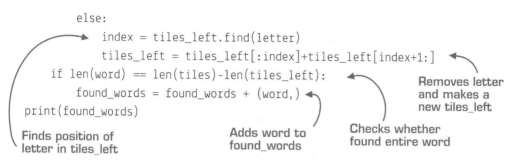

```
        else:
            index = tiles_left.find(letter)
            tiles_left = tiles_left[:index]+tiles_left[index+1:]
        if len(word) == len(tiles)-len(tiles_left):
            found_words = found_words + (word,)
    print(found_words)
```

Finds position of letter in tiles_left

Adds word to found_words

Checks whether found entire word

Removes letter and makes a new tiles_left

At the end, you print all the words you can make. But you can tweak the results you get to choose words that are only a certain length, or only words that are the longest, or words that contain a certain letter (whatever you prefer).

 ## Summary

In this lesson, my objective was to show you how to think about approaching complicated problems and to walk you through a real-life problem for which you could use programming to write a custom program for your situation. Understanding a problem before coding can be a major confidence boost. You can use pictures or simple input values and expected outputs to help refine your understanding of the problem.

When you understand the problem, you should write a few pieces of pseudocode. You can use a mixture of English and code to see whether you'll have to break up the problem further before starting to code.

The final step is to look at the visual representation and the abstractions you came up with and use these as natural divisions in your code. These smaller pieces are easier to ⟨ ⟩ dle when coding, and they also provide natural points for taking a break from coding to test and debug the code.

Here are the key takeaways:

- Understand the problem being asked by drawing a couple of relevant pictures.
- Understand the problem being asked by coming up with a few simple test cases that you can write out.
- Generalize parts of the problem to come up with formulas or the logic for accomplishing each part.
- Pseudocode can be useful, especially for writing algorithm logic that includes conditionals or looping constructs.
- Think in terms of code pieces and ask whether the code has any natural divisions—for example, initializing variables, implementing one or more algorithms, and cleanup code.

Organizing your code into reusable blocks

In the preceding unit, you learned how to write code that automatically repeats tasks. Your programs are now getting pretty complicated!

In this unit, you'll see how to start organizing your code into functions. *Functions* are reusable blocks of code that can be called upon at any point in your program to do a certain task. Functional code blocks can take in input, perform operations, and send back their results to whatever part of the program needs it. Using functions will make your code look much neater and easier to read.

In the capstone project, you'll write a program that reads in data from two files: one file has names and phone numbers of your friends, and the other file has area codes and the states that they're from. Your program will tell you the number of friends you have and the states they're from.

20

BUILDING PROGRAMS TO LAST

After reading lesson 20, you'll be able to

- Understand how a bigger task is divided into modules
- Understand why you should hide away details of complicated tasks
- Understand what it means for tasks to be dependent on or independent of other tasks

You saw how useful loops are at getting the computer to repeat a certain group of statements many times. As you're writing code, it's important to be aware of how you can harness the power of computers to make life easier for you. In this lesson, you'll take this idea a step further to see how to divide a larger program into smaller mini-programs, each one constructed to achieve a specific task.

For example, if you think about the process of building a car as a large program, you'd never build one machine that builds the entire car. That would be one extremely complicated machine. Instead, you'd build various machines and robots that focus on doing different and specific tasks: one machine might assemble the frame, one might paint the frame, and another might program the on-board computer.

20.1   Breaking a big task into smaller tasks

The main idea behind taking one task and breaking it into smaller tasks is to help you write programs more effectively. If you start with a smaller problem, you can debug it quicker. If you know that a few smaller problems work as expected, you can focus on making sure they work well together as opposed to trying to debug a large and complex one all at once.

20.1.1   Ordering an item online

Think about what happens when you order an item online. You start by putting your personal information on a website order form, and you end with getting the item delivered to your house. This entire process can be broken into a few steps, as you can see in figure 20.1:

1   You fill in a web form to place the order. The order information goes to the seller, who extracts the important details: what item, how many, and your name/address.
2   Using the item type and number, the seller (a person or a robot) finds the item in a warehouse and gives it to the packer.
3   The packer takes the item(s) and puts them in a box.
4   Using your name/address, someone else makes a shipping label.
5   The box is matched with a label, and the package is sent to the post office, which takes care of finding your house and delivering the package.

Figure 20.1 shows how to divide the big task of ordering an item into five other subtasks. Each subtask might be handled by separate people or machines and represent different specialties in the process of ordering an item online.

This example also illustrates a few other important ideas. The first idea is *task dependence/independence*.

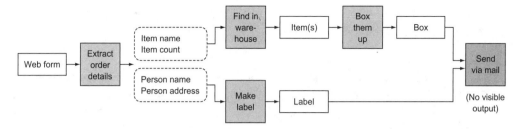

Figure 20.1   One possible way to divide the task of ordering an item online into smaller, self-contained, and reusable subtasks. Each gray box represents a task. Things to the left of the box are the inputs to a task, and things to the right are outputs of the task.

DEFINITION   A task depends on another one if it can't start before the other one completes. Two tasks are independent if they can be performed at the same time.

Some tasks depend on the completion of others, whereas some tasks are completely independent. You first do the task "extract order details." You use its output to do the "find item in warehouse" and the "make label" tasks. Notice that these last two tasks are independent of each other and can be done in any order. The task "box them up" depends on the task "find in warehouse." The "send via mail" task depends on both "box them up" and "make label" tasks to be finished before it can begin.

Quick check 20.1   Are the following actions dependent or independent?
1   (1) Eating pie and (2) writing 3.1415927 on a piece of paper.
2   (1) You don't have an internet connection and (2) you can't check your email.
3   (1) It's January 1 and (2) it's sunny.

DEFINITION   Abstraction of a task is a way to simplify the task such that you understand it by using the least amount of information; you hide all unnecessary details.

To understand what happens when you order an item online, you don't need to understand every detail behind the scenes. This brings us to the second idea: abstraction. In the warehouse example, you don't need to know the details of how to find an item in a warehouse; whether the seller employs a person to get your item or whether they use a sophisticated robot doesn't matter to you. You need to know only that you supply it an "item name" and an "item count" and that you get back the items requested.

Broadly speaking, to understand a task, you need to know only what input a task needs before starting (for example, personal information on a form) and what the task will do (for example, items show up at your door). You don't need to know the details of each step in the task to understand what it does.

> **Quick check 20.2**   For each of the following, what are possible inputs and outputs (if any)? Ask what items you need in order to perform each action and what items you get out of doing the action:
>
> 1   Writing a wedding invitation
> 2   Making a phone call
> 3   Flipping a coin
> 4   Buying a dress

The third idea is of *reusable subtasks*.

> **DEFINITION**   Reusable subtasks are tasks whose steps can be reused with different inputs to produce different output.

Sometimes you want to do a task that's slightly different from another one. In the warehouse example, you might want to find a book in the warehouse or you might want to find a bicycle. It wouldn't make sense to have a separate robot for every item that you might want to retrieve. That would lead to too many robots that kind of do the same thing! It's better to make one robot that can find any item you want. Or to make two robots: one that can retrieve big items and one for small items. This trade-off between creating subtasks while making the subtasks generic enough to be reusable can be subjective. With a little bit of practice in the next few lessons, you'll get the hang of striking a good balance.

> **Quick check 20.3**   Divide the following task into smaller subtasks: "Research the history of crayons, write a five-page paper, and give a presentation." Draw diagrams similar to figure 20.1.

20.1.2 Understanding the main points

When you deal with tasks, consider each one a *black box*.

> **DEFINITION**   A black box is a way to visualize a system that does a certain task. A black box on top of the system reminds you that you don't get to (or need to) see inside the box in order to understand what the system does.

Right now, you don't need to know how that task is accomplished; you're only trying to visualize your overall system in terms of these smaller tasks without getting bogged down in their details.

Take the task "find in warehouse" from figure 20.1 and look at figure 20.2 to see one way the task could look under the black box. Without a black box, you get more details on how the task is implemented—what steps and actions are done using the inputs. But these details don't help you understand the task itself; the details of the task implementation aren't important or necessary to understand what the task does. In some situations, seeing these details might even create more confusion. Ultimately, the inputs and outputs to the overall system are the same with and without the black box over the system.

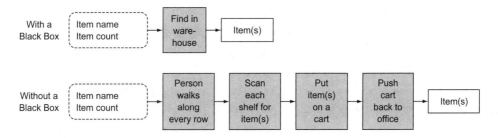

Figure 20.2 "Find in warehouse" shown with and without a black box over the task. Seeing the details of how the item is found and retrieved in the warehouse doesn't add any more understanding of the task itself.

Each task is a sequence of actions or steps. These steps should be generic enough that they can be repeated for any appropriate inputs. How do you determine what's an appropriate input? You need to document your black boxes so that whoever wants to use them knows exactly what's expected of them in terms of inputs to supply and outputs they'll get back.

20.2 Introducing black boxes of code in programming

The programs you've seen so far have been simple enough that the entire program is a black box. The tasks you've been given aren't complex enough to warrant having specialized pieces of code to do different tasks; your entire programs have been pieces of code to each do one task.

Your programs so far have mostly done the following: (1) ask the user for input, (2) do some operations, and (3) show some output. From now on, you'll find it helpful and necessary to divide the program into smaller and more manageable pieces. Each piece will solve part of the puzzle. You can put all the pieces together to implement a larger program.

In programming, these tasks are considered black boxes of code. You don't need to know how each block of code works. You only need to know what inputs go into the box, what the box is supposed to do, and what output the box gives you. You're abstracting the programming task to these three pieces of information. Each black box becomes a *module* of code.

> **DEFINITION**   A code module is a piece of code that achieves a certain task. A module is associated with input, a task, and output.

20.2.1 Using code modules

Modularity is the division of a big program into smaller tasks. You write code for each task separately, independent of other tasks. In general, each code module is supposed to stand on its own. You should be able to quickly test whether the code that you wrote for this module works. Dividing a larger task in this way makes the larger problem seem easier and will reduce the time it takes you to debug.

20.2.2 Abstracting code

You likely watch TV and use a remote to change the channel. If I gave you all the parts necessary to build a TV and a remote, would you know how to put them together? Probably not. But if I assembled the TV and the remote for you, would you know how to use the two to achieve a task such as changing the channel? Probably. This is because you know the inputs of each item, what each item is supposed to do, and what each item outputs. Figure 20.3 and table 20.1 show inputs, behavior, and output for the process of using a remote with a TV.

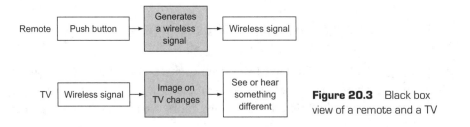

Figure 20.3   Black box view of a remote and a TV

Table 20.1 Input, behavior, and output of a TV and remote for changing the channel or the volume

Item	Input	Behavior	Output
Remote	Push a button	Generates a signal depending on the button pressed	A wireless signal
TV	A wireless signal from a remote	Image on the screen changes (whole image or a volume bar appears) or volume changes	What you see or hear changes

In programming, abstraction aims to present ideas at a *high level*. It's the process of documenting what a piece of code does, with three key bits of information: inputs, the task, and outputs. You've seen black boxes represented using this information.

Abstraction in code eliminates the details of how the code for a task/module is implemented; instead of looking at the code for a module, you look at its documentation. To document the module, you use a special type of code comment, called a *docstring*. A docstring contains the following information:

- *All inputs to the module*—Represented by variables and their types.
- *What the module is supposed to do*—Its function.
- *What output the module gives you*—This might be an object (variable) or it might be something that the module prints.

You'll see examples of code and docstrings in the next lesson.

20.2.3 Reusing code

Suppose someone gives you two numbers, and you want to be able to do four operations on the numbers: add, subtract, multiply, and divide. The code might look like the following listing.

Listing 20.1 Code to add, subtract, multiply, and divide two numbers

```
a = 1            Variables a and b are used to
b = 2            do a + b, a - b, a * b, and a / b.
print(a+b)
print(a-b)
print(a*b)
print(a/b)
```

In addition to this code, you also want to add, subtract, multiply, and divide a different pair of numbers. Then yet another pair of numbers. To write a program that does the same four operations on many pairs of numbers, you'd have to copy and paste the code in listing 20.1 and change the values of a and b a bunch of times. That sounds tedious, and looks ugly, as you can see in the following listing! Notice that the code to do the operations themselves is the same no matter what variables a and b are.

Listing 20.2 Code to add, subtract, multiply, and divide for three pairs of numbers

```
a = 1
b = 2
print(a+b)          Code to do operations
print(a-b)          on a = 1 and b = 2
print(a*b)
print(a/b)
a = 3
b = 4
print(a+b)          Code to do operations
print(a-b)          on a = 3 and b = 4
print(a*b)
print(a/b)
a = 5
b = 6
print(a+b)          Code to do operations
print(a-b)          on a = 5 and b = 6
print(a*b)
print(a/b)
```

This is where the idea of reusability comes into play. The part where you do operations and print the results of the operations is common across any pairs of numbers a and b. It doesn't make sense to copy and paste it every time. Instead, think of this common set of operations as a black box; the inputs to this black box change (as does the output). Figure 20.4 shows a black-box view of a task that can do four simple mathematical operations on any two numbers, a and b, where a and b are now inputs to the black box.

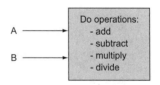

Figure 20.4   Black-box view of code that adds, subtracts, multiplies, and divides any two numbers

Now, instead of copying and pasting code in a program and changing a small part of it, you can write a black box around the code, which is reusable. The box is a *code wrapper* that adds a piece of functionality to the program. You can write programs that are more complex by reusing wrappers you already wrote. The code in listing 20.2 can be abstracted away using the black-box concept to become something like the following. Variables a and b still change, but now you're using code wrapped up in a black box. The four lines of code to do the four mathematical operations are simplified as one bundle under a black box.

Listing 20.3 Code to add, subtract, multiply, and divide for three pairs of numbers

```
a = 1
b = 2
< wrapper for operations_with_a_and_b >
a = 3
b = 4
< wrapper for operations_with_a_and_b >
a = 5
b = 6
< wrapper for operations_with_a_and_b >
```

(Not actual code) placeholder for a black box that does four operations

In the next lesson, you'll see the details on how to write the wrappers for the black boxes around code. You'll also see how to use these wrappers in your program. These wrappers are called functions.

20.3 Subtasks exist in their own environments

Think about doing a group project with two other people; you must research the history of telephones and give a presentation. You're the leader. Your job is to assign tasks to the other two people and to give the final presentation. As the leader, you don't have to do any research. Instead, you call upon the two other group members to do research, and they relay their results to you.

The other two people are like smaller worker modules helping you with the project. They're in charge of doing the research, coming up with results, and giving you a summary of their findings. This demonstrates the idea of *dividing a larger task into subtasks*.

Notice that you, as the leader, aren't concerned with the details of their research. You don't care whether they use the internet, go to the library, or interview a random group of people. You just want them to tell you their findings. The summary they give you demonstrates the idea of *abstraction of details*.

Each person doing the research might use an item that has the same name. One might read a children's picture book named *Telephone* and one might read a reference book named *Telephone*. Unless these two people pass a book to each other or communicate with each other, they have no idea what information the other is gathering. Each researcher is in their own environment, and any information they gather stays only with them—unless they share it. You can think of a code module as a mini-program to achieve a certain task. Each module exists in its own environment, independent from the environment of other modules. Any item created inside the module is specific to the module, unless explicitly passed on to another module. Modules can pass items through output and input. You'll see many examples of how this looks in code in the next lesson.

In the group project example, the group project is like the main program. Each person is like a separate module, each in charge of doing a task. Some tasks may communicate with each other, and some may not. For larger group projects, some people in the group might not need to share information with others if they're in charge of independent pieces. But all group members communicate with the leader to relay information gathered.

Each person does the research in a separate environment. They might use different objects or methods to do the research, each being useful only in the environment of that one person. The leader doesn't need to know the details of how the research takes place.

> **Quick check 20.4**   Draw a black-box system for the task of researching the telephone in a group project setting described in this section. Draw a black box for each person and indicate what each person may take as input and may output.

 ## Summary

In this lesson, my objective was to teach you why it's important to view tasks as black boxes and, ultimately, as code modules. You saw that different modules can work together to pass information to each other to achieve a larger goal. Each module lives in its own environment, and any information it creates is private to that module, unless explicitly passed around through outputs. In the bigger picture, you don't need to know the details of how modules accomplish their specific tasks. Here are the major take-aways:

- Modules are independent and in their own self-contained environments.
- Code modules should be written only once and be reusable with different inputs.
- Abstracting away module details allows you to focus on the way many modules work together to accomplish a larger task.

Let's see if you got this...

Q20.1 Divide the following task into smaller subtasks: "A couple orders at a restaurant and gets drinks and food." Draw a diagram.

21

ACHIEVING MODULARITY AND ABSTRACTION WITH FUNCTIONS

After reading lesson 21, you'll be able to

- Write code that uses functions
- Write functions with (zero or more) parameters
- Write functions that (may or may not) return a specified value
- Understand how variable values change in different function environments

In lesson 20, you saw that dividing larger tasks into modules can help you to think about problems. The process of breaking up the task leads to two important ideas: modularity and abstraction. *Modularity* is having smaller (more or less independent) problems to tackle, one by one. *Abstraction* is being able to think about the modules themselves at a higher level, without worrying about the details of implementing each. You already do this a lot in your day-to-day life; for example, you can use a car without knowing how to build one.

These modules are most useful for decluttering your larger tasks. They *abstract* certain tasks. You have to figure out the details of how to implement a task only once. Then you can reuse a task with many inputs to get outputs without having to rewrite it again.

Consider this   For each of the following scenarios, figure out what set of steps would make sense to abstract into a module:

- You're in school. Your teacher is taking attendance. She calls a name. If the student is there, that student says their name. Repeat this process for every student taking that class.
- A car manufacturer is assembling 100 cars a day. The assembly process is made up of (1) assembling the frame, (2) putting in the engine, (3) adding the electronics, and (4) painting the body. There are 25 red, 25 black, 25 white, and 25 blue cars.

Answer:

- Module: Call a name
- Module: Assemble the frame
  Module: Put in the engine
  Module: Add electronics
  Module: Paint each car

 **21.1 Writing a function**

In many programing languages, a *function* is used to stand for a module of code that achieves a simple task. When you're writing a function, you have to think about three things:

- What input the function takes in
- What operations/calculations the function does
- What the function returns

Recall the attendance example from the preceding "Consider this" exercise. Here's a slight modification of that situation, along with one possible implementation using functions. Functions start with a keyword `def`. Inside the function, you document what the function does between triple quotes—mention what the inputs are, what the function does, and what the function returns. Inside the function shown in listing 21.1, you check whether every student in the classroom roster is also physically present in the classroom, with a `for` loop. Anyone matching this criteria gets their name printed. At the end of the `for` loop, you return the string `finished taking attendance`. The word `return` is also a keyword associated with functions.

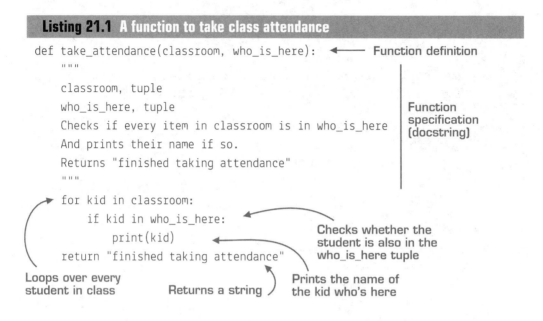

Listing 21.1 A function to take class attendance

```
def take_attendance(classroom, who_is_here):    ◄—— Function definition
    """
    classroom, tuple
    who_is_here, tuple                                       Function
    Checks if every item in classroom is in who_is_here      specification
    And prints their name if so.                             (docstring)
    Returns "finished taking attendance"
    """
    for kid in classroom:
        if kid in who_is_here:
            print(kid)
    return "finished taking attendance"
```

Loops over every student in class

Checks whether the student is also in the who_is_here tuple

Prints the name of the kid who's here

Returns a string

Listing 21.1 shows a Python function. When you tell Python that you want to define a function, you use the def keyword. After the def keyword, you name your function. In this example, the name is take_attendance. Function names abide by the same rules that variables do. After the function name, you put in parentheses all inputs to the function, separated by a comma. You end the function definition line with a colon character.

How does Python know which lines of code are part of a function and which aren't? All lines that you want to be a part of the function are indented—the same idea used with loops and conditionals.

Quick check 21.1   Write a line to define functions with the following specifications:

1   A function named set_color that takes in two inputs: a string named name (representing the name of an object) and a string named color (representing the name of a color)
2   A function named get_inverse that takes in one input: a number named num
3   A function named print_my_name that doesn't take in any inputs

21.1.1 Function basics: what the function takes in

You use functions to make your life easier. You write a function so you can reuse its guts with different inputs. This allows you to avoid having to copy and paste the implementation with only a couple of variable values changed.

All inputs to a function are variables called *parameters*, or *arguments*. More specifically, they're called *formal parameters*, or *formal arguments*, because inside the function definition these variables don't have any value. A value is assigned to them only when you make a call to a function with some values, which you'll see how to do in a later section.

> **Quick check 21.2** For the following function definitions, how many parameters does each take in?
>
>   1 def func_1(one, two, three):
>   2 def func_2():
>   3 def func_3(head, shoulders, knees, toes):

21.1.2 Function basics: what the function does

When you write the function, you write the code inside the function assuming that you have values for all the parameters to the function. The implementation of a function is just Python code, except it starts out indented. Programmers can implement the function in any way they want.

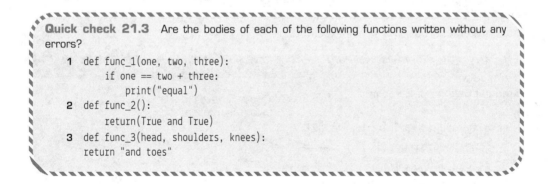

> **Quick check 21.3** Are the bodies of each of the following functions written without any errors?
>
>   1 def func_1(one, two, three):
>   if one == two + three:
>   print("equal")
>   2 def func_2():
>   return(True and True)
>   3 def func_3(head, shoulders, knees):
>   return "and toes"

21.1.3 Function basics: what the function returns

Functions should do something. You use them to repeat the same action on a slightly different input. As such, function names are generally descriptive action words and phrases: get_something, set_something, do_something, and others like these.

> **Quick check 21.4**   Come up with an appropriate name for functions that do each of the following:
>
>   1   A function that tells you the age of a tree
>   2   A function that translates what your dog is saying
>   3   A function that takes a picture of a cloud and tells you the closest animal it resembles
>   4   A function that shows you what you'll look like in 50 years

A function creates its own environment, so all variables created inside this environment aren't accessible anywhere outside the function. The purpose of a function is to perform a task and pass along its result. In Python, passing results is done using the return keyword. A line of code that contains the return keyword indicates to Python that it has finished with the code inside the function and is ready to pass the value to another piece of code in the larger program.

In listing 21.2, the program concatenates two string inputs together and returns the length of the resulting concatenation. The function takes in two strings as parameters. It adds them and stores the concatenation into the variable named word. The function returns the value len(word), which is an integer corresponding to the length of whatever value the variable word holds. You're allowed to write code inside the function after the return statement, but it won't be executed.

Listing 21.2 A function to tell you the length of the sum of two strings

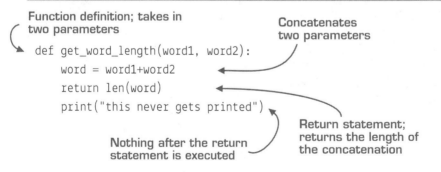

Function definition; takes in two parameters

Concatenates two parameters

```
def get_word_length(word1, word2):
    word = word1+word2
    return len(word)
    print("this never gets printed")
```

Return statement; returns the length of the concatenation

Nothing after the return statement is executed

Quick check 21.5 What does each function return? What is the type of the return variable?

```
1  def func_1(sign):
       return len(sign)
2  def func_2():
       return (True and True)
3  def func_3(head, shoulders, knees):
       return("and toes")
```

21.2 Using functions

In section 21.1, you learned how to define a function. Defining a function in your code only tells Python that there's now a function with this name that's going to do something. The function doesn't run to produce a result until it's called somewhere else in the code.

Assume that you've defined the function word_length in your code, as in listing 21.2. Now you want to use the function to tell you the number of letters in a full name. Listing 21.3 shows how to call the function. You type in the name of the function and give it *actual parameters*—variables that have a value in your program. This is in contrast to the formal parameters you saw earlier, which are used when defining the function.

Listing 21.3 How to make a call to a function

```
def word_length(word1, word2):
    word = word1+word2
    return len(word)
    print("this never gets printed")
```
Function definition
code for word_length

```
length1 = word_length("Rob", "Banks")
length2 = word_length("Barbie", "Kenn")
length3 = word_length("Holly", "Jolley")
```
Each line calls the function with different inputs and assigns the return from the function to a variable.

```
print("One name is", length1, "letters long.")
print("Another name is", length2, "letters long.")
print("The final name is", length3, "letters long.")
```
Each line prints the variables.

Figure 21.1 shows what happens with the function call word_length("Rob", "Banks"). A new *scope* (or environment) is created whenever a function call is made and is associated with that specific function call. You can think of the scope as a separate mini-program that contains its own variables, not accessible to any other part of the program.

After the scope is created, every actual parameter is mapped to the function's formal parameter, preserving the order. At this point, the formal parameters have values. As the function progresses and executes its statements, any variables that are created exist only in the scope of this function call.

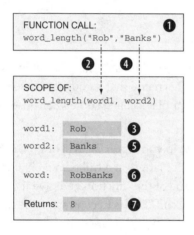

Figure 21.1   What happens when you make a function call in ❶? With ❷ and ❸, the first parameter is mapped in the function's scope. With ❹ and ❺, the second parameter is mapped. ❻ is another variable created inside the function. ❼ is the return value. After the function returns, the function scope disappears along with all its variables.

21.2.1 Returning more than one value

You may have noticed that a function can return only one object. But you can "trick" the function into returning more than one value by using tuples. Each item in the tuple is a different value. This way, the function returns only one object (a tuple), but the tuple has as many different values (through its elements) as you want. For example, you can have a function that takes in the name of a country and returns one tuple whose first element is the latitude of the country's center and whose second element is the longitude of the country's center.

Then, when you call the function, you can assign each item in the returned tuple to a different variable, as in the following listing. The function add_sub adds and subtracts the two parameters, and returns one tuple consisting of these two values. When you call the function, you assign the return result to another tuple (a,b) so that a gets the value of the addition and b gets the value of the subtraction.

Listing 21.4 Returning a tuple

```
def add_sub(n1, n2):
    add = n1 + n2              Returns a tuple with
    sub = n1 - n2              addition and
                              subtraction values
    return (add, sub)    ←

(a, b) = add_sub(3,4)    ←——— Assigns result to a tuple
```

Quick check 21.6

1 Complete the following function that tells you whether the number and suit match the secret values and the amount won:

```
def guessed_card(number, suit, bet):
    money_won = 0
    guessed = False
    if number == 8 and suit == "hearts":
        money_won = 10*bet
        guessed = True
    else:
        money_won = bet/10
    # write one line to return two things:
    # how much money you won and whether you
    # guessed right or not
```

2 Use the function you wrote in [1]. If executed in the following order, what do the following lines print?

- `print(guessed_card(8, "hearts", 10))`
- `print(guessed_card("8", "hearts", 10))`
- `guessed_card(10, "spades", 5)`
- `(amount, did_win) = guessed_card("eight", "hearts", 80)`
  `print(did_win)`
  `print(amount)`

21.2.2 Functions without a return statement

You may want to write functions that print a message and don't explicitly return any value. Python allows you to skip the return statement inside a function. If you don't write a return statement, Python automatically returns the value None in the function. None is a special object of type NoneType that stands for the absence of a value.

Look through the example code in listing 21.5. You're playing a game with kids. They're hiding, and you can't see them. You call their names in order:

- If they come out from their hiding spot to you, that's like having a function that returns an object to the caller.
- If they yell out "here" and don't show themselves, that's like having a function that doesn't return the kid object but does print something to the user. You need to get an object back from them, so they all agree that if they don't show themselves, they throw at you a piece of paper with the word *None* written on it.

Listing 21.5 defines two functions. One prints the parameter given (and implicitly returns None). Another returns the value of the parameter given. There are four things going on here:

- The first line in the main program that's executed is say_name("Dora"). This line prints Dora because the function say_name has a print statement inside it. The result of the function call isn't printed.
- The next line, show_kid("Ellie"), doesn't print anything because nothing is printed inside the function show_kid, nor is the result of the function call printed.
- The next line, print(say_name("Frank")), prints two things: Frank and None. It prints Frank because the function say_name has a print statement inside it. None is printed because the function say_name has no return statement (so by default returns None), and the result of the return is printed with the print around say_name("Frank").
- Finally, print(show_kid("Gus")), prints Gus because show_kid returns the name passed in, and the print around show_kid("Gus") prints the returned value.

Listing 21.5 Function with and without a return

```
def say_name(kid):        ←———— Takes in a string with kid name
    print(kid)      ←————  Doesn't explicitly return anything,
                           so Python returns None

def show_kid(kid):        ←———— Takes in a string with kid name
    return kid      ←———— Returns a string

say_name("Dora")          ←———— Prints "Dora" to the console
show_kid("Ellie")         ←———— Doesn't print anything to the console
print(say_name("Frank"))  ←———— Prints Frank, then None, to the console
print(show_kid("Gus"))    ←———— Prints Gus to the console
```

One particularly interesting line is print(say_name("Frank")). The function call itself prints the name of the kid, Frank. Because there's no return statement, Python returns None automatically. The line print(say_name("Frank")) is then replaced with the return value to give print(None), which then prints the value None to the console. It's important to understand that None isn't an object of type string. It's the only value for an object of type NoneType. Figure 21.2 shows which returned value replaces each function call.

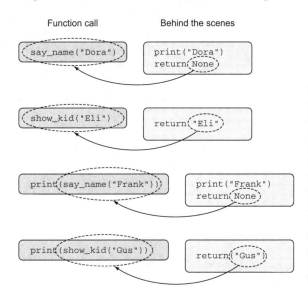

Figure 21.2 Four combinations, representing calling a function that doesn't return a value, calling a function that returns something, printing the result of calling a function that doesn't return a value, and printing the result of calling a function that returns something. The black box is the function call, and the gray box is what happens behind the scenes when the function is called. If the function doesn't have an explicit return statement, return None is automatically added. The black dotted line indicates the value that will replace the function call.

Quick check 21.7 Given the following function and variable initializations, what will each line print, if executed in the following order?

```
def make_sentence(who, what):
    doing = who+" is "+what
    return doing

def show_story(person, action, number, thing):
    what = make_sentence(person, action)
    num_times = str(number) + " " + thing
    my_story = what + " " + num_times
    print(my_story)

who = "Hector"
what = "eating"
thing = "bananas"
number = 8
  1  sentence = make_sentence(who, thing)
  2  print(make_sentence(who, what))
  3  your_story = show_story(who, what, number, thing)
  4  my_story = show_story(sentence, what, number, thing)
  5  print(your_story)
```

21.3 Documenting your functions

In addition to functions being a way to modularize your code, they're also a way to abstract chunks of code. You saw how abstraction is achieved by passing in parameters so that the function can be used more generally. Abstraction is also achieved through function *specifications*, or *docstrings*. You can quickly read the docstrings to get a sense of what inputs the function takes in, what it is supposed to do, and what it returns. Scanning the text of a docstring is much quicker than reading the function implementation.

Here's an example of a docstring for a function whose implementation you saw in listing 21.1:

```
def take_attendance(classroom, who_is_here):
    """

    classroom, tuple of strings
    who_is_here, tuple of strings
    Prints the names of all kids in class who are also in who_is_here
    Returns a string, "finished taking attendance"
    """
```

A docstring starts inside the function, indented. The triple quotes """ denote the start and end of the docstring. A docstring includes the following:

- Each input parameter name and type
- A brief overview of what the function does
- The meaning of the return value and the type

Summary

In this lesson, my objective was for you to write simple Python functions. Functions take in input, perform an action, and return a value. They're one way that you can write reusable code in your programs. Functions are modules of code written in a generic way. In your programs, you can call a function with specific values to give you back a value. The returned value can then be used in your code. You write function specifications to document your work so that you don't have to read an entire piece of code to figure out what the function does. Here are the major takeaways:

- Function definitions are just that—definitions. The function is executed only when it's called somewhere else in the code.

- A function call is replaced with the value returned.
- Functions return one object, but you can use tuples to return more than one value.
- Function docstrings document and abstract details of the function implementation.

Let's see if you got this…

Q21.1

1 Write a function named `calculate_total` that takes in two parameters: a float named `price`, and an integer named `percent`. The function calculates and returns a new number representing the price plus the tip: total = price + percent * price.

2 Make a function call to your function with a price of 20 and a percent of 15.

3 Complete the following code in a program to use your function:

```
my_price = 78.55
my_tip = 20
# write a line to calculate and save the new total
# write a line to print a message with the new total
```

22

ADVANCED OPERATIONS WITH FUNCTIONS

After reading lesson 22, you'll be able to

- Pass functions (as an object) as a parameter to another function
- Return a function (as an object) from another function
- Understand which variables belong to which scope based on certain rules

Before formally learning about functions in lesson 21, you saw and used functions in simple code. Here are some of the functions you've been using already:

- `len()`–For example, `len("coffee")`
- `range()`–For example, `range(4)`
- `print()`–For example, `print("Witty message")`
- `abs(),sum(),max(),min(),round(),pow()`–For example, `max(3,7,1)`
- `str(),int(),float(),bool()`–For example, `int(4.5)`

Consider this For each of the following function calls, how many parameters does the function take in, and what's the value of type returned?

- `len("How are you doing today?")`
- `max(len("please"), len("pass"), len("the"), len("salt"))`
- `str(525600)`
- `sum((24, 7, 365))`

Answer:

- Takes in one parameter, returns 24
- Takes in four parameters, returns 6
- Takes in one parameter, returns "525600"
- Takes in one parameter, returns 396

 ## 22.1 Thinking about functions with two hats

Recall that a function definition defines a series of commands that can be called later in a program with different inputs. Think of this idea like building a car and driving a car: someone has to build a car in the first place, but after they build it, the car sits in a garage until someone wants to use it. And someone who wants to use the car doesn't need to know how to build one, and that person can use it more than once. It may help to think about functions from two perspectives: someone writing a function, and someone who wants to use a function. Sections 22.1.1 and 22.1.2 briefly review the main ideas you should have picked up in the previous lesson.

22.1.1 Writer hat

You write the function in a general way so that it can work with various values. You generalize the function by pretending that the inputs given are named variables. The inputs are called *formal parameters*. You do the operations inside the function, assuming you have values for these parameters.

Parameters and variables defined inside a function exist only in the scope (or environment) of the function. The function scope exists from the time that the function is called to the time that the function returns a value.

The way you abstract a module is by a function specification, or *docstring*. A docstring is a multiline comment starting with triple quotes and ending with triple quotes, `"""`.

Inside the docstring, you typically write (1) what inputs the function is supposed to take in and their type, (2) what the function is supposed to do, and (3) what the function returns. Assuming the inputs are according to the specification, the function is assumed to behave correctly and guaranteed to return a value according to the specification.

22.1.2 User hat

Using a function is easy. A function is called in another statement in your main program code. When you call a function, you call it with values. These values are the *actual parameters* and replace the function's formal parameters. The function performs the operations it's supposed to by using the actual parameter values.

The output from the function is what the function returns. The function return is given back to whichever statement called the function. The expression for the function call is replaced with the value of the return.

22.2 Function scope

The phrase "what happens in Vegas stays in Vegas" is an accurate representation of what happens behind the scenes during a function call; what happens in a function code block stays in a function code block. Function parameters exist only within the scope of the function. You can have the same name in different function scopes because they point to different objects. You get an error if you try to access a variable outside the function in which it's defined. Python can be in only one scope at a time and knows only about variables whose scope it's currently in.

22.2.1 Simple scoping example

It's possible for a function to create a variable with the same name as another variable in another function, or even in the main program. Python knows that these are separate objects; they just happen to have the same name.

Suppose you're reading two books, and each has a character named *Peter*. In each book, Peter is a different person, even though you're using the same name. Take a look at listing 22.1. The code prints two numbers. The first number is 5, and the second is 30. In this code, you see two variables named `peter` defined. But these variables exist in different scopes: one in the scope of the function `fairy_tale`, and one in the main program scope.

Listing 22.1 Defining variables with the same name in different scopes

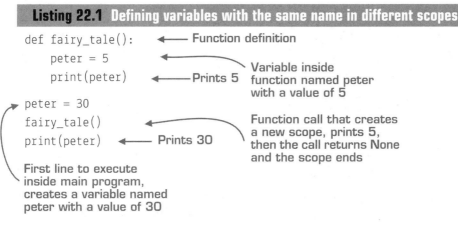

22.2.2 Scoping rules

Here are the rules for deciding which variable to use (if you have more than one with the same name in your program):

- Look in the current scope for a variable with that name. If it's there, use that variable. If it's not, look in the scope of whatever line called the function. It's possible that another function called it.
- If there's a variable with that name in the caller's scope, use that.
- Successively keep looking in outer scopes until you get to the main program scope, also called the *global scope*. You can't look further outside of the global scope. All variables that exist in the global scope are called *global variables*.
- If a variable with that name isn't in the global scope, show an error that the variable doesn't exist.

The code in the next four listings show a few scenarios for variables with the same name in different scopes. There are a couple of interesting things to note:

- You can *access* a variable inside a function without defining it inside a function. As long as a variable with that name exists in the main program scope, you won't get an error.
- You can't *assign* a value to a variable inside a function without defining it inside the function first.

In the following listing, function e() shows that you can create and access a new variable with the same name as a variable in your global scope.

Listing 22.2 A function that initializes a variable

```
def e():
    v = 5
    print(v)        ◀────── Uses v from function

v = 1                        Function call OK; uses
e()             ◀──          v inside the function
```

In the next listing, function f() shows that it's OK to access a variable even if it's not created inside the function, because a variable of that same name exists in the global scope.

Listing 22.3 A function that accesses a variable outside its scope

```
def f():
    print(v)     ◀────── Access variables outside scope

v = 1
f()          ◀────── Function call OK; uses v from the program
```

In the following listing, function g() shows that it's OK to do operations with variables not defined in the function, because you're only accessing their values and not trying to change them.

Listing 22.4 A function that accesses more than one variable outside its scope

```
def g():
    print(v+x)      ◀────── Access only variables

v = 1                   Function call OK; uses v and
x = 2                   x from the global scope
g()         ◀──
```

In the following listing, function h() shows that you're trying to add to the value to a variable inside the function without defining it first. This leads to an error.

Listing 22.5 A function that tries to modify a variable defined outside its scope

```
                        Performs an operation on
def h():            ╱   variable v before defining
    v += 5      ◀──     it inside the function

v = 1
h()          ◀────── Function call gives an error
```

Functions are great because they break your problem into smaller chunks rather than having hundreds or thousands of lines to look at all at once. But functions also introduce scope; with this, you can have variables with the same name in different scopes without them interfering with each other. You need to be mindful of the scope you're currently looking at.

> **Thinking like a programmer**
> You should start to get in the habit of *tracing* through a program. To trace through a program, you should go line by line, draw the scope you're in, and write any variables and their values currently in the scope.

The following listing shows a simple function definition and a couple of function calls. In the code, you have one function that returns "odd" if a number is odd, and "even" if it's even. The code within the function doesn't print anything, it only returns the result. The code starts running at the line num = 4 because everything above it is a function definition. This variable is in the global scope. The function call odd_or_even(num) creates a scope and maps the value 4 to the formal parameter in the function definition. You do all the calculations and return "even" because the remainder when 4 is divided by 2 is 0. print(odd_or_even(num)) prints the returned value, "even". After printing, you calculate odd_or_even(5). The return from this function call isn't used (isn't printed), and no operations are performed on it.

Listing 22.6 Functions showing different scoping rules

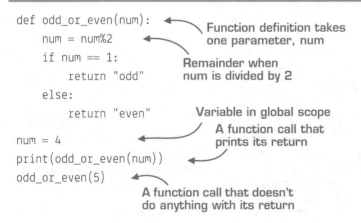

```
def odd_or_even(num):          ← Function definition takes
    num = num%2                   one parameter, num
    if num == 1:          Remainder when
        return "odd"      num is divided by 2
    else:
        return "even"     Variable in global scope
                          A function call that
num = 4                   prints its return
print(odd_or_even(num))
odd_or_even(5)
        A function call that doesn't
        do anything with its return
```

Figure 22.1 shows how you might draw a trace of a program. The one tricky thing is that you have two variables named num. But because they're in different scopes, they don't interfere with each other.

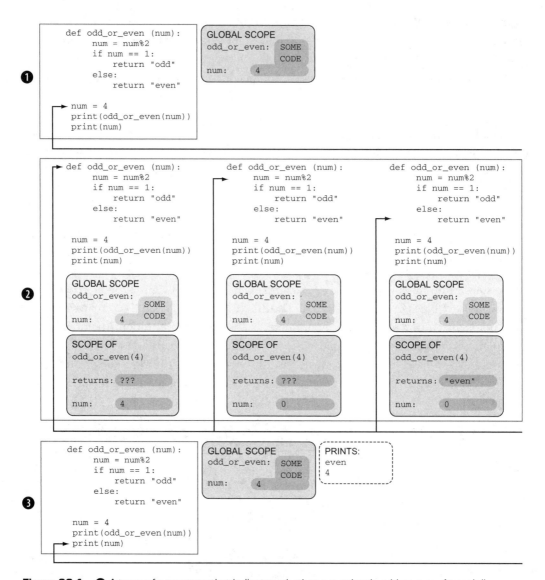

Figure 22.1 ❶ A trace of a program that indicates whether a number is odd or even. At each line, you draw the scope you're in along with all variables existing in that scope. In ❶ you start the program and are at the line with the arrow. After that line executes, the scope of the program contains a function definition and a variable named num. In ❷ you just made the function call print(odd_or_even(num)). You create a new scope. Notice that the global scope still exists but isn't in focus right now. In the left panel of ❷, you have the parameter num as a variable with the value 4. In the middle panel of ❷ you're executing the line num=num%2 inside the function call and reassign, only in the function call scope, the variable num to be 0. In the right panel of ❷ you make the decision and return "even". In ❸ the function returned "even" and the scope of the function call disappeared. You're back in the global scope and perform the two prints. Printing the function call shows "even" and printing the num shows 4 because you're using the num variable from the global scope.

```
def f(a, b):
    x = a+b
    y = a-b
    print(x*y)
    return x/y

a = 1
b = 2
x = 5
y = 6
  1  print(f(x, y))
  2  print(f(a, b))
  3  print(f(x, a))
  4  print(f(y, b))
```

22.3 Nesting functions

Just as you can have nested loops, you can have nested functions. These are function definitions inside other functions. Python knows only about an inner function inside the scope of the outer function—and only when the outer function is being called.

Listing 22.7 shows a nested function stop() inside the function sing(). The global scope is the main program scope. It has one function definition for sing(). The function definition at this point is just some code. The function doesn't execute until you make a function call. When you try to say stop() in the main program scope, you get an error.

Inside the definition of sing(), you define another function named stop() that also contains code. You don't care what that code is until you make a function call. Inside sing(), the stop() call doesn't cause an error because stop() is defined inside sing(). As far as the main program is concerned, only function sing is its scope.

Listing 22.7 Nesting functions

```
def sing():
    def stop(line):                    Function definition
        print("STOP",line)             inside sing()
    stop("it's hammer time")
    stop("in the name of love")        Calls inside sing() to
    stop("hey, what's that sound")     the stop function
```

```
stop()
sing()        Error because stop() doesn't
              exist in the global scope
```

Quick check 22.2   For the following code, what will each line print?

```
def add_one(a, b):
    x = a+1
    y = b+1
    def mult(a,b):
        return a*b
    return mult(x,y)

a = 1
b = 2
x = 5
y = 6
  1  print(add_one(x, y))
  2  print(add_one(a, b))
  3  print(add_one(x, a))
  4  print(add_one(y, b))
```

22.4 Passing functions as parameters

You've seen objects of type int, string, float, and Boolean. In Python, everything is an object, so any function you define is an object of type function. Any object can be passed around as a parameter to a function, even other functions!

You want to write code to make one of two sandwiches. A BLT sandwich tells you it has bacon, lettuce, and tomato in it. A breakfast sandwich tells you it has egg and cheese in it. In listing 22.8, blt and breakfast are both functions that return a string.

A function sandwich takes in a parameter named kind_of_sandwich. This parameter is a function object. Inside the sandwich function, you can call kind_of_sandwich as usual by adding parentheses after it.

When you call the sandwich function, you call it with a function object as a parameter. You give it the name of a function for the sandwich you want to make. You don't put parentheses after blt or breakfast as the argument because you want to pass the function object itself. If you use blt() or breakfast(), this will be a string object because this is a function call that returns a string.

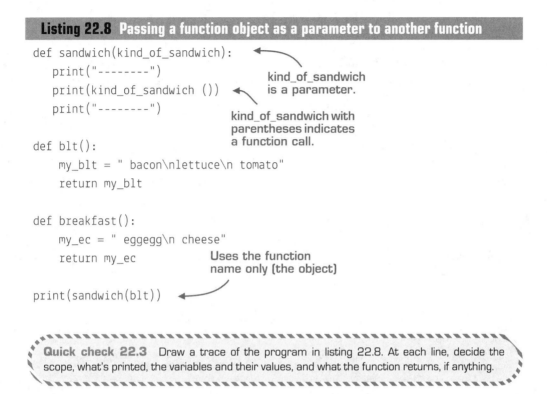

Listing 22.8 Passing a function object as a parameter to another function

```python
def sandwich(kind_of_sandwich):
    print("--------")
    print(kind_of_sandwich ())
    print("--------")


def blt():
    my_blt = " bacon\nlettuce\n tomato"
    return my_blt


def breakfast():
    my_ec = " eggegg\n cheese"
    return my_ec


print(sandwich(blt))
```

kind_of_sandwich is a parameter.

kind_of_sandwich with parentheses indicates a function call.

Uses the function name only (the object)

> **Quick check 22.3** Draw a trace of the program in listing 22.8. At each line, decide the scope, what's printed, the variables and their values, and what the function returns, if anything.

22.5 Returning a function

Because a function is an object, you can also have functions that return other functions. This is useful when you want to have specialized functions. You typically return functions when you have nested functions. To return a function object, you return only the function name. Recall that putting parentheses after the function name makes a function call, which you don't want to do.

Returning a function is useful when you want to have specialized functions inside other functions. In listing 22.9, you have a function named grumpy, and it prints a message. Inside the function grumpy, you have another function named no_n_times. It prints a message, and then inside that function you define another function, named no_m_more_times. The innermost function no_m_more_times prints a message and then prints no n + m times.

You're using the fact that no_m_more_times is nested inside no_n_times and therefore knows about the variable n, without having to send that variable in as a parameter.

The function no_n_times returns the function no_m_more_times itself. The function grumpy returns the function no_n_times.

When you make a function call with grumpy()(4)(2), you work from left to right and replace function calls as you go with whatever they return. Notice the following:

- You don't have to print the return of grumpy because you're printing things inside the functions.
- A function call to grumpy() gets replaced with whatever grumpy returns, which is the function no_n_times.
- Now no_n_times(4) is replaced with whatever it returns, which is the function no_m_more_times.
- Finally, no_m_more_times(2) is the last function call, which prints out all the nos.

Listing 22.9 **Returning a function object from another function**

```
def grumpy():                        ←——— Function definition
    print("I am a grumpy cat:")
    def no_n_times(n):               ←——— Nested function definition
        print("No", n,"times...")
        def no_m_more_times(m):             ←——— Nested function definition
            print("...and no", m,"more times")
            for i in range(n+m):      ←——  Loop to print the word
                print("no")                "no" n + m times
        return no_m_more_times        ←——
    return no_n_times  ←                  Function no_n_times
                                          returns the function
grumpy()(4)(2)  ←                         no_m_more_times

Function call in  /    Function grumpy returns
main program          the function no_n_times
```

This example shows that the function call is left-associative, so you replace the calls left to right with the functions they return. For example, you use f()()()() if you have four nested functions, each returning a function.

Quick check 22.4 Draw a trace of the program in listing 22.9. At each line, decide the scope, what gets printed, the variables and their values, and what the function returns, if anything.

 **22.6 Summary**

In this lesson, my objective was to teach you about the subtleties of functions. These ideas only begin to scratch the surface of what you can do with functions. You created functions that had variables with the same name and saw that they didn't interfere with each other because of function scopes. You learned that functions are Python objects and that they can be passed in as parameters to or returned by other functions. Here are the major takeaways:

- You've been using built-in functions already, and now you understand why you wrote them in that way. They take parameters and return a value after doing a computation.
- You can nest functions by defining them inside other functions. The nested functions exist only in the scope of the enclosing function.
- You can pass around function objects like any other object. You can use them as parameters, and you can return them.

Let's see if you got this…

Q22.1 Fill the missing parts to the following code:

```python
def area(shape, n):
    # write a line to return the area
    # of a generic shape with a parameter of n

def circle(radius):
    return 3.14*radius**2
def square(length):
    return length*length

print(area(circle,5))  # example function call
```

1 Write a line to use area() to find the area of a circle with a radius of 10.
2 Write a line to use area() to find the area of a square with sides of length 5.
3 Write a line to use area() to find the area of a circle with diameter of length 4.

Q22.2 Fill the missing parts to the following code:

```python
def person(age):
    print("I am a person")
    def student(major):
        print("I like learning")
```

```
def vacation(place):
    print("But I need to take breaks")
    print(age,"|",major,"|",place)
# write a line to return the appropriate function
# write a line to return the appropriate function
```

For example, the function call

```
person(12)("Math")("beach")  # example function call
```

should print this:

```
I am a person
I like learning
But I need to take breaks
12 | Math | beach
```

1 Write a function call with age of 29, major of "CS", and vacation place of "Japan".

2 Write a function call so that the last line of its printout is as follows:

```
23 | "Law" | "Florida"
```

23

CAPSTONE PROJECT: ANALYZE YOUR FRIENDS

After reading lesson 23, you'll be able to

- Write a function to read a file line by line
- Save numbers and strings from the file in variables
- Write a function to analyze the stored information

The only two ways you've seen so far to input data are to (1) to predefine variables in your program or (2) to ask the user to input data one-by-one. But when users have a lot of information to input into your program, you can't expect them to enter it in real time. It's often useful to have them give you the information in a file.

Computers are great at doing many computations quickly. A natural use for computers is to write programs that can read in large amounts of data from files and to perform simple analyses on that data. For example, you can export your own data from Microsoft Excel spreadsheets as files, or you can download data (such as weather or election data). After you're given a file structured in a certain way, you can use knowledge of the structure to write a program to sequentially read and store the information from the file. With the data stored in your program, you can analyze it (for example, to find averages, maximums/minimums, and duplicates).

In addition to reviewing the concepts in this unit, this lesson will show you how to read data from a file.

THE PROBLEM   Write a program that reads input from a file in a specific format, regarding all your friends' names and phone numbers. Your program should store that information and analyze it in some way. For example, you can show the user where their friends live based on the area code of the phone numbers, and the number of states where they live.

23.1 Reading a file

You'll write a function named read_file to go through each line and put the information from each line into a variable.

23.1.1 File format

This function assumes that the user gives you information in the following format, with a different piece of information on each line:

```
Friend 1 name
Friend 1 phone number
Friend 2 name
Friend 2 phone number
<and so on>
```

It's important that each piece of information is on a separate line, implying that your program will have a newline character as the final character on each line. Python has a way to deal with this, as you'll soon see. Knowing this is the format, you can read the file line by line. You store every other line, starting with the first line, in a tuple. Then you store every other line, starting with the second line, in another tuple. The tuples look like this:

```
(Friend 1 name, Friend 2 name, <and so on>)
(Friend 1 phone, Friend 2 phone, <and so on>)
```

Notice that at index 0, both tuples store information regarding Friend 1; at index 1, both tuples store info regarding Friend 2, and so on.

You have to go through every line. This should trigger the idea to use a loop that goes through each line. The loop reads each line from the file as a string.

23.1.2 The newline character

A special hidden character is at the end of every line, the newline character. The representation of this character is \n. To see the effect of this character, type the following in your console:

```
print("no newline")
```

The console prints the phrase no newline and then gives you the prompt to type something in again. Now type in the following:

```
print("yes newline\n")
```

Now you see an extra empty line between what was printed and the next prompt. This is because the special character combination of the backslash and the letter *n* tells Python that you want a new line.

23.1.3 Remove the newline character

When you're reading a line from the file, the line contains all the characters you can see plus the newline character. You want to store everything except that special character, so you need to remove it before storing the information.

Because each line you read in is a string, you can use a string method on it. The easiest thing to do is to replace every occurrence of \n with the empty string "". This will effectively remove the newline character.

The following listing shows how to replace a newline character with an empty string and save the result into a variable.

Listing 23.1 Remove the newline character

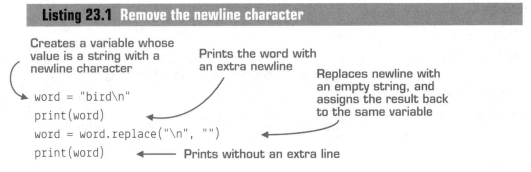

Creates a variable whose value is a string with a newline character

Prints the word with an extra newline

Replaces newline with an empty string, and assigns the result back to the same variable

```
word = "bird\n"
print(word)
word = word.replace("\n", "")
print(word)
```

Prints without an extra line

> **Thinking like a programmer**
> What's intuitive to one programmer may not be to another. Often there's more than one way to write a piece of code. When faced with writing a line of code, browse the Python documentation to see what functions you can use before writing your own. For example, listing 23.1 replaces newline characters with the empty space character, using `replace` on strings. The Python documentation has another function that would be appropriate to use: `strip`. The `strip` function removes all instances of a certain character from the beginning and end of a string. The following two lines do the same thing:
>
> ```
> word = word.replace("\n", "")
> word = word.strip("\n")
> ```

23.1.4 Using tuples to store information

Now that each line is cleaned up of newline characters, you're left with the pure data, as strings. The next step is to store it in variables. Because you'll have a collection of data, you should use one tuple to store all the names together and another tuple to store all the phone numbers together.

Every time you read in a line, add the new information to the tuple. Recall that adding an item to a tuple gives you a tuple that contains the old information, with the thing you just added at the end of the tuple. Now you have what the old tuple had, plus the new information you just read in that line. Figure 23.1 shows which lines of the file are stored in which tuple. In the next section, you'll see the code for this.

23.1.5 What to return

You're writing a function that does the simple task of reading a file, organizing the information, and giving the organized information back. Now that you have two tuples (one with all the names and the other with all the phone numbers, as shown in figure 23.1), return a tuple of tuples, like so:

```
((Friend1 Name, Friend2 Name, ...), (Friend1 phone, Friend2 phone, ...))
 --------------------------------    ----------------------------------
          one tuple                             other tuple
```

You have to return a tuple of tuples because a function can return only one thing. Recall from lesson 21 that returning a tuple with multiple elements allows you to get around this!

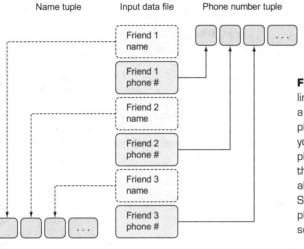

Figure 23.1 The input data contains lines of data. The first line is the name of a friend, and the second is that friend's phone number. The third is the name of your second friend, and the fourth is their phone number, and so on. Starting from the first line, take every other line to store all the names of your friends in a tuple. Starting from the second line, take all the phone numbers and store those in a separate tuple.

The following listing shows you the code for the function to read in the data. The function `read_file` takes in a file object; you'll see what this means later in this lesson. It iterates through every line in the file and strips the line of the newlines. If you're looking at an even numbered line, you add to your tuple of names. If you're looking at an odd numbered line, you add to your tuple of phone numbers. In both cases, notice that you're adding a singleton tuple, so you need to put an extra comma in the parentheses. Lastly, the function returns a tuple of tuples so that you can hand off the information parsed from the file.

Listing 23.2 Read names and phone numbers from a file

```
def read_file(file):
    """

    file, a file object
    Starting from the first line, it reads every 2 lines
    and stores them in a tuple.
    Starting from the second line, it reads every 2 lines
    and stores them in a tuple.
    Returns a tuple of the two tuples.
    """

    first_every_2 = ()
    second_every_2 = ()
```

docstring

Empty tuples for names and phone numbers

```
line_count = 0                  ◀────── Counter for line number
for line in file:               ◀────── Loops through every line
    stripped_line = line.replace("\n", "")  ◀──── Removes newline character
    if line_count%2 == 0:               ◀────── Odd-numbered lines
        first_every_2 += (stripped_line,)  ◀──── Adds to the names tuple
    elif line_count%2 == 1:            ◀──────── Even-numbered lines
        second_every_2 += (stripped_line,)  ◀────── Adds to the phone tuple
    line_count += 1                  ◀────── Increments line number
return (first_every_2, second_every_2)  ◀────── Returns a tuple of tuples
```

23.2 Sanitizing user inputs

Now you have the information the user gave you, in two tuples: one tuple contains people names, and the other tuple contains phone numbers.

You never specified the format of phone numbers, so the user can have a file that contains phone numbers in any format; users might have dashes, parentheses, spaces, or any other weird characters. Before you can analyze the numbers, you have to get them into a consistent form. This means removing all the special characters and leaving the digits all together.

This seems like a good job for a function. The function sanitize does this by using the replace method you learned about to replace all the special characters with the empty string "". The following listing shows a possible implementation. You iterate through each string and replace unnecessary characters that might be found in phone numbers. After removing dashes, spaces, and parentheses, you put the cleaned-up phone number (as a string) into the new tuple that you return.

Listing 23.3 Remove spaces, dashes, and parentheses from phone numbers

```
def sanitize(some_tuple):
    """

    phones, a tuple of strings
    Removes all spaces, dashes, and open/closed parentheses
    in each string
    Returns a tuple with cleaned up string elements
    """

    clean_string = ()       ◀─────  Replaces unnecessary
                                     characters with empty string
```

```
for st in some_tuple:
    st = st.replace(" ", "")
    st = st.replace("-", "")
    st = st.replace("(", "")
    st = st.replace(")", "")
    clean_string += (st,)
return clean_string
```

Empty tuple

Adds cleaned number to new tuple

Returns new tuple

23.3 Testing and debugging what you have so far

The remainder of the larger task is to do analysis on this data. Before moving on to this, it's a good idea to do a little testing (and debugging, if necessary) to make sure the two functions you wrote work well together.

At this point, you have two functions that do a couple of interesting tasks. Recall that functions don't run until they're called somewhere in a larger program. Now you'll write code that integrates these functions together.

23.3.1 File objects

When you're working with files, you have to create file *objects*. As with other objects you've seen so far, Python knows how to work with these file objects to do specialized operations. For example, in the read_file function you wrote, you were able to write for line in file to iterate over each line in a specific file object.

23.3.2 Writing a text file with names and phone numbers

In Spyder, create a new file. Type in a few lines of data in the format that read_file expects. Start with a name; on the next line, put in a phone number, then another name, then another phone number, and so on. For example,

```
Bob
000 123-4567
Mom Bob
(890) 098-7654
Dad Bob
321-098-0000
```

Now save the file as friends.txt or any other name you want. Make sure you save the file in the same folder as the Python program you're writing. This file will be read by your program, so it's a plaintext file.

23.3.3 Opening files for reading

You create file objects by opening a filename. You use a function named open, which takes in a string with the filename you want to read. The file must be located in the same folder as your .py program file.

Listing 23.4 shows how to open a file, run the functions you wrote, and check that the functions return the correct thing. You use the open function to open a file named friends.txt. This creates a file object, which is the parameter to the function read_file(). read_file() returns a tuple of tuples. You store the return in two tuples: one for the names and one for the phones.

You can test that your sanitize function works by calling it with the phones tuple as its parameter. At each step, you can print variables and see that the output is as you expect it to be.

Listing 23.4 **Read names and phone numbers from a file**

```
friends_file = open('friends.txt')          ←——— Opens the file
(names, phones) = read_file(friends_file)    ←——— Calls function

print(names)                                 Outputs printed
print(phones)                                to the user
clean_phones = sanitize(phones)              ←——— Sees whether your function worked

print(clean_phones)                          ←——— Outputs printed to the user
friends_file.close()                         ←——— Closes the file
```

It's good practice to test functions one by one before moving on to write more. Occasionally, you should test to make sure that the data being passed around from the output of one function to the input of another function works well together.

23.4 Reusing functions

The great thing about functions is that they're reusable. You don't have to write them to work for a specific kind of data; for example, if you write a program that adds two numbers, you can call the function to add two numbers representing temperatures, or ages, or weights.

You already wrote a function to read in data. You used the function to read in and store names and phone numbers into two tuples. You can reuse that function to read in a different set of data organized in the same format.

Because the user is going to give you phone numbers, suppose you have a file that contains area codes and the states to which they belong. The lines in this file are going to be in the same format as the file containing people names and their phone numbers:

```
Area code 1
State 1
Area code 2
State 2
<and so on>
```

The first few lines of a file called map_areacodes_states.txt are as follows:

```
201
New Jersey
202
Washington D.C.
203
Connecticut
204
<and so on>
```

With this file, you can call the same function, read_data, and store the returned value:

```
map_file = open('map_areacodes_states.txt')
(areacodes, places) = read_file(map_file)
```

23.5 Analyzing the information

Now it's time to put everything together. You gathered all your data and stored it into variables. The data you now have is as follows:

- Names of people
- Phone numbers corresponding to each name
- Area codes
- States corresponding to the area codes

23.5.1 The specification

Write a function named `analyze_friends` that takes in your four tuples: the first is the names of friends, the second is their phone numbers, the third is all the area codes, and the fourth is all the places corresponding to the area codes.

The function prints information. It doesn't return anything. Say the friends given in the file are as follows:

```
Ana
801-456-789
Ben
609 4567890
Cory
(206)-345-2619
Danny
6095648765
```

Then the function will print this:

```
You have 4 friends!
They live in ('Utah', 'New Jersey', 'Washington')
```

Notice that even though you have four friends, two live in the same state, so you'll print only the unique states. The following is the docstring of the function you'll write:

```
def analyze_friends(names, phones, all_areacodes, all_places):
    """

    names, a tuple of friend names
    phones, a tuple of phone numbers without special symbols
    all_areacodes, a tuple of strings for the area codes
    all_places, a tuple of strings for the US states
    Prints out how many friends you have and every unique
    state that is represented by their phone numbers.
    """
```

23.5.2 Helper functions

The task of analyzing the information is complicated enough that you should write helper functions. *Helper functions* are functions that help another function achieve its task.

Unique area codes

The first helper function you'll write is get_unique_area_codes. It doesn't take in any parameters and returns a tuple of only the unique area codes, in any order. In other words, it doesn't duplicate area codes in a tuple of area codes.

Listing 23.5 shows the function. This function will be nested in the analyze_friends function. Because it's nested, this function knows of all parameters given to analyze_friends. This includes the phones tuple, meaning that you don't have to pass in this tuple as a parameter again to get_unique_area_codes.

The function iterates through every number in phones and looks only at the first three digits (the area code). It keeps track of all the area codes it has seen so far and adds it to the unique area codes tuple only if it isn't already in there.

Listing 23.5   Helper function to keep only unique area codes

```
def get_unique_area_codes():
    """

    Returns a tuple of all unique area codes in phones
    """
    area_codes = ()                                 ← Tuple to contain
    for ph in phones:                                 unique area codes
        if ph[0:3] not in area_codes:    ← Goes through every area
            area_codes += (ph[0:3],)       code, variable phones is a
                                           parameter to analyze_friends
    return area_codes
```

Checks that area code isn't there

Concatenates tuple of unique codes with a singleton tuple

Mapping area codes to states

Two of the inputs to analyze_friends are tuples containing area codes and states. Now you want to use these tuples to map each unique area code to its state. You can write another function that does this; call it get_states. The function takes in a tuple of area codes and returns a tuple of states corresponding to each area code. This function is also nested inside analyze_friends, so it will know of all the parameters given to analyze_friends.

Listing 23.6 shows how to do this. You use a loop to go through every area code. With a valid area code, you now have to figure out the position in the area code tuple where the given area code is. You use the index method on tuples to get this value. Recall that the area code tuple and the states tuples match up (that's how we created them when we read them in from the file). You use the index you get from the area code tuple to look up the state at that same position in the state tuple.

A good programmer anticipates any possible problems with inputs from the user and tries to deal with them gracefully. For example, sometimes the user might enter a bogus area code. You anticipate that by writing code to the effect of something like "if you give me a bad area code, I will associate a state with it named BAD AREACODE."

Listing 23.6 Helper function to look up states from unique area codes

```
def get_states(some_areacodes):
    """

    some_areacodes, a tuple of area codes
    Returns a tuple of the states associated with those area codes
    """
    states = ()
    for ac in some_areacodes:
        if ac not in all_areacodes:
            states += ("BAD AREACODE",)
        else:
            index = all_areacodes.index(ac)
            states += (all_places[index],)
    return states
```

User gave you a bogus value; variable all_areacodes is a parameter to analyze_friends

Finds the position of the area code in tuple

Uses position to look up the state

And that's it for the helper functions nested within the analyze_friends function. Now you can use them so that the code inside the analyze_friends function is simple and readable, as shown in the following listing. You just call the helper functions and print the information they return.

Listing 23.7 Body of the analyze_friends function

```
def analyze_friends(names, phones, all_areacodes, all_places):
    """

    names, a tuple of friend names
    phones, a tuple of phone numbers without special symbols
    all_areacodes, a tuple of strings for the area codes
    all_places, a tuple of strings for the US states
    Prints out how many friends you have and every unique
    state that is represented by their phone numbers.
    """
```

```
def get_unique_area_codes():
    """
    Returns a tuple of all unique area codes in phones
    """
    area_codes = ()
    for ph in phones:
        if ph[0:3] not in area_codes:
            area_codes += (ph[0:3],)

    return area_codes

def get_states(some_areacodes):
    """
    some_area_codes, a tuple of area codes
    Returns a tuple of the states associated with those area codes
    """
    states = ()
    for ac in some_areacodes:
        if ac not in all_areacodes:
            states += ("BAD AREACODE",)
        else:
            index = all_areacodes.index(ac)
            states += (all_places[index],)
    return states
```

```
num_friends = len(names)                                    ◄──── Number of friends
unique_area_codes = get_unique_area_codes()    ◄──── Keeps only unique area codes
unique_states = get_states(unique_area_codes)  ◄──  Gets states corresponding
                                                     to the unique area codes
print("You have", num_friends, "friends!")  ◄──
                                                ──◄  Prints number of friends
print("They live in", unique_states)  ◄──
                                        ──  Prints the unique states
```

◄──── Nothing to return ────►

The final step of the program is to read the two files, call the function to analyze the
data, and close the files. The following listing shows this.

Listing 23.8 Commands to read files, analyze content, and close files

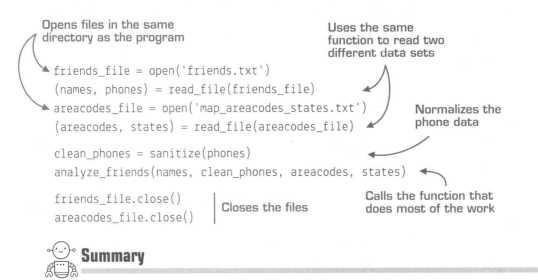

Opens files in the same
directory as the program

Uses the same
function to read two
different data sets

```
friends_file = open('friends.txt')
(names, phones) = read_file(friends_file)
areacodes_file = open('map_areacodes_states.txt')
(areacodes, states) = read_file(areacodes_file)

clean_phones = sanitize(phones)
analyze_friends(names, clean_phones, areacodes, states)

friends_file.close()
areacodes_file.close()
```

Normalizes the
phone data

Closes the files

Calls the function that
does most of the work

Summary

In this lesson, my objective was to teach you how to take on the problem of analyzing your friends' data. You wrote a few functions that specialized in doing certain tasks. One function read data from a file. You used that function twice: once to read in names and phone numbers, and another time to read in area codes and states. Another function cleaned up data by removing unnecessary characters from phone numbers. A final function analyzed the data you collected from the files. This function comprised two helper functions: one to return unique area codes from a set of area codes, and one to convert the unique area codes to their respective states. Here are the major takeaways:

- You can open files in Python to work with their contents (to read lines as strings).
- Functions are useful for organizing code. You can reuse any function you wrote with different inputs.
- You should test your functions often. Write a function and immediately test it. When you have a couple of functions, make sure they work well together.
- You can nest functions inside other functions if the nested functions are relevant to only a specific task, as opposed to the program as a whole.

Working with mutable data types

In the previous unit, you learned how to organize your code with functions. Functions are used to write modular code whose parts can be reused in different sections of a bigger program.

In this unit, you'll learn about two new data types in Python: lists and dictionaries. These data types are *mutable* because you can modify them directly rather than having to make copies of them. Mutable data types are commonly used when writing complex programs, especially ones in which you store larger collections of data that's likely to change. For example, you want to maintain inventory of your company's products or all the employees who work there and their information. Mutable objects don't have the extra overhead of having to copy the object with every change.

In the capstone project, you'll write a program that assigns a similarity score to two documents. You'll read two files and use a metric to determine how similar the two pieces of work are based on the number of words in the two documents and the number of words that they have in common. You'll use dictionaries to pair words to how often they occur. Then you'll use a formula to calculate the difference between the documents based on these frequencies.

24

MUTABLE AND IMMUTABLE OBJECTS

After reading lesson 24, you'll be able to

- Understand what an immutable object is
- Understand what a mutable object is
- Understand how objects are stored in computer memory

Consider the following scenario. You buy a house that's just the right size for you; it's big enough for one person to live in. Then you get married, and there's no space for your spouse. You have two choices: build an addition to the house, or tear the whole house down and build a new larger house to hold two people. Building an addition makes more sense than demolishing a perfectly good house and making an exact copy of it just to make an addition. Now, you have a kid and decide you need more room. Again, do you build an addition or tear the house down to build a new one to hold three people? Again, it makes more sense to build an extension. As you're adding more people to your house, it's quicker and less costly to keep the same structure and modify it.

In some situations, it helps to be able to put your data in some sort of container so you can modify the data within the container instead of having to create a new container and put the modified data in the new one.

> **Consider this**   This exercise requires a piece of paper and your computer. Think of the names of all the countries you've visited. If you need inspiration, suppose you've visited Canada, Brazil, Russia, and Iceland:
>
> - On a piece of paper, use a pen to write all the countries you've visited in alphabetical order, one on each line.
> - On a text editor on your computer, type the same list of countries.
> - Suppose you realize that you visited Greenland, not Iceland. Modify your list on paper so you have Canada, Brazil, Russia, and Greenland in alphabetical order. Can you modify the list (keeping one country per line) without having to rewrite it all? Can you modify the list on the computer (keeping one country per line) without having to rewrite it all?
>
> Answer:
>
> Using a pen, I'd have to rewrite the list. Otherwise, it'd be too messy to scratch out and write the new country name beside it. On the text editor, I can replace the name directly.

24.1 Immutable objects

All Python objects that you've seen (Booleans, integers, floats, strings, and tuples) are immutable. After you create the object and assign a value to it, you can't modify that value.

> **DEFINITION**   An *immutable object* is an object whose value can't change.

What does this mean behind the scenes, in computer memory? An object created and given a value is assigned a space in memory. The variable name bound to the object points to that place in memory. Figure 24.1 shows the memory locations of objects and what happens when you bind the same variable to a new object by using the expressions a = 1 and then a = 2. The object with value 1 still exists in memory, but you've lost the binding to it.

You can see the value of the memory location to which the object has been assigned, using the id() function. Type the following in the console:

```
a = 1
id(a)
```

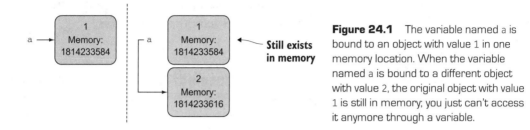

Figure 24.1 The variable named a is bound to an object with value 1 in one memory location. When the variable named a is bound to a different object with value 2, the original object with value 1 is still in memory; you just can't access it anymore through a variable.

The value shown represents the location in memory of the object with value 1, accessed by the variable named a. Now, type the following:

```
a = 2
id(a)
```

As before, the value shown represents the location in memory of the object with value 2, accessed by the variable named a. Why are these values different if you're using variable name a in both cases? We come back to the idea that the variable name is a name bound to an object. The name points to an object; in the first case, the variable points to the integer object with value 1 and then to the object with value 2. The id() function tells you the memory location of the object pointed to by the variable name, not anything about the variable name itself.

Objects of the types you've seen so far can't be modified after they're created. Suppose you have the following lines of code, which are executed in the order shown. You initialize two variables, a and b, to two objects with values 1 and 2, respectively. Then you change the binding of variable a to a different object with a value of 3:

```
a = 1
b = 2
a = 3
```

Figure 24.2 shows the objects that exist in your program's memory with each line of code:

- When you create the object with value 1, you bind the object to the variable named a.
- When you create the object with value 2, you bind the object to the variable named b.
- In the final line, you're rebinding the variable name a to a completely new object, one whose value is 3.

The old object with a value of 1 may still exist in computer memory, but you lost the binding to it; you don't have a variable name as a way to refer to it anymore.

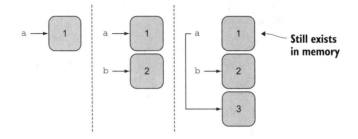

Figure 24.2   Progression of binding variables to objects. On the left, a = 1 shows that object 1 is at some memory location. In the middle, a = 1 and then b = 2. Objects with values 1 and 2 are at different memory locations. On the right, a = 1 and then b = 2 and then a = 3. The variable named a is bound to a different object, but the original object still exists in memory.

After an immutable object loses its variable handle, the Python interpreter may delete the object to reclaim the computer memory it took up and use it for something else. Unlike some other programming languages, you (as the programmer) don't have to worry about deleting old objects; Python takes care of this for you through a process called *garbage collection*.

> **Quick check 24.1**   Draw a diagram similar to the one in figure 24.2 to show variables and objects that they point to (and any leftover objects) for the following sequence of statements:
> ```
> sq = 2 * 2
> ci = 3.14
> ci = 22 / 7
> ci = 3
> ```

24.2 The need for mutability

After you lose the variable binding to an object, there's no way to get back to that object. If you want the program to remember its value, you need to store its value in a temporary variable. Using a temporary variable to store values that you don't need right now, but may need in the future, isn't an efficient way of programming. It wastes memory and leads to cluttered code filled with variables that, for the most part, will never be used again.

If immutable objects are objects whose value can't change after they're created, a mutable object is an object whose value can change after it's created. Mutable objects are often objects that can store a collection of data. In later lessons in this unit, you'll see lists (Python type list) and dictionaries (Python type dict) as examples of mutable objects.

> **DEFINITION** A *mutable object* is an object whose value can change.

For example, you can make a list of items you'll need from the grocery store; as you decide what you need, you add items to the list. As you buy things, you remove them from the list. Notice that you're using the same list and modifying it (crossing out or adding to the end), as opposed to having many lists in which you copy over items every time you want to make a change. As another example, you can keep your grocery needs in a dictionary that maps every item you need from the store to a number representing the quantity that you need.

Figure 24.3 shows what happens in memory when you bind variables to mutable objects. When you modify the object, you keep the same variable binding, and the object at the same memory location is directly modified.

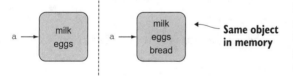

Figure 24.3 On the left, you have a grocery list at a certain memory location. On the right, you add another item to your grocery list, and the object at the same memory location is directly modified.

Mutable objects are more flexible when programming, because you can modify the object itself without losing the binding to it.

First, a mutable object can behave the same way as an immutable object. If you rebind a sample grocery list to a variable a and check its memory location, you see that the memory location changes and the binding to the original list is lost:

```
a = ["milk", "eggs"]
id(a)
a = ["milk", "eggs", "bread"]
id(a)
```

But you have the option to modify the original object directly without losing the binding to it, using operations that work only on mutable objects. In the following code, you append one more item (add it to the end of the list). The memory location of the object that the variable a is bound to remains unchanged. The behavior of the following code is shown in figure 24.3:

```
a = ["milk", "eggs"]
id(a)
a.append("bread")
id(a)
```

Mutable objects are useful in programing for several reasons.

First, you can store data that's part of a collection (for example, lists of people or mappings of people to phone numbers) in an object, and you can keep the object for use later.

After the object is created, you can add data to and remove data from the object itself, without creating a new object. When you have the object, you can also modify elements in the collection by modifying the elements in the object itself instead of creating a new copy of the object with only one of its values modified.

Finally, you can rearrange data in the collection by keeping the same object and making the rearrangement in place—for example, if you have a list of people and you want to sort it alphabetically.

With large collections of data, copying your collection into a new object every time you make a change to it would be inefficient.

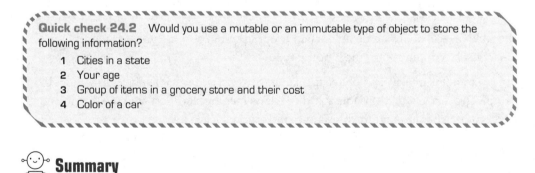

Quick check 24.2   Would you use a mutable or an immutable type of object to store the following information?

1   Cities in a state
2   Your age
3   Group of items in a grocery store and their cost
4   Color of a car

Summary

In this lesson, my objective was to teach you how an object exists in computer memory. The values of some objects can't change after they're created (immutable objects). The values of some objects can change after they're created (mutable objects). You may use one kind or another kind of object, depending on the task you're trying to accomplish using programming. Here are the major takeaways:

- Immutable objects can't change their value (for example, strings, integers, floats, Booleans).
- Mutable objects can change their value (in this unit, you'll see lists and dictionaries).

Let's see if you got this...

Q24.1   In the following diagram, each panel is showing a new operation of code. Which of the following variables are bound to immutable objects? Which are bound to mutable objects?

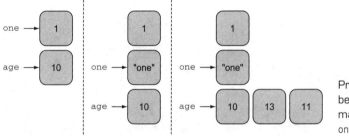

Progression of expressions being added to code that manipulates two variables: one and age

WORKING WITH LISTS

After reading lesson 25, you'll be able to

- Build Python lists
- Add items, remove items, and modify items in Python lists
- Perform operations on list elements

Mutable data types are types of objects on which you can perform operations, such that the object's value is modified; the modification is done in place, so to speak, so no copy of the object is made. There's a need for data types that are mutable, especially when working with large amounts of data; it's more efficient to modify data stored directly instead of copying it into a new object with every operation.

Instead of creating new objects, it's sometimes useful to reuse an object and modify its value. This is especially true when you have an object that represents an ordered collection of other objects. Most programming languages have a data type to represent this type of ordered collection that you can mutate. In Python, this is called a *list*. A list is a new type of object that you haven't seen before. It represents an ordered collection of other object types. Among many others, you can have lists of numbers, lists of strings, or even a list of a mix of object types.

Often you'll find that you need to store objects in a certain order. For example, if you keep a list of grocery items, the first item will be on the first line, the second on the next line, and so on. The fact that a list is ordered comes from the idea that each item has a specific place in the list, and that your first item will always be at the first place in the list, and the last item will be at the final place in the list. This lesson will show you how to create lists and perform operations to mutate the lists; these operations may move items around in the list, but a list will always have an item in its first place and in its final place. Dictionaries, which are covered in lesson 27, are data types that store objects in an unordered fashion.

Consider this   You maintain a list of all people who work at your company. The list is in a document on the computer. Which one of these events would require you to start a new document, copy over all information, and then act on the event?

- Someone joins the company.
- Someone leaves the company.
- Someone changes their name.
- The list will be sorted by first name, not last name.

Answer:

None.

25.1 Lists vs. tuples

A list is a collection of any object type; it's like a tuple, which you've seen and worked with already. A tuple and a list both have an order to them, in that the first element in the collection is at index 0, the second element is at index 1, and so on. The main difference is that lists are mutable objects, whereas tuples aren't. You can add elements to, remove elements from, and modify elements in the same list object. With a tuple, every time you do an operation, you create a new tuple object whose value is the changed tuple.

Tuples are generally used to store data that's more or less fixed. Examples of data you'd store in a tuple are a pair of coordinate points in a 2D plane, or the page number and line number where a word occurs in a book. Lists are used to store data that's more dynamic. You use them when you're storing data that changes often as you need to add, change values, remove, reorder, sort, and so on. For example, you can use a list to store student grade scores or items in your fridge.

25.2 Creating lists and getting elements at specific positions

You create a Python list by using square brackets. The line L = [] creates an object representing an empty list (a list with no elements), and binds the name L to that empty list object. L is a variable name, and you can use any variable name you want. You can also create a list with items initially in it. The following line creates a list of three items and binds the variable name grocery to that list:

```
grocery = ["milk", "eggs", "bread"]
```

As with strings and tuples, you can get the length of a list with len(). The command len(L), where L is a list, tells you the number of elements that are in list L. The empty list has 0 elements. The length of the preceding list named grocery is 3.

Recall that in programming, we start counting from 0. As with strings and tuples, the first element in a list is at index 0, the second element is at index 1, and so on. The last element in the list is at len(L) - 1. If you have a grocery list grocery = ["milk" "eggs", "bread"], you can get the value of each element by indexing into the list by using the square brackets, as with tuples and strings. The following code indexes into the list and prints each element:

```
grocery = ["milk", "eggs", "bread"]
print(grocery[0])
print(grocery[1])
print(grocery[2])
```

What happens if you try to index farther than the length of the list? Say you have the following code:

```
grocery = ["milk", "eggs", "bread"]
print(grocery[3])
```

You'll get this error, which tells you that you're trying to index into a list farther than the length of the list:

```
Traceback (most recent call last):
  File "<ipython-input-14-c90317837012>", line 2, in <module>
    print(grocery[3])

IndexError: list index out of range
```

Recall that because the list contains only three elements and the first element is at index 0, then the last element in grocery is at index 2. An index position of 3 is beyond the limits of the list.

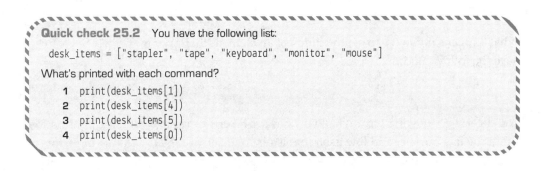

Quick check 25.2   You have the following list:

```
desk_items = ["stapler", "tape", "keyboard", "monitor", "mouse"]
```

What's printed with each command?

   1 `print(desk_items[1])`
   2 `print(desk_items[4])`
   3 `print(desk_items[5])`
   4 `print(desk_items[0])`

25.3 Counting and getting positions of elements

In addition to counting all elements in the list with the len() command, you can also count the number of times a particular element occurs by using the count() operation. The command L.count(e) tells you the number of times the element e occurs in the list L. For example, if you're looking at your grocery list, you could count the word *cheese* to make sure you have five kinds of cheeses on your list for your five-cheese pizza recipe.

You can also determine the index of the first element in the list that matches a value with the index() operation. The command L.index(e) tells you the index (starting from 0) of the first time the element e occurs in list L. The following listing shows how count() and index() work.

Listing 25.1 **Using** count **and** index **with a list**

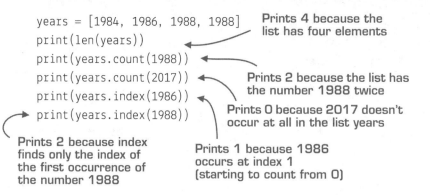

```
years = [1984, 1986, 1988, 1988]
print(len(years))
print(years.count(1988))
print(years.count(2017))
print(years.index(1986))
print(years.index(1988))
```

Prints 4 because the list has four elements

Prints 2 because the list has the number 1988 twice

Prints 0 because 2017 doesn't occur at all in the list years

Prints 1 because 1986 occurs at index 1 (starting to count from 0)

Prints 2 because index finds only the index of the first occurrence of the number 1988

What happens if you try to get the index of an element that's not in the list? Say you have the following code:

```
L = []
L.index(0)
```

You'll get the following error when you run it. The error message contains information about the line number and line itself that leads to the error. The last line of the error message contains the reason the command failed: ValueError: 0 is not in list. This is the expected behavior of the index operation on a value that's not in the list:

```
Traceback (most recent call last):

  File "<ipython-input-15-b3f3f6d671a3>", line 2, in <module>
    L.index(0)

ValueError: 0 is not in list
```

Quick check 25.3   What's printed by the following code? If there's an error, write *error*.

```
L = ["one", "three", "two", "three", "four", "three", "three", "five"]
print(L.count("one"))
print(L.count("three"))
print(L.count("zero"))
print(len(L))
print(L.index("two"))
print(L.index("zero"))
```

25.4 Adding items to lists: append, insert, and extend

An empty list isn't useful. Nor is a list that you have to populate as soon as you create it. After you create a list, you'll want to add more items to it. For example, given an empty piece of paper representing you weekly grocery list, you'll want to add items to the end of the list as you think of them instead of transcribing everything on a new piece of paper every time you want to add an item.

To add more elements to the list, you can use one of three operations: append, insert, and extend.

25.4.1 Using append

`L.append(e)` adds an element `e` to the end of your list `L`. Appending to a list always tacks on the element to the end of the list, at the highest index. You can append only one element at a time. The list `L` is mutated to contain the one extra value.

Say you have an initially empty grocery list:

```
grocery = []
```

You can add an item as follows:

```
grocery.append("bread")
```

The list now contains one element in it: the string `"bread"`.

25.4.2 Using insert

`L.insert(i, e)` adds element `e` at index `i` in list `L`. You can insert only one element at a time. To find the position for the insert, start counting elements in `L` from 0. When you insert, all elements at and after that index are shifted toward the end of the list. The list `L` is mutated to contain the one extra value.

Say you have this grocery list:

```
grocery = ["bread", "milk"]
```

You can insert an item between the two existing items:

```
grocery.insert(1, "eggs")
```

The list then contains all the items:

```
["bread", "eggs", "milk"]
```

25.4.3 Using extend

L.extend(M) appends all elements from list M to the end of list L. You effectively append all the elements from list M, preserving their order, to the end of list L. The list L is mutated to contain all the elements in M. The list M remains unchanged.

Say you have an initial grocery list and a list of fun things to buy:

```
grocery = ["bread", "eggs", "milk"]
for_fun = ["drone", "vr glasses", "game console"]
```

You can extend the two lists:

```
grocery.extend(for_fun)
```

This gives you a master shopping list:

```
["bread", "eggs", "milk", "drone", "vr glasses", "game console"]
```

Listing 25.2 Adding items to a list

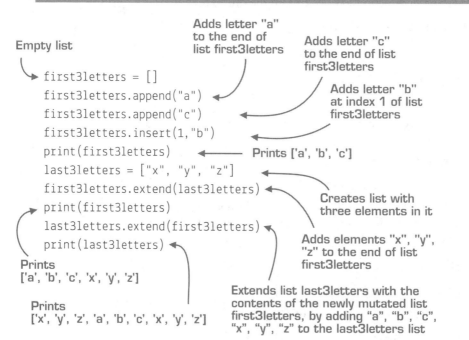

With lists being mutable objects, certain actions you do on a list lead to the list object being changed. In listing 25.2, the list first3letters is mutated every time you append to, insert to, and extend it. Similarly, the list last3letters is mutated when you extend it by the first3letters list.

Quick check 25.4   What's printed after each code snippet is executed?

```
1  one = [1]
   one.append("1")
   print(one)

2  zero = []
   zero.append(0)
   zero.append(["zero"])
   print(zero)

3  two = []
   three = []
   three.extend(two)
   print(three)

4  four = [1,2,3,4]
   four.insert(len(four), 5)
   print(four)
   four.insert(0, 0)
   print(four)
```

 ## 25.5 Removing items from a list: pop

Lists aren't useful if you can only add items to them. They'll keep growing and quickly become unmanageable. Having mutable objects when removing items is also useful so you don't make copies with every change. For example, as you keep your grocery list, you want to remove items from it as you purchase them so you know that you don't need to look for them anymore. Each time you remove an item, you can keep the same list instead of transcribing all items you still need to a new list.

You can remove items from a list with the operation pop(), as shown in listing 25.3. The command L.pop() will remove the element at the last position in list L. Optionally, you can specify a number in the parentheses representing the index whose value you want to remove with L.pop(i). When removed, the list that the element is removed from is mutated. All elements after the one removed are shifted by one spot to replace the one removed. This operation is a function and returns the element removed.

Listing 25.3 Removing from a list

```
polite = ["please", "and", "thank", "you"]          List of four elements
print(polite.pop())
print(polite)
print(polite.pop(1))
print(polite)
```

Prints "you" because pop() returns the value of the element at the last index

Prints ['please', 'and', 'thank'] because pop() removed the last element

Prints ['please', 'thank'] because the preceding line removed the element at index 1 (second element in the list)

Prints "and" because pop(1) returns the value of the element at index 1

As with adding items to a list, removing items from the list also mutates the list. Every operation that removes an item changes the list on which the operation is performed. In listing 25.3, every time you print the list, you print the mutated list.

> **Quick check 25.5**   What's printed when this code snippet is executed?
> ```
> pi = [3, ".", 1, 4, 1, 5, 9]
> pi.pop(1)
> print(pi)
> pi.pop()
> print(pi)
> pi.pop()
> print(pi)
> ```

25.6 Changing an element value

So far, you can add and remove items in a list. With mutability, you can even modify existing object elements in the list to change their values. For example, in your grocery list, you realize that you need cheddar instead of mozzarella cheese. As before, because of the mutability property, instead of copying the list over to another paper with the one item changed, it makes more sense to modify the list you currently have by replacing *mozzarella cheese* with *cheddar cheese*.

To modify an element in a list, you first need to access the element itself and then assign it a new value. You access an element by using its index. For example L[0] refers to the first element. The square brackets you used when you created a list now have this new purpose when placed to the right of the list variable name. The following listing shows how to do this.

Listing 25.4 Modifying an element value

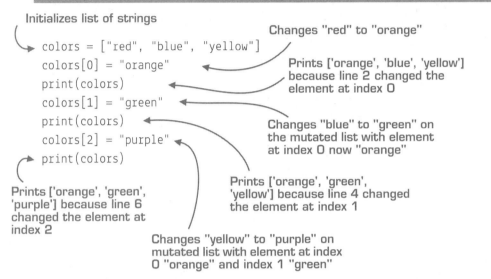

Initializes list of strings

```
colors = ["red", "blue", "yellow"]
colors[0] = "orange"
print(colors)
colors[1] = "green"
print(colors)
colors[2] = "purple"
print(colors)
```

Changes "red" to "orange"

Prints ['orange', 'blue', 'yellow'] because line 2 changed the element at index 0

Changes "blue" to "green" on the mutated list with element at index 0 now "orange"

Prints ['orange', 'green', 'yellow'] because line 4 changed the element at index 1

Prints ['orange', 'green', 'purple'] because line 6 changed the element at index 2

Changes "yellow" to "purple" on mutated list with element at index 0 "orange" and index 1 "green"

Elements in mutable lists can be modified to contain different values. After a list is mutated, every operation you do from then on is done on the mutated list.

Quick check 25.6 If L is a list of integers that initially contains the numbers shown in the first line of code that follows, what's the value of L after each of the four subsequent operations are done in order?

```
L = [1, 2, 3, 5, 7, 11, 13, 17]
```

   1 L[3] = 4
   2 L[4] = 6
   3 L[-1] = L[0] (Recall how negative indices work from lesson 7.)
   4 L[0] = L[1] + 1

Summary

In this lesson, my objective was to teach you a new data type, a Python list. A list is a mutable object whose value can change. A list contains elements, and you can add to it, remove from it, change element values, and perform operations on the entire list. Here are the major takeaways:

- Lists can be empty or can contain elements.
- You can add an element to the end of a list, at a specific index, or you can extend it by more than one element.
- You can remove elements from the list, from the end or from a specific index.
- You can change element values.
- Every action mutates the list, so the list object changes without you having to reassign it to another variable.

Let's see if you got this…

Q25.1   You start out with the following empty list, intending to contain the items in a restaurant menu:

```
menu = []
```

1   Write one or more commands that mutate the list, so that the list menu contains `["pizza", "beer", "fries", "wings", "salad"]`.
2   Continuing on, write one or more commands that mutate the list to contain `["salad", "fries", "wings", "pizza"]`.
3   Finally, write one or more commands that mutate the list, so that it contains `["salad", "quinoa", "steak"]`.

Q25.2   Write a function named `unique`. It takes in one parameter, a list named `L`. The function doesn't mutate `L` and returns a new list containing only the unique elements in `L`.

Q25.3   Write a function named `common`. It takes in two parameters, lists named `L1` and `L2`. The function doesn't mutate `L1` or `L2`. It returns `True` if every unique element in `L1` is in `L2` and if every unique element in `L2` is in `L1`. It returns `False` otherwise. Hint: try to reuse your function from Q25.2. For example,

- `common([1,2,3], [3,1,2])` returns `True`
- `common([1,1,1], [1])` returns `True`
- `common([1], [1, 2])` returns `False`

26

ADVANCED OPERATIONS WITH LISTS

After reading lesson 26, you'll be able to

- Build lists whose elements are lists
- Sort and reverse list elements
- Convert a string into a list by splitting on a character

A list is typically used to represent a collection of items, frequently but not necessarily of the same type. You'll see that it may be useful for the list elements to be lists themselves. For example, suppose you want to keep a list of all the items in your house. Because you have many items, it'll be more organized to have sublists, where each sublist represents a room, and a sublist's elements are all the items in that room.

At this point, it's important to take a step back and understand what has been going on with this new mutable object, a list. Lists are directly modified by any actions you do on them. Because the list is directly modified, you don't reassign the list to a new variable after an operation; the list itself now contains the changed values. To see the value of the modified list, you can print it.

> **Consider this** Your friend can recite the number pi up to 100 digits. You add each digit into a list as he tells it to you. You want to figure out how many zeros are in the first 100 digits. How can you quickly do this?
>
> Answer:
>
> If you sort the list, you can count the zeros at the beginning of the list.

26.1 Sorting and reversing lists

After you have a list of elements, you can perform operations that rearrange elements in the whole list. For example, if you have a list of students in your class, you don't need to keep two lists of the same students: one sorted and one unsorted. You can start out with an unsorted list and then sort it directly when needed. When you care only about the contents of the list, storing it in a sorted manner may be preferred. But note that after it's sorted, you can't go back to the unsorted version of the list unless you re-create it from scratch.

Because lists are mutable, you can sort a list, using the operation sort(), so that the list elements of the original list are now in sorted order. The command L.sort() will sort the list L in ascending order (for numbers) and lexicographically (for letters or strings). In contrast, if you wanted to sort items in an immutable tuple object, you'd be creating many intermediary objects as you're concatenating the items from end to beginning (take the last item and put it at index 0, take the second-to-last item and put it at index 1, and so on).

Reversing a list may also be useful. For example, if you have a list of the names of your students and you sorted them alphabetically, you can reverse the list and have them sorted in reverse alphabetical order. The command L.reverse() reverses the list L so that the element at the front is now at the end, and so on.

Listing 26.1 **Sorting and reversing a list**

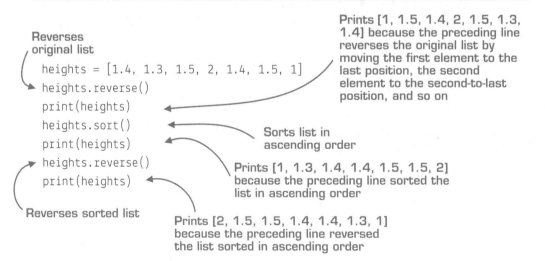

Reverses original list

```
heights = [1.4, 1.3, 1.5, 2, 1.4, 1.5, 1]
heights.reverse()
print(heights)
heights.sort()
print(heights)
heights.reverse()
print(heights)
```

Reverses sorted list

Prints [1, 1.5, 1.4, 2, 1.5, 1.3, 1.4] because the preceding line reverses the original list by moving the first element to the last position, the second element to the second-to-last position, and so on

Sorts list in ascending order

Prints [1, 1.3, 1.4, 1.4, 1.5, 1.5, 2] because the preceding line sorted the list in ascending order

Prints [2, 1.5, 1.5, 1.4, 1.4, 1.3, 1] because the preceding line reversed the list sorted in ascending order

You've seen lists whose elements are floats, integers, or strings. But a list can contain elements of any type, including other lists!

26.2 Lists of lists

If you want to program a game, especially a game that relies on the user being in a certain position, you'll often want to think about the position on a board represented in a two-dimensional coordinate plane. Lists can be used to help you represent the two-dimensional coordinate plane by using one list whose elements are also lists. The following listing creates a list L whose three elements are empty lists, and then populates the list with elements.

Listing 26.2 Creating and populating a list of lists

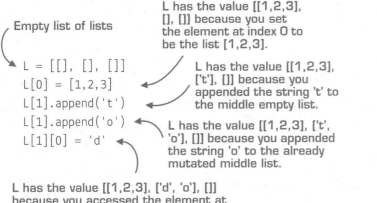

Empty list of lists

L has the value [[1,2,3], [], []] because you set the element at index 0 to be the list [1,2,3].

```
L = [[], [], []]
L[0] = [1,2,3]
L[1].append('t')
L[1].append('o')
L[1][0] = 'd'
```

L has the value [[1,2,3], ['t'], []] because you appended the string 't' to the middle empty list.

L has the value [[1,2,3], ['t', 'o'], []] because you appended the string 'o' to the already mutated middle list.

L has the value [[1,2,3], ['d', 'o'], []] because you accessed the element at index 1 (a list) and then accessed that object's element at index 0 (letter t) to change it (to the letter d).

Working with lists of lists adds another layer of indirection when indexing into the list to work with its elements. The first time you index a list of lists (or even a list of lists of lists of lists), you access the object at that position. If the object at that position is a list, you can index into that list as well, and so on.

You can represent a tic-tac-toe board with a list of lists. Listing 26.3 shows the code for setting up the board with lists. Because lists are one-dimensional, you can consider each element of the outer list to be a row in the board. Each sublist will contain all the elements for each column in that row.

Listing 26.3   Tic-tac-toe board with lists of lists

```
x = 'x'          ◄──────── Variable x       Replaces every variable with its value.
                                            Variable board has three rows (one
o = 'o'          ◄──────── Variable o       for each sublist) and three columns
empty = '_'      ◄──────── Empty space      (each sublist has three elements).
board = [[x, empty, o], [empty, x, o], [x, empty, empty]]  ◄──╯
```

This tic-tac-toe board represented in code looks like this:

```
X _ O
_ X O
X _ _
```

Using lists inside lists, you can represent any size tic-tac-toe board by adjusting the number of sublists you have and the number of elements each sublist contains.

> **Quick check 26.2**   Using the variables set up in listing 26.3, write the line of code to set up a board that looks like this:
>
>   **1**   A 3 × 3 board
>
>   _ _ _
>   x x x
>   o o o
>
>   **2**   A 3 × 4 board
>
>   x o x o
>   o o x x
>   o _ x x

26.3 Converting a string to a list

Suppose you're given a string that contains email data separated by commas. You'd like to separate out each email address and keep each address in a list. The following sample string shows how the input data might look:

```
emails = "zebra@zoo.com,red@colors.com,tom.sawyer@book.com,pea@veg.com"
```

You could solve this problem by using string manipulations, but in a somewhat tedious way. First, you find the index of the first comma. Then you save the email as the substring from the beginning of the string emails until that index. Then you save the rest of the string from that index until the end of emails in another variable. And finally, you repeat the process until you don't have any more commas left to find. This solution uses a loop and forces you to create unnecessary variables.

Using lists provides a simple, one-line solution to this problem. With the preceding emails string, you can do this:

```
emails_list = emails.split(',')
```

This line uses the operation split() on the string named emails. In the parentheses to split(), you can put the element on which you'd like to split the string. In this case, you want to split on the comma. The result from running that command is that emails_list is a list of strings that contains every substring between the commas, as shown here:

```
['zebra@zoo.com', 'red@colors.com', 'tom.sawyer@book.com', 'pea@veg.com']
```

Notice that each email is now a separate element in the list emails_list, making it easy to work with.

> **Quick check 26.3** Write a line of code to achieve the following tasks:
> 1 Split the string " abcdefghijklmnopqrstuvwxyz" by the space character.
> 2 Split the string "spaces and more spaces" by words.
> 3 Split the string "the secret of life is 42" on the letter s.

With the operations you saw on lists in lesson 25 (sorting and reversing a list), you're now able to simulate real-life phenomena: stacks and queues of items.

26.4 Applications of lists

Why would you need to simulate a stack or a queue by using a list? This is a somewhat philosophical question, and it hints at what you'll see in the next unit. A more basic question is why do I need a list object when I can just create a bunch of integer/float/string objects and remember the order I want them in? The idea is that you use simpler objects to create more complex objects that have more specific behaviors. In the same way that a list is made up of an ordered group of objects, a stack or a queue is made up of a list. You can make up your own stack or queue object so that their construction is the same (you use a list) but their behavior is different.

26.4.1 Stacks

Think of a stack of pancakes. As they're being made, new pancakes are added to the top of the stack. When a pancake is eaten, it's taken from the top of the stack. You can mimic this behavior with a list. The top of the stack is the end of the list. Every time you have a new element, you add it to the end of the list with append(). Every time you want to take an element out, you remove it from the end of the list with pop().

Listing 26.4 shows an implementation of a pancake stack in Python. Suppose you have blueberry and chocolate pancakes. A blueberry pancake is represented by the element 'b' (letter *b* as a string) and a chocolate pancake as 'c' (letter *c* as a string). Your pancake stack is originally an empty list (no pancakes made yet). One cook makes batches of pancakes; the cook is also a list with pancake elements. As soon as a batch is made by the cook, the batch is added to the stack by using extend(). Someone eating a pancake can be represented by using the pop() operation on the stack.

Listing 26.4 A stack of pancakes represented with a list

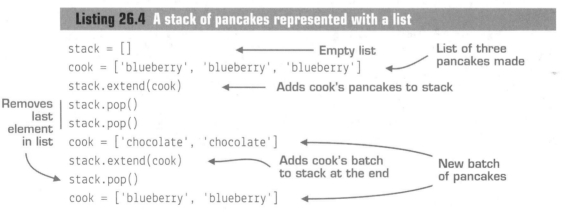

```
stack = []                                        Empty list            List of three
cook = ['blueberry', 'blueberry', 'blueberry']                          pancakes made
stack.extend(cook)              Adds cook's pancakes to stack
stack.pop()
stack.pop()
cook = ['chocolate', 'chocolate']
stack.extend(cook)              Adds cook's batch                       New batch
stack.pop()                     to stack at the end                     of pancakes
cook = ['blueberry', 'blueberry']
```

Removes last element in list

```
stack.extend(cook)  ◄──────────  Adds cook's batch
stack.pop()         │            to stack at the end
stack.pop()         │ Removes last
stack.pop()         │ element in list
```

Stacks are a *first-in-last-out* structure because the first item added to the stack is the last one taken out. Queues, on the other hand, are *first-in-first-out* because the first item added to a queue is the first one taken out.

26.4.2 Queues

Think of a grocery store queue. When a new person arrives, they stand at the end of the line. As people are being helped, the ones that have been in the queue the longest (at the front of the line) are going to be helped next.

You can simulate a queue by using a list. As you get new elements, you add to the end of the list. When you want to take out an element, you remove the one at the beginning of the list.

Listing 26.5 shows an example of a simulated queue in code. Your grocery store has one line, represented by a list. As customers come in, you use append() to add them to the end of the list. As customers are helped, you use pop(0) to remove them from the front of the line.

Listing 26.5 A queue of people represented by a list

```
line = []                ◄────── Empty list
line.append('Ana')       ◄─────── List of one person now in queue
line.append('Bob')       ◄─────── List of two people now in queue
line.pop(0)              ◄─────── First person removed from the queue
line.append('Claire')   │ New people added
line.append('Dave')     │ to the end of list
line.pop(0)             │
line.pop(0)             │ People removed from
line.pop(0)             │ beginning of list
```

Using more complex object types, such as lists, you can simulate real-life actions. In this case, you can use specific sequences of operations to simulate stacks and queues of objects.

> **Quick check 26.4** Are the following situations best representative of a queue, a stack, or neither?
>
> 1 The Undo mechanism in your text editor
> 2 Putting tennis balls in a container and then taking them out
> 3 Cars in a line waiting for inspection
> 4 Airport luggage entering the carousel and being picked up by its owner

Summary

In this lesson, my objective was to teach you more operations that you can do with lists. You sorted a list, reversed a list, created lists that contained other lists as elements, and converted a string into a list by splitting it on a character. Here are the major takeaways:

- Lists can contain elements that are other lists.
- You can sort or reverse a list's elements.
- Behaviors of stacks and queues can be implemented using lists.

Let's see if you got this...

Q26.1 Write a program that takes in a string containing city names separated by commas, and then prints a list of the city names in sorted order. You can start with this:

```
cities = "san francisco,boston,chicago,indianapolis"
```

Q26.2 Write a function named is_permutation. It takes in two lists, L1 and L2. The function returns True if L1 and L2 are permutations of each other. It returns False otherwise. Every element in L1 is in L2, and vice versa, only arranged in a different order. For example,

- is_permutation([1,2,3], [3,1,2]) returns True.
- is_permutation([1,1,1,2], [1,2,1,1]) returns True.
- is_permutation([1,2,3,1], [1,2,3]) returns False.

GA 719 3664

27

DICTIONARIES AS MAPS BETWEEN OBJECTS

After reading lesson 27, you'll be able to

- Understand what a dictionary object data type is
- Add to, remove from, and look up objects in dictionaries
- Understand when to use a dictionary object
- Understand the difference between a dictionary and a list

In the previous lesson, you learned about lists as collections of data with elements at a certain position in the list. Lists are useful when you want to store one group of objects; you saw that you could store a group of names or a group of numbers. But in real life, you often have pairs of data: a word and its meaning, a word and a list of synonyms, a person and their phone number, a movie and its rating, a song and its artist, and many others.

Figure 27.1 takes the grocery list metaphor from the previous lesson and shows you one way to apply it to dictionaries. In a list, your grocery items are enumerated; the first item is on the first line, and so on. You can think of a list as mapping the numbers 0, 1, 2, and so on, in that order, to each item in your list. With a dictionary, you get additional flexibility in what you can map, and to what. In figure 27.1, the grocery dictionary now maps an item to its quantity.

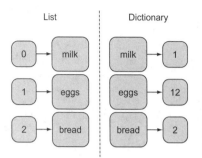

Figure 27.1 A list puts the first item at position 0, the second item at position 1, and the third at position 2. A dictionary doesn't have positions, but rather maps one object to another; here it maps a grocery item to its quantity.

You can think of a list as a structure that maps an integer (index 0, 1, 2, 3 …) to an object; a list can be indexed only by an integer. A dictionary is a data structure that can map any object, not just an integer, to any other object; indexing using any object is more useful in situations when you have pairs of data. Like lists, dictionaries are mutable so that when you make a change to a dictionary object, the object itself changes without having to make a copy of it.

Consider this   A word dictionary maps words from one language to their equivalent in another language. For each of the following scenarios, are you able to map one thing to another?

- Your friends and their phone numbers
- All the movies you've seen
- The number of times each word occurs in your favorite song
- Each coffee shop in the area and its Wi-Fi availability
- All the names of the paints available at the hardware store
- Your coworkers and their arrival and leave times

Answer:

- Yes
- No
- Yes
- Yes
- No
- Yes

27.1 Creating dictionaries, keys, and values

Many programming languages have a way to map objects to each other or to look up one object using another. In Python, such an object is called a *dictionary* with the object type `dict`.

A dictionary maps one object to another; we can also say that you look up one object by using another object. If you think of a traditional word dictionary, you look up a word to find its meaning. In programming, the item you look up (in a traditional dictionary, the *word*) is called the *key*, and what the item lookup returns (in a traditional dictionary, the *meaning*) is called the *value*. In programming, a dictionary stores entries, and each entry is a key-value pair. You use one object (the key) to look up another object (the value).

You create an empty Python dictionary with curly braces:

```
grocery = {}
```

This command creates an empty dictionary with no entries and binds the dictionary object to a variable named `grocery`.

You can also create a dictionary with items already in it. In your grocery list, you map a grocery item to its quantity. In other words, the keys to `grocery` will be strings representing the grocery items, and the values to `grocery` will be integers representing the quantity:

```
grocery = {"milk": 1, "eggs": 12, "bread": 2}
```

This line creates a dictionary with three items, as shown in figure 27.2. Each item in a dictionary is separated by a comma. The keys and values for an item are separated by a colon. The key is to the left of the colon, and the value for that key is to the right of the colon.

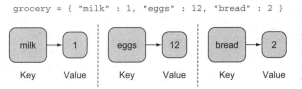

Figure 27.2 A dictionary initialized with three entries. Entries are separated by commas. Each entry has a key to the left of a colon, and the key's corresponding value to the right of the colon.

Both keys and values to a dictionary are single objects. A dictionary entry can't have more than one object as its key or more than one object as its value. If you'd like to store more than one object as the value, you could store all the objects inside a tuple, because a tuple is one object. For example, your grocery list could have the string key `"eggs"` and the tuple value `(1, "carton")` or `(12, "individual")`. Notice that the values in both situations are one Python object, a tuple.

Quick check 27.1   For each of the following situations, write a line of code that creates a dictionary and binds it to a variable with an appropriate name. For each, also indicate the keys and values:

1   Empty dictionary of employee names and their phone numbers and addresses
2   Empty dictionary of cities and the number of inches of snow each city got in 1990 and 2000
3   Dictionary of items in a house and their value: a TV worth $2,000 and a sofa worth $1,500

Quick check 27.2   For each of the following, how many entries are in the dictionary? What's the type of the keys, and what's the type of the values?

1   `d = {1:-1, 2:-2, 3:-3}`
2   `d = {"1":1, "2":2, "3":3}`
3   `d = {2:[0,2], 5:[1,1,1,1,1], 3:[2,1,0]}`

27.2 Adding key-value pairs to a dictionary

Empty dictionaries or dictionaries with a fixed number of entries aren't useful. You'll want to add more entries to store more information. To add a new key-value pair, you use square brackets, much as with lists:

```
d[k] = v
```

This command adds the key `k` and its associated value `v` into the dictionary `d`. If you try to add to the same key again, the previous value associated with that key will be overwritten.

At any point, you can use the `len()` function to tell you the number of entries in the dictionary. The following listing adds items to a dictionary.

Listing 27.1 Adding pairs to a dictionary

```
legs = {}              ◄──── Empty dictionary
legs["human"] = 2      ◄──── Adds key "human" with value 2
legs["cat"] = 4        ◄──── Adds key "cat" with value 4
legs["snake"] = 0      ◄──── Adds key "snake" with value 0
```

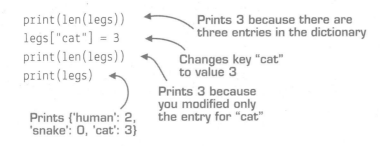

```
print(len(legs))
legs["cat"] = 3
print(len(legs))
print(legs)
```

Prints 3 because there are three entries in the dictionary

Changes key "cat" to value 3

Prints 3 because you modified only the entry for "cat"

Prints {'human': 2, 'snake': 0, 'cat': 3}

The preceding code shows the output using Python 3.5. If you use a different version of Python, you may see a different order in the dictionary. Using the output from Python 3.5, you may have noticed that the items you added to the dictionary were a human, then a cat, and then a snake. But when you printed the dictionary in listing 27.1, the dictionary printed a different order. This is normal behavior with dictionaries, and section 27.4.1 discusses this further.

27.2.1 Short diversion into restrictions on keys

When you try to insert an object key into a dictionary that already contains that key, the value for the existing key is overwritten. This leads to an interesting point about the kinds of objects you can store as keys in a dictionary.

You can't have the same key multiple times in a dictionary; if you did, Python wouldn't know which key you're referring to when you want to retrieve a value. For example, if you have the word box as a key that maps to container, and the word box that also maps to fight, then which definition do you give to someone who wants the definition of box? The first one you find? The last one? Both? The answer isn't so clear. Instead of dealing with this situation, Python guarantees that all keys in a dictionary are unique objects.

How and why does the Python language make this guarantee? Python enforces that a key is an immutable object. This decision is because of the way that Python implements the dictionary object.

Given a key, Python uses a formula based on the key value to calculate the location to store the value. The formula is called a *hash function*. This method is used so that when you want to look up a value, you can quickly retrieve the value by running the formula instead of iterating through all the keys to find the one you want. Because the result of the hash function should be the same when inserting or when looking up an item, the location where the value is stored is fixed. Using an immutable object, you'll get the same location value because the immutable object's value doesn't change. But if you used a mutable object, it's possible (and likely) that the hash function would give a different location value when applied to the mutated key value, as opposed to the original key value.

> **Quick check 27.3**   What's the value of the dictionary after each line is executed?
>
> ```
> city_pop = {}
> city_pop["LA"] = 3884
> city_pop["NYC"] = 8406
> city_pop["SF"] = 837
> city_pop["LA"] = 4031
> ```

27.3 Removing key-value pairs from a dictionary

As with lists, you can remove items after you put them into a dictionary by using the pop() operation. The command d.pop(k) will remove the key-value entry in the dictionary d corresponding to the key k. This operation is like a function and returns the value from the dictionary associated with the key k. After the pop operation in the next listing, the dictionary household will have the value {"person":4, "cat":2, "dog":1}.

> **Listing 27.2 Removing pairs from a dictionary**

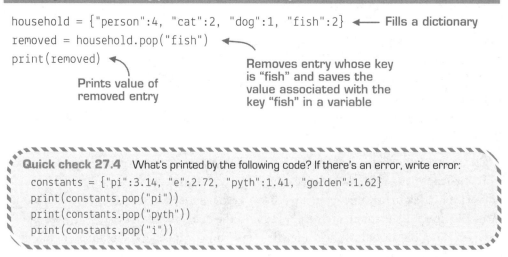

```
household = {"person":4, "cat":2, "dog":1, "fish":2}     ◄── Fills a dictionary
removed = household.pop("fish")   ◄─┐
print(removed)   ◄─┐                │
                  │                 │
       Prints value of      Removes entry whose key
       removed entry        is "fish" and saves the
                            value associated with the
                            key "fish" in a variable
```

> **Quick check 27.4**   What's printed by the following code? If there's an error, write error:
>
> ```
> constants = {"pi":3.14, "e":2.72, "pyth":1.41, "golden":1.62}
> print(constants.pop("pi"))
> print(constants.pop("pyth"))
> print(constants.pop("i"))
> ```

27.4 Getting all the keys and values in a dictionary

Python has two operations that allow you to get all the keys in the dictionary and all the values in the dictionary. This is useful if you need to look through all the pairs to find entries that match certain criteria. For example, if you have a dictionary that maps a song name to its rating, you may want to retrieve all the pairs, and keep only the ones whose rating is 4 or 5.

If a dictionary named songs contains pairs of songs and ratings, you can use songs.keys() to get all the keys in the dictionary. The following code prints dict_keys(['believe', 'roar', 'let it be']):

```
songs = {"believe": 3, "roar": 5, "let it be": 4}
print(songs.keys())
```

The expression dict_keys(['believe', 'roar', 'let it be']) is a Python object that contains all the keys in the dictionary.

You can iterate over the returned keys directly by using a for loop, as in this line:

```
for one_song in songs.keys():
```

Alternatively, you can save the keys in a list by casting the returned keys into a list via this command:

```
all_songs = list(songs.keys())
```

Similarly, the command songs.values() gives you all the values in the dictionary songs. You can either iterate over them directly or cast them into a list if you need to use them later in your code. It's most often useful to iterate over the keys in a dictionary because after you know a key, you can always look up the value corresponding to that key.

Let's look at a different example. Suppose you have data for the following students in your class:

```
Name        Quiz 1 Grade   Quiz 2 Grade
Chris       100            70
Angela      90             100
Bruce       80             40
Stacey      70             70
```

Listing 27.3 shows an example of how to use dictionary commands to keep track of students and their grades in your class. First, you create a dictionary that maps student names to their grades on exams. Assuming each student took two exams, the value in the dictionary for each student will be a list containing two elements. Using the dictionary, you can print all the names of the students in the class by iterating through all the keys, and you can also iterate through all the values and print all the averages for the quizzes. Lastly, you can even modify the values for each key by adding to the end of the list the average of the two quizzes.

Listing 27.3 Keeping track of student grades by using a dictionary

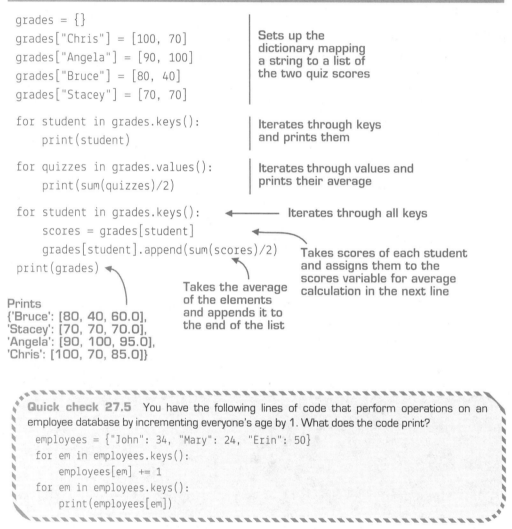

```
grades = {}
grades["Chris"] = [100, 70]
grades["Angela"] = [90, 100]
grades["Bruce"] = [80, 40]
grades["Stacey"] = [70, 70]

for student in grades.keys():
    print(student)

for quizzes in grades.values():
    print(sum(quizzes)/2)

for student in grades.keys():
    scores = grades[student]
    grades[student].append(sum(scores)/2)
print(grades)
```

Sets up the
dictionary mapping
a string to a list of
the two quiz scores

Iterates through keys
and prints them

Iterates through values and
prints their average

Iterates through all keys

Takes scores of each student
and assigns them to the
scores variable for average
calculation in the next line

Takes the average
of the elements
and appends it to
the end of the list

Prints
{'Bruce': [80, 40, 60.0],
'Stacey': [70, 70, 70.0],
'Angela': [90, 100, 95.0],
'Chris': [100, 70, 85.0]}

Quick check 27.5 You have the following lines of code that perform operations on an employee database by incrementing everyone's age by 1. What does the code print?

```
employees = {"John": 34, "Mary": 24, "Erin": 50}
for em in employees.keys():
    employees[em] += 1
for em in employees.keys():
    print(employees[em])
```

27.4.1 No ordering to dictionary pairs

In this lesson, I mentioned that you may see different results depending on the version of Python you're using. If you use Python 3.5 to run the code in listing 27.3, you may notice something odd. The output from printing all the keys is as follows:

```
Bruce
Stacey
Angela
Chris
```

But when you added items to the dictionary, you added Chris, then Angela, then Bruce, then Stacey. These orders don't seem to match. Unlike lists, a Python dictionary forgets the order in which items were added to the dictionary. When you ask for keys or values, you have no guarantee about the order in which they're returned. You can see this by typing in the following code that checks for equality between two dictionaries and then between two lists:

```
print({"Angela": 70, "Bruce": 50} == {"Bruce": 50, "Angela": 70})
print(["Angela", "Bruce"] == ["Bruce", "Angela"])
```

The two dictionaries are equal, even though the order that the entries are put in aren't the same. In contrast, a list of the two names must be in the same order to be considered equal.

27.5 Why should you use a dictionary?

By now, it should be clear that dictionaries can be fairly useful objects because they map objects (keys) to other objects (values), and you can later look up values given a key. Dictionaries have two common uses: keeping count of the number of times something occurs, and using dictionaries to map items to functions.

27.5.1 Keeping count with frequency dictionaries

Possibly one of the most common uses of dictionaries is to keep track of the quantity of a certain item. For example, if you're writing a Scrabble game, you may use a dictionary to keep track of the quantity of each letter in your hand. If you have a text document, you may want to keep track of the number of times you use each word. In listing 27.4, you'll build a frequency dictionary that maps a word to the number of times it occurs in a song. The code takes a string and makes a list of words by splitting on the space. With an initially empty dictionary, you go through all the words in the list and do one of two things:

- If you haven't added the word to the dictionary yet, add it with a count of 1.
- If you've already added the word to the dictionary, increase its count by 1.

Listing 27.4 Building a frequency dictionary

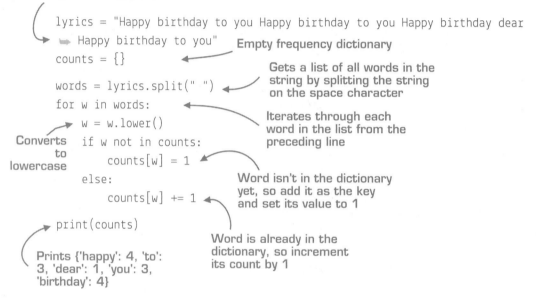

String with song lyrics

```
lyrics = "Happy birthday to you Happy birthday to you Happy birthday dear
         Happy birthday to you"
counts = {}                    Empty frequency dictionary

words = lyrics.split(" ")       Gets a list of all words in the
                                string by splitting the string
                                on the space character
for w in words:
    w = w.lower()               Iterates through each
                                word in the list from the
Converts  if w not in counts:   preceding line
   to
lowercase     counts[w] = 1     Word isn't in the dictionary
                                yet, so add it as the key
    else:                       and set its value to 1
        counts[w] += 1

print(counts)                   Word is already in the
                                dictionary, so increment
Prints {'happy': 4, 'to':       its count by 1
3, 'dear': 1, 'you': 3,
'birthday': 4}
```

A frequency dictionary is a useful application of Python dictionaries, and you'll write a function to build a frequency dictionary in the capstone project in lesson 29.

27.5.2 Building unconventional dictionaries

A Python dictionary is a useful data structure. It allows easy access to one object's value by looking it up using another object's value. Anytime you need to map two items and access them later, a dictionary should be the first thing you try to use. But there are some less obvious scenarios for using a dictionary. One use is to map common names to functions. In listing 27.5, you define three functions that, given an input variable, find the area of three common shapes: a square, circle, and equilateral triangle.

You can build a dictionary that maps a string to the function itself, referenced by the function name. When you look up each string, you'll get back the function object. Then, using the function object, you can call it using a parameter. In listing 27.5, when you access the dictionary using "sq" in the line print(areas["sq"](n)), the value retrieved by areas["sq"] is the function named square. The function is then called on the number n = 2 when you use areas["sq"](n).

Listing 27.5 **Dictionaries and functions**

```
def square(x):
    return x*x
```
Known function to calculate area of a square

```
def circle(r):
    return 3.14*r*r
```
Known function to calculate area of a circle

```
def equilateraltriangle(s):
    return (s*s)*(3**0.5)/4
```
Known function to calculate area of an equilateral triangle

```
areas = {"sq": square, "ci": circle, "eqtri": equilateraltriangle}
```
Dictionary maps string to function

```
n = 2
print(areas["sq"](n))
```
Calls function mapped in dictionary by key "sq" on n where n is 2

```
print(areas["ci"](n))
```
Calls function mapped in dictionary by key "ci" on n where n is 2

```
print(areas["eqtri"](n))
```
Calls function mapped in dictionary by key "eqtri" on n where n is 2

Summary

In this lesson, my objective was to teach you a new data type, the Python dictionary. A dictionary maps one object to another. Like lists, dictionaries are mutable objects in which you can add to, remove from, and change elements. Unlike lists, dictionaries don't have an order, and they allow only certain object types to be the keys. Here are the major takeaways:

- Dictionaries are mutable.
- Dictionary keys must be immutable objects.
- Dictionary values can be mutable or immutable.
- A dictionary doesn't have an order.

Let's see if you got this…

Q27.1   Write a program that uses dictionaries to accomplish the following task. Given a dictionary of song names (strings) mapped to ratings (integers), print the song names of all songs that are rated exactly 5.

Q27.2   Write a function named replace. It takes in one dictionary, d, and two values, v and e. The function doesn't return anything. It mutates d such that all the values v in d are replaced with e. For example,

- replace({1:2, 3:4, 4:2}, 2, 7) mutates d to {1: 7, 3: 4, 4: 7}.
- replace({1:2, 3:1, 4:2}, 1, 2) mutates d to {1: 2, 3: 2, 4: 2}.

Q27.3   Write a function named invert. It takes in one dictionary, d. The function returns a new dictionary, d_inv. The keys in d_inv are the unique values in d. The value corresponding to a key in d_inv is a list. The list contains all the keys in d that mapped to the same value in d. For example,

- invert({1:2, 3:4, 5:6}) returns {2: [1], 4: [3], 6: [5]}.
- invert({1:2, 2:1, 3:3}) returns {1: [2], 2: [1], 3: [3]}.
- invert({1:1, 3:1, 5:1}) returns {1: [1, 3, 5]}.

28

ALIASING AND COPYING LISTS AND DICTIONARIES

After reading lesson 28, you'll be able to

- Make aliases for mutable objects (lists and dictionaries)
- Make copies of mutable objects (lists and dictionaries)
- Make sorted copies of lists
- Remove elements from mutable objects based on certain criteria

Mutable objects are great to use because they allow you to modify the object itself without making a copy. When your mutable objects are large, this behavior makes sense because otherwise, making a copy of a large item every time you make a change to it is expensive and wasteful. But using mutable objects introduces a side effect that you need to be aware of: you can have more than one variable bound to the same mutable object, and the object can be mutated via both names.

> **Consider this**   Think of a famous person. What aliases do they have, or what other names or nicknames do they go by?
>
> Answer: Bill Gates
>
> Nicknames: Bill, William, William Gates, William Henry Gates III

Suppose you have data on the famous computer scientist Grace Hopper. Let's say Grace Hopper is an object, and her value is a list of labels: `["programmer", "admiral", "female"]`. To friends she might be known as *Grace*, to others as *Ms. Hopper*, and her nickname is *Amazing Grace*. All these names are aliases for the same person, the same object with the same string of labels. Now suppose that someone who knows her as Grace adds another value to her list of labels: `"deceased"`. To people who know her as Grace, her list of labels is now `["programmer", "admiral", "female", "deceased"]`. But because the labels refer to the same person, every other one of her aliases now also refers to the new list of labels.

28.1 Using object aliases

In Python, *variable names* are names that point to an object. The object resides at a specific location in computer memory. In lesson 24, you used the `id()` function to see a numerical representation of the memory location of an object.

28.1.1 Aliases of immutable objects

Before looking at mutable objects, let's look at what happens when you use the assignment operator (equal sign) between two variable names that point to immutable objects. Type the following commands in the console and use the `id()` function to see the memory locations of the variables a and b:

```
a = 1
id(a)
Out[2]: 1906901488

b = a
id(b)
Out[4]: 1906901488
```

The `Out` lines tell you the output of the `id()` function. Notice that both a and b are names that point to the same object (an integer with value 1). What happens if you change the object that a points to? In the following code, you reassign variable name a to point to a different object:

```
a = 2
id(a)
Out[6]: 1906901520

id(b)
Out[7]: 1906901488
```

```
a
Out[8]: 2

b
Out[9]: 1
```

Notice that the variable named a now points to a completely different object with a different memory location. But this operation doesn't change the variable name to which b points, so the object that b points to is at the same memory location as before.

> **Quick check 28.1** You have a variable named x that points to an immutable object with x = "me". Running id(x) gives 2899205431680. For each of the following lines, determine whether the ID of that variable will be the same as id(x). Assume that the lines are executed one after another:
>
> ```
> 1  y = x     # what is id(y)
> 2  z = y     # what is id(z)
> 3  a = "me"  # what is id(a)
> ```

28.1.2 Aliases of mutable objects

You can do the same sequence of commands as in section 28.1.1 on a mutable object, such as a list. In the following code, you can see that using the assignment operator between a variable name that points to a list behaves in the same way as with an immutable object. Using the assignment operator on a mutable object doesn't make a copy; it makes an alias. An *alias* is another name for the same object:

```
genius = ["einstein", "galileo"]
id(genius)
Out[9]: 2899318203976

smart = genius
id(smart)
Out[11]: 2899318203976
```

The memory location that objects genius and smart point to are the same because they point to the same object. Figure 28.1 shows how the variables smart and genius point to the same object.

Figure 28.1   In the left panel, you create the variable genius pointing to the list ["einstein", "galileo"]. In the right panel, the variable smart points to the same object as genius.

Quick check 28.2   You have a variable named x that points to a mutable object with x = ["me", "I"]. Running id(x) gives 2899318311816. For each of the following lines, determine whether the ID of that variable will be the same as id(x). Assume that the lines are executed one after another:

   1 y = x # what is id(y)
   2 z = y # what is id(z)
   3 a = ["me", "I"] # what is id(a)

The difference between mutable and immutable objects is evident in the next set of commands, when you mutate the list:

```
genius.append("shakespeare")
id(genius)
Out[13]: 2899318203976

id(smart)
Out[14]: 2899318203976

genius
Out[16]: ["einstein", "galileo", "shakespeare"]

smart
Out[15]: ["einstein", "galileo", "shakespeare"]
```

When you modify a mutable object, the object itself is changed. When you append a value to the list pointed to by genius, the list object itself is changed. Variable names genius and smart still point to the same object at the same memory location. The object pointed to by variable name smart is also changed (because it points to the same thing as the variable genius). This is shown in figure 28.2.

Using the equal sign between mutable lists implies that if you modify the list through one variable name, all other variable names pointing to the same list will point to the mutated value.

Figure 28.2 When the list object ["einstein", "galileo"] is modified through the variable genius, the variable smart also points to the modified list object.

> **Quick check 28.3** You have a variable named x that points to a mutable object with x = ["me", "I"]. For each of the following points, answer the question:
>
> 1 Does x change after the following lines are executed?
>    ```
>    y = x
>    x.append("myself")
>    ```
> 2 Does x change after the following lines are executed?
>    ```
>    y = x
>    y.pop()
>    ```
> 3 Does x change after the following lines are executed?
>    ```
>    y = x
>    y.append("myself")
>    ```
> 4 Does x change after the following lines are executed?
>    ```
>    y = x
>    y.sort()
>    ```
> 5 Does x change after the following lines are executed?
>    ```
>    y = [x, x]
>    y.append(x)
>    ```

28.1.3 Mutable objects as function parameters

In unit 5, you saw that variables inside a function are independent of variables outside the function. You could have a variable named x outside the function and a variable named x as a parameter to the function. They don't interfere with each other because of scoping rules. When working with mutable objects, passing mutable objects as actual parameters to a function implies that the actual parameter to the function will be an alias.

Listing 28.1 shows code that implements a function. The function is named add_word(). Its input parameters are a dictionary, a word, and a definition. The function mutates the dictionary so that even when accessed outside the function, the dictionary contains the newly added word. The code then calls the function with a dictionary named words as the actual parameter. In the function call, the dictionary named d is the formal parameter and is now an alias for the dictionary words. Any changes made to d inside the function reflect when you access the dictionary words.

Listing 28.1 Function that mutates a dictionary

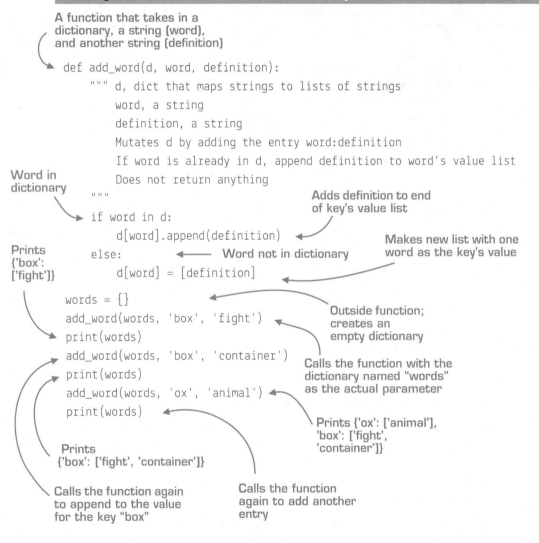

A function that takes in a dictionary, a string (word), and another string (definition)

```
def add_word(d, word, definition):
    """ d, dict that maps strings to lists of strings
        word, a string
        definition, a string
        Mutates d by adding the entry word:definition
        If word is already in d, append definition to word's value list
        Does not return anything
    """
    if word in d:
        d[word].append(definition)
    else:                           ← Word not in dictionary
        d[word] = [definition]

words = {}
add_word(words, 'box', 'fight')
print(words)
add_word(words, 'box', 'container')
print(words)
add_word(words, 'ox', 'animal')
print(words)
```

Word in dictionary

Adds definition to end of key's value list

Makes new list with one word as the key's value

Prints {'box': ['fight']}

Outside function; creates an empty dictionary

Calls the function with the dictionary named "words" as the actual parameter

Prints {'ox': ['animal'], 'box': ['fight', 'container']}

Prints {'box': ['fight', 'container']}

Calls the function again to append to the value for the key "box"

Calls the function again to add another entry

 **28.2 Making copies of mutable objects**

When you want to make a copy of a mutable object, you need to use a function that makes it clear to Python that you want to make a copy. There are two ways to do this: make a new list with the same elements as another list, or use a function.

28.2.1 Commands to copy mutable objects

One way to make a copy is to make a new list object with the same values as the other one. Given a list artists with some elements, the following command creates a new list object and binds the variable name painters to it:

```
painters = list(artists)
```

The new list object has the same elements as artists. For example, the following code shows that the objects that lists painters and artists point to are different because modifying one doesn't modify the other:

```
artists = ["monet", "picasso"]
painters = list(artists)
painters.append("van gogh")

painters
Out[24]: ["monet", "picasso", "van gogh"]

artists
Out[25]: ["monet", "picasso"]
```

The other way is to use the copy() function. If artists is a list, the following command creates a new object that has the same elements as artists, but copied into the new object:

```
painters = artists.copy()
```

The following code shows how to use the copy command:

```
artists = ["monet", "picasso"]
painters = artists.copy()
painters.append("van gogh")

painters
Out[24]: ["monet", "picasso", "van gogh"]

artists
Out[25]: ["monet", "picasso"]
```

From the console output, you can see that the list objects pointed to by painters and artists are separate because making changes to one doesn't affect the other. Figure 28.3 shows what it means to make a copy.

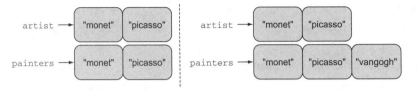

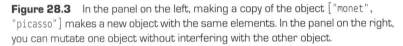

Figure 28.3 In the panel on the left, making a copy of the object ["monet", "picasso"] makes a new object with the same elements. In the panel on the right, you can mutate one object without interfering with the other object.

28.2.2 Getting copies of sorted lists

You saw that you can sort a list so that the list itself is modified directly. For a list L, the command is L.sort(). In some situations, you'd like to keep your original list and get a sorted copy of the list, while keeping the original unchanged.

Instead of making a copy of the list and then sorting the copy, Python has a function that allows you to do it in one line. The following command shows a function that returns a sorted version of a list and stores it in another list:

```
kid_ages = [2,1,4]
sorted_ages = sorted(kid_ages)

sorted_ages
Out[61]: [1, 2, 4]

kid_ages
Out[62]: [2, 1, 4]
```

You can see that the variable sorted_ages points to a sorted list, but the original list kid_ages remains unchanged. Previously, when you wrote the command kid_ages.sort(), kid_ages would be changed so that it got sorted without a copy being made.

> **Quick check 28.4** Write a line of code that achieves each of the following:
> 1. Creates a variable named order that's a sorted copy of a list named chaos
> 2. Sorts a list named colors
> 3. Sorts a list named deck and aliases it to a variable named cards

28.2.3 A word of caution when iterating over mutable objects

Often you want to have code that removes items from a mutable object, provided they meet some sort of criteria. For example, suppose you have a dictionary of songs and their ratings. You want to remove all songs from the dictionary that have a rating of 1.

Listing 28.2 tries (but fails) to accomplish this. The code iterates through every key in the dictionary. It checks whether the value associated with that key is a 1. If so, it removes the pair from the dictionary. The code fails to run and shows the error message `RuntimeError: dictionary changed size during iteration`. Python doesn't allow you to change the size of a dictionary as you're iterating over it.

Listing 28.2 Attempt to remove elements from a dictionary while iterating over it

```
songs = {"Wannabe": 1, "Roar": 1, "Let It Be": 5, "Red Corvette": 4}    ← songs dictionary

for s in songs.keys():      ←─── Iterates through every pair
    if songs[s] == 1:       ←─── If the rating value is 1...
        songs.pop(s)        ←─── ...removes the song with that value
```

Suppose you try to do the same thing, except that instead of a dictionary, you have a list. The following listing shows how you might accomplish this, but also fails to do the right thing. The code doesn't fail this time. But it has a behavior different from what you expected; it gives the wrong value for songs: [1, 5, 4] instead of [5, 4].

Listing 28.3 Attempt to remove elements from a list while iterating over it

```
songs = [1, 1, 5, 4]        ←─── Song rating list

for s in songs:             ←─── Iterates through every rating
    if s == 1:              ←─── If the rating value is 1...
        songs.pop(s)        ←─── ...removes the song with that value
print(songs)                ←─── Prints [1,5,4]
```

You can see the buggy effect of removing items from a list while iterating over it. The loop gets to the element at index 0, sees that it's a 1, and removes it from the list. The list is now [1, 5, 4]. Next, the loop looks at the element at index 1. This element is now from the mutated list [1, 5, 4], so it looks at the number 5. This number isn't equal to 1, so it doesn't remove it. Then it finally looks at the element at index 2 from the list [1, 5, 4], the number 4. It's also not equal to 1, so it keeps it. The issue here is that when you popped the first 1 you saw, you decreased the length of the list. Now the index count is one off from the original list. Effectively, the second 1 in the original list [1, 1, 5, 4] was skipped.

If you ever need to remove (or add) items to a list, you'll first make a copy. You can iterate over the list copy and then start fresh on the original list by adding items you want to keep, as you iterate over the copied list. The following listing shows how to modify the code in listing 28.3 to do the right thing. This code doesn't cause an error, and the correct value for songs is now [5, 4].

> **Listing 28.4 A correct way to remove elements from a list while iterating over it**

```
songs = [1, 1, 5, 4]          ◄——— Original ratings list
songs_copy = songs.copy()     ◄——— Makes a copy of the object
songs = []                    ◄——————— Sets original list to be empty
for s in songs_copy:          ◄——————— For every rating in the list
    if s != 1:                ◄——————— If the rating is one to keep...
        songs.append(s)       ◄——— ...adds the rating to the original list
print(songs)                  ◄——————— Prints [5,4]
```

28.2.4 Why does aliasing exist?

If aliasing an object introduces the problem of inadvertently mutating an object you didn't intend to change, why use aliasing in the first place? Why not just make copies all the time? All Python objects are stored in computer memory. Lists and dictionaries are "heavy" objects, unlike an integer or a Boolean. If you make copies, for example, every time you make a function call, this can severely cripple the program with many function calls. If you have a list of the names of all people in the United States, copying that list every time you want to add someone new can be slow.

Summary

In this lesson, my objective was to teach you about subtleties of dealing with mutable objects. Mutable objects are useful because they can store a lot of data that can easily be modified in place. Because you're dealing with mutable objects that contain many elements, making copies with every operation becomes inefficient in terms of computer time and space. By default, Python aliases objects so that using the assignment operator makes a new variable that points to the same object; this is called an *alias*. Python recognizes that in some situations you want to make a copy of a mutable object, and it allows you to explicitly tell it that you want to do so. Here are the major takeaways:

- Python aliases all object types.
- Aliasing a mutable object may lead to unexpected side effects.
- Modifying a mutable object through one alias leads to seeing the change through all other aliases of that object.
- You can make a copy of a mutable object by making a new object and copying over all elements of the original one.

Let's see if you got this…

Q28.1 Write a function named `invert_dict` that takes as input a dictionary. The function returns a new dictionary; the values are now the original keys, and the keys are now the original values. Assume that the values of the input dictionary are immutable and unique.

Q28.2 Write a function named `invert_dict_inplace` that takes as input a dictionary. The function doesn't return anything. It mutates the dictionary passed in so that the values are now the original keys, and the keys are now the original values. Assume that the values of the input dictionary are immutable and unique.

CAPSTONE PROJECT: DOCUMENT SIMILARITY

After reading lesson 29, you'll be able to

- Take as input two files and determine their similarity
- Write organized code by using functions
- Understand how to work with dictionaries and lists in a real-life setting

How similar are two sentences? Paragraphs? Essays? You can write a program incorporating dictionaries and lists to calculate the similarity of two pieces of work. If you're a teacher, you could use this to check for similarity between essay submissions. If you're making changes to your own documents, you can use this program as a sort of version control, comparing versions of your documents to see where major changes were made.

THE PROBLEM   You're given two files containing text. Using the names of the files, write a program that reads the documents and uses a metric to determine how similar they are. Documents that are exactly the same should get a score of 1, and documents that don't have any words in common should get a score of 0.

Given this problem description, you need to decide a few things:

- Do you count punctuation from the files or only words?
- Do you care about the ordering of the words in files? If two files have the same words but in different order, are they still the same?
- What metric do you use to assign a numerical value to the similarity?

These are important questions to answer, but when given a problem, a more important action is to break it into subtasks. Each subtask will become its own module, or a *function* in Python terms.

29.1 Breaking the problem into tasks

If you reread the problem statement, you can see that a few natural divisions exist for self-contained tasks:

1. Get the filename, open the file, and read the information.
2. Get all the words in a file.
3. Map each word to how often it occurs. Let's agree that order doesn't matter for now.
4. Calculate the similarity.

Notice that in breaking down the tasks, you haven't made any specific decisions about implementations. You have only broken down your original problem.

> **Thinking like a programmer**
> When thinking about how to break down your problem, choose and write tasks in such a way that they can be reusable. For example, make a task that reads a filename and gives you back the file contents, as opposed to a task that reads exactly two filenames and gives you back their contents. The idea is that the function that reads one filename is more versatile and, if needed, you can call it two (or more) times.

29.2 Reading file information

The first step is to write a function that takes in a filename, reads the contents, and gives you back the contents in useable form. A good choice for the return would be to give you back all the contents of the file as a (possibly large) string. Listing 29.1 shows you the function to do this. It uses Python functions to open the file by using the filename given, read the entire contents into a string, and return that string. When the function is called on the name of a file, it'll return a string with all the file contents.

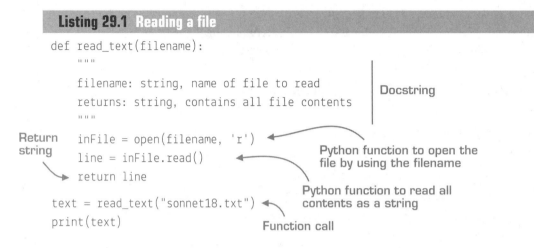

Listing 29.1 Reading a file

```
def read_text(filename):
    """

    filename: string, name of file to read
    returns: string, contains all file contents
    """
    inFile = open(filename, 'r')
    line = inFile.read()
    return line

text = read_text("sonnet18.txt")
print(text)
```

Docstring

Return string

Python function to open the file by using the filename

Python function to read all contents as a string

Function call

After you write a function, you should test and, if necessary, debug it. To test this function, you need to create a file with contents. Create an empty text document in the same folder where you have your .py file for this lesson. Populate the text file with content and save it; I used Shakespeare's "Sonnet 18." Now, in the .py file, you can call the function with

```
print(read_text("sonnet18.txt"))
```

When you run the file, the console should print the entire contents of the file.

> **Thinking like a programmer**
>
> The point of writing functions is to make your life easier. Functions should be self-contained pieces of code that you need to debug only once but that you can reuse many times. When you're integrating more than one function, you need to debug only the way they interact as opposed to debugging the functions themselves.

29.3 Saving all words from the file

Now you have a function that returns a string containing all the contents of a file. One giant string isn't helpful to a computer. Remember that Python works with objects, and a large string containing a bunch of text is one object. You'd like to break this large string into parts. If you're comparing two documents, a natural breakdown of the string would be to separate it into words.

> **Thinking like a programmer**
> When faced with a task, you'll often need to decide which data structures (types) to use. Before beginning to code, think about each data type you've learned about and decide whether it's an appropriate one to use. When more than one may work, pick the simplest one.

This task of breaking down a string will be done using a function. Its input is a string. Its output can be one of many things. With more coding practice, you'll more quickly recognize when to use certain object types and why. In this case, you'll separate all the words in the string into a list, with each word being an element in the list. Listing 29.2 shows the code. It first does a bit of cleanup by replacing newlines with a space and removes all special characters. The expression string.punctuation is a string itself whose value is the set of all the punctuation characters that a string object could have:

```
"!#$%&\'()*+,-./:;<=>?@[\\] _ {|}~
```

After the text has been cleaned up, you use the split operation to split the string on the space character and give back a list of all words (because all words are separated by a space).

Listing 29.2 Finding words from a string

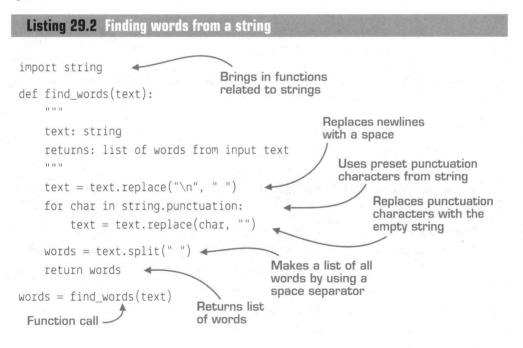

```python
import string

def find_words(text):
    """
    text: string
    returns: list of words from input text
    """
    text = text.replace("\n", " ")
    for char in string.punctuation:
        text = text.replace(char, "")
    words = text.split(" ")
    return words

words = find_words(text)
```

Brings in functions related to strings

Replaces newlines with a space

Uses preset punctuation characters from string

Replaces punctuation characters with the empty string

Makes a list of all words by using a space separator

Returns list of words

Function call

> **Thinking like a programmer**
> Before running a function on large input files, try it on a smaller test file with a couple of words. That way, if anything goes wrong, you don't have to look through hundreds of lines to figure out what's wrong.

You run this function on the text file sonnet18.txt:

```
Shall I compare thee to a summer's day?
Thou art more lovely and more temperate:
Rough winds do shake the darling buds of May,
And summer's lease hath all too short a date:
Sometime too hot the eye of heaven shines,
And often is his gold complexion dimmed,
And every fair from fair sometime declines,
By chance, or nature's changing course untrimmed:
But thy eternal summer shall not fade,
Nor lose possession of that fair thou ow'st,
Nor shall death brag thou wander'st in his shade,
When in eternal lines to time thou grow'st,
So long as men can breathe, or eyes can see,
So long lives this, and this gives life to thee.
```

If you type the following code, you'll get back a list of all the words in the console:

```
print(find_words(text))
```

This prints the following list for sonnet18.txt:

```
['Shall', 'I', 'compare', ... LIST TRUNCATED ..., 'life', 'to', 'thee']
```

29.4 Mapping words to their frequency

Now that you have a list of words, you have a Python object with which you can work more in-depth to analyze its contents. At this point, you should be thinking about how to find the similarity between two documents. At the very least, you'll probably want to know the quantity of each word in the document.

Notice that when you created the list of words, the list contained all the words, in order, from the original string. If there were duplicate words, they were added in as another list element. To give you more information about the words, you'd like to pair up each word to how often it occurs. Hopefully, the phrase *pair up* led you to believe that a

Python dictionary would be an appropriate data structure. In this particular case, you'll be building a frequency dictionary. The following listing shows you the code to accomplish this.

Listing 29.3 Making a frequency dictionary for words

```
def frequencies(words):
    """

    words: list of words
    returns: frequency dictionary for input words
    """

    freq_dict = {}              ◄──── Initially empty dictionary

    for word in words:          ◄──────── Looks at each word in list
        if word in freq_dict:       ◄──────── If word already in dictionary...
            freq_dict[word] += 1    ◄──── ...adds one to its count
        else:                   ◄──────── Word not in dictionary yet
            freq_dict[word] = 1    ◄──────── Adds word and sets its count to 1
        return freq_dict       ◄──────── Returns dictionary

freq_dict = frequencies(words)  ◄────── Function call
```

A frequency dictionary is a useful application of dictionaries in this problem. It maps a word to the number of times you see it in the text. You can use this information when you compare two documents.

29.5 Comparing two documents by using a similarity score

Now you have to decide which formula you'd like to use to compare two documents, given the number of times each word occurs. To begin with, the formula doesn't need to be too complicated. As an initial pass, you can use a simple metric to make the comparison and see how well it does. Suppose these steps will calculate the score, by using a running sum over each word:

- Look for a word in both frequency dictionaries (one for each document).
- If it's in both, add the difference between the counts. If it appears in only one of them, add the count for that one (effectively adding the difference between the count from one dictionary and 0 from the other one).

- The score is the division between the total difference and the total number of words in both documents.

After coming up with a metric, it's important to do a sanity check. If the documents are exactly the same, the difference between all the word counts in both frequency dictionaries is 0. Dividing this by the total number of words in both dictionaries gives 0. If the documents don't have any words in common, the difference summed up will be "total words in one document" + "total words in other document." Dividing this by the total number of words in both documents gives a ratio of 1. The ratios make sense except that you want documents that are exactly the same to have a ratio of 1, and ones that are completely different to have a ratio of 0. To solve this, subtract the ratio from 1.

Listing 29.4 shows the code to calculate the similarity, given two input dictionaries. The code iterates over the keys of one dictionary; it doesn't matter which one, because you'll iterate over the other dictionary in another loop.

As you're going through the keys of one dictionary, you check whether the key is also in the other dictionary. Recall that you're looking at the value for each key; the value is the number of times the word occurs in one text. If the word is in both dictionaries, take the difference between the two frequency counts. If it isn't, take the count from the one dictionary in which it exists.

After you finish going through one dictionary, go through the other dictionary. You no longer need to look at the difference between the two dictionary values because you already counted that previously. Now you're just looking to see whether any words in the other dictionary weren't in the first one. If so, add up their counts.

Finally, when you have the sum of the differences, divide that by the total number of words in both dictionaries. Take 1 minus that value to match the original problem specifications for scoring.

Listing 29.4 Calculate similarity given two input dictionaries

```
def calculate_similarity(dict1, dict2):
    """

    dict1: frequency dictionary for one text
    dict2: frequency dictionary for another text
    returns: float, representing how similar both texts are to each other
    """

    diff = 0
    total = 0
```

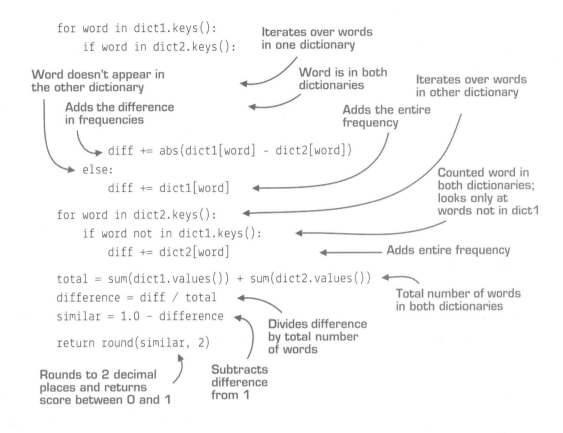

The function returns a float number between 0 and 1. The lower the number, the less similar the documents are, and vice versa.

29.6 Putting it all together

The final step is to test the code on text files. Before using your program on two separate files, do a sanity check: first, use the same file as both texts to check that the score you get is 1.0, and then use the sonnet file and an empty file for the other to check that the score you get is 0.0.

Now, use Shakespeare's "Sonnet 18" and "Sonnet 19" to test two pieces of work, and then modify "Sonnet 18" by changing the word *summer* to *winter* to see if the program found them to be almost exactly the same.

The text of "Sonnet 18" was shown earlier. Here's the text for "Sonnet 19":

```
Devouring Time, blunt thou the lion's paws,
And make the earth devour her own sweet brood;
Pluck the keen teeth from the fierce tiger's jaws,
And burn the long-lived phoenix in her blood;
Make glad and sorry seasons as thou fleet'st,
And do whate'er thou wilt, swift-footed Time,
To the wide world and all her fading sweets;
But I forbid thee one most heinous crime:
O! carve not with thy hours my love's fair brow,
Nor draw no lines there with thine antique pen;
Him in thy course untainted do allow
For beauty's pattern to succeeding men.
Yet, do thy worst old Time: despite thy wrong,
My love shall in my verse ever live young.
```

The following listing opens two files, reads their words, makes the frequency dictionary, and calculates their similarity.

Listing 29.5 Code to run the document similarity program

```
text_1 = read_text("sonnet18.txt")
text_2 = read_text("sonnet19.txt")
words_1 = find_words(text_1)
words_2 = find_words(text_2)
freq_dict_1 = frequencies(words_1)
freq_dict_2 = frequencies(words_2)
print(calculate_similarity(freq_dict_1, freq_dict_2))
```

When I run the program on "Sonnet 18" and "Sonnet 19" the similarity score is 0.24. It makes sense that it's closer to 0 because they're two different pieces of work. When I run the program on "Sonnet 18" and my modified "Sonnet 18" (with three instances of the word *summer* changed to *winter*), the score is 0.97. This also makes sense because the two pieces are almost the same.

29.7 One possible extension

You can make your program more robust by looking at pairs of words instead of single words. After you read the file as a string, look at pairs of words, called *bigrams*, and save them in a list. Looking at bigrams instead of words can improve your program because pairs of words often give a better indication of similarity in languages. This could lead to a more accurate setup and a better model of written text. If you want, you could also use a mixture of bigrams and words when you calculate a similarity score.

 ## Summary

In this lesson, my objective was to teach you how to write a program that reads in two files, converts their content to a string, uses a list to store all the words in a file, and then makes a frequency dictionary to store each word and the number of times it occurred in a file. You compared two frequency dictionaries by counting the differences between the word counts in each dictionary to come up with a score for how similar the files were. Here are the major takeaways:

- You wrote modular code by using functions that could be reused.
- You used lists to store individual elements.
- You used a dictionary to map a word to its count.

Making your own object types by using object-oriented programming

In the previous units, you used various Python object types. You wrote programs that created multiple objects of different, and of the same, types. Your objects interacted with each other to exchange information and work together to achieve a certain task.

In this unit, you'll learn how to make your own object types. An object is defined by two attributes: a set of properties and a set of behaviors. For example, an integer has one property, a whole number. An integer's set of behaviors is all the operations you can do on an integer (add, subtract, take the absolute value, and so forth). Object types offer programmers a way to package properties and behaviors together and allow you to create objects of your own custom type to use in your programs.

In the capstone project, you'll write a program that simulates playing a card game, War. It's a two-player game using one deck of cards. Every player takes turns flipping a card; the one with the higher card wins and gives their card to the other player. The game ends when the deck has no more cards. You'll create two new object types, one to represent a player playing the game and one to represent a card deck. You'll decide what properties and what behaviors each object type will have, and then you'll use your object types to play the game.

MAKING YOUR OWN OBJECT TYPES

After reading lesson 30, you'll be able to

- Understand that an object has properties
- Understand that an object has operations associated with it
- Understand what dot notation means when working with objects

You use objects all the time in your daily life. You use computers and phones, handle boxes and envelopes, and interact with people and animals. Even numbers and words are basic objects.

Every object you use is made up of other objects. Except for the basic building blocks of matter, every object you interact with can be decomposed into smaller objects. For example, your calculator can be decomposed into a few basic components: the logic chip, screen, and buttons (and each of these into smaller components). Even a sentence can be decomposed into individual words arranged in a certain order.

Every object you interact with has certain behaviors. For example, a basic calculator can do mathematical operations but can't check email. The calculator has been programmed to work in a certain way depending on which key or button is pressed. Words in different languages can be arranged differently, according to the rules of the language, to form sentences that make sense.

As you build complex systems, you can reuse objects you've already built without going back to the basic building blocks of matter. For example, a computer may have the same logic chip that a calculator already has, to do basic arithmetic. In addition to that, a computer may also have components already built into it that allow it to access the internet or to display color graphics.

The same idea can be applied to programming! You can create more-complex object types to use in your programs, made up from other object types. In fact, you may have noticed that lists and dictionaries are object types that are made up of other object types: a list contains a set of objects, and a dictionary contains a set of pairs of objects.

Consider this   Here are some properties and behaviors of two objects. Can you separate properties from behaviors? What are the objects?

Two eyes
Sleeps on a keyboard
No eyes
Any color
Scratches
Bounces
Fur
Round
Rolls
Hides
Four limbs

Answer:

A cat.
Characteristics: Two eyes, fur, four limbs
Behaviors: Sleeps on a keyboard, scratches, hides

A ball.
Characteristics: No eyes, round, any color
Behaviors: Bounces, rolls

30.1 Why do you need new object types?

You've been working with object types since you wrote your first line of code. Integers, floats, strings, Booleans, tuples, lists, and dictionaries are all types of objects. They're objects that are built into the Python language, meaning that they're available to use by default when you start Python. As you were working with lists (and dictionaries), you may have noticed that they're object types made up of other object types. For example, the list L = [1,2,3] is a list made up of integers.

Integers, floats, and Booleans are atomic objects because they can't be separated into smaller object types; these types are the basic building blocks of the Python language. Strings, tuples, lists, and dictionaries are nonatomic objects because they can be decomposed into other objects.

Using different object types helps organize your code and make it more readable. Imagine how confusing code would look if all you had to use were the atomic data types. If you wanted to write code that contained your grocery list, you might have to create a string variable for each of the list items. That would quickly make your program messy. You'd have to make variables as you realize you have more items to add.

As you continue to build more complex programs, you'll find that you want to create your own object types. These object types "save" a set of properties and a set of behaviors under this new type of object. The properties and behaviors are things that you, as the programmer, get to decide on and define. As you build programs, you can create new object types from other types, even ones that you create yourself.

> **Quick check 30.1** For each of the following scenarios, would you need to create a new object type or can you represent it with an object type you already know?
>
> 1 Someone's age
> 2 Latitude and longitude of a group of map points
> 3 A person
> 4 A chair

30.2 What makes up an object?

An object type is defined by two things: a set of properties and a set of behaviors.

30.2.1 Object properties

Object type *properties* are data that define your object. What characteristics can be used to explain the "look" of your object?

Let's say you want to create an object type that represents a car. What data can describe a generic car? As the creator of the car type, you get to decide on how much or how little data defines the generic car. The data can be things like the length, width, height, or the number of doors.

After you decide on the properties for a specific object type, these choices will define your type and will be fixed. When you start adding behaviors to your type, you may manipulate these properties.

Here are a few more examples of properties for object types. If you have a circle type, its data may be its radius. If you have a "point on map" type, the data may be the values of the latitude and longitude. If you have a room type, its data may be its length, width, height, number of items that are in it, and whether it has an occupant.

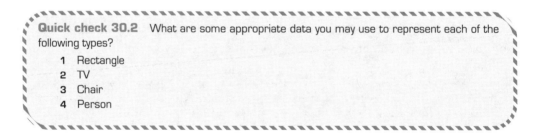

Quick check 30.2   What are some appropriate data you may use to represent each of the following types?

    1   Rectangle
    2   TV
    3   Chair
    4   Person

30.2.2 Object behaviors

Object type *behaviors* are operations that define your object. What are some ways that someone can interact with your type?

Let's go back to the generic car type. How can someone interact with a car? Once again, as the creator of the car object, you get to decide the number of ways you'll allow someone to interact with it. A car's behaviors may be things like changing the color of the car, getting the car to make a noise, or making the car's wheels turn.

These operations are actions that objects of this type, and only this type, can do. These can be actions done by the objects themselves, or ways that an object can interact with other objects.

How do other object types behave? For a circle, one action could be to get its area or its circumference. For a point on a map, one action could be to get the country it's in and another action could be to get the distance between two points. For a room, one action might be to add an item, which increases the item count by 1, or to remove an item to decrease the item count, and another could be to get the volume of the room.

Quick check 30.3 What are some appropriate behaviors you may add for each of the following object types?

1 Rectangle
2 TV
3 Chair
4 Person

 ## 30.3 Using dot notation

You already have an idea of what an object type is. An object type has properties and operations. Here are some object types that you've already worked with:

- An integer is a whole number. Its operations are addition, subtraction, multiplication, division, casting to a float, and many more.
- A string is a sequence of characters. Its operations are addition, indexing, slicing, finding a substring, replacing a substring by another, and many more.
- A dictionary has a key, a value, and a formula to map a key to a memory location to put the value there. Its operations are getting all the keys, getting all the values, indexing using a key, and many more.

Properties and behaviors are defined for, and belong to, a particular object type; other object types don't know about them.

In lesson 7, you used dot notation on strings. Dot notation indicates that you're accessing data or behaviors for a particular object type. When you use dot notation, you indicate to Python that you want to either run a particular operation on, or to access a particular property of, an object type. Python knows how to infer the object type on which this operation is being run because you use dot notation on an object. For example, when you created a list named L, you appended an item to the list with L.append(). The dot notation leads Python to look at the object, L, that the operation, append, is being applied to. Python knows that L is of type list and checks to make sure that the list object type has an operation named append defined.

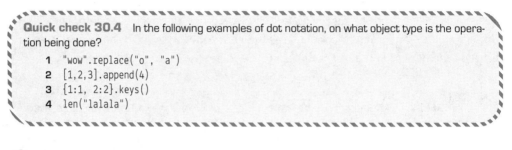

Quick check 30.4   In the following examples of dot notation, on what object type is the operation being done?
1   "wow".replace("o", "a")
2   [1,2,3].append(4)
3   {1:1, 2:2}.keys()
4   len("lalala")

Summary

In this lesson, my goal was to teach you that an object type is represented by two things: its data properties and its behaviors. You've been using objects built into Python and have even seen dot notation used on more-complex types including strings, lists, and dictionaries. Here are the major takeaways:

- An object type has data properties: other objects that make up the type.
- An object type has behaviors: operations that allow interactions with objects of this type.
- Objects of the same type know the properties and behaviors that define them.
- Dot notation is used to access properties and behaviors of an object.

31

CREATING A CLASS FOR AN OBJECT TYPE

After reading lesson 31, you'll be able to

- Define a Python class
- Define data properties for a class
- Define operations for a class
- Use a class to create objects of that type and perform operations

You can create your own types of objects to suit whatever your program needs. Except for atomic object types (`int`, `float`, `bool`), any object that you create is made up of other preexisting objects. As someone who implements a new object type, you get to define the properties that make up the object and the behaviors that you'll allow an object to have (on its own or when interacting with other objects).

You usually define your own objects in order to have customized properties and behaviors, so that you can reuse them. In this lesson, you'll view code you write from two points of view, just as when you wrote your own functions. You'll separate yourself from a programmer/writer of a new object type and from the programmer/user of a newly created object type.

Before defining an object type by using a class, you should have a general idea of how you'll implement it by answering two questions:

- What is your object made up of (its characteristics, or properties)?
- What do you want your object to do (its behaviors, or operations)?

31.1 Implementing a new object type by using a class

The first part of creating your own object type is to define the class. You use the `class` keyword to do this. A simple object type you may want to create is an object representing a circle. You tell Python that you want to define a new object type through a class. Consider the following line:

```
class Circle(object):
```

The keyword `class` starts the definition. The word `Circle` is the name of your class as well as the name of the object type that you want to define. In the parentheses, the word `object` means that your class is going to be a Python object. All classes you define are going to be Python objects. As such, objects created using your class will inherit all basic behaviors and functionality that any Python object has—for example, binding a variable to your object by using the assignment operator.

31.2 Data attributes as object properties

After you start defining the class, you'll have to decide how your object will be initialized. For the most part, this involves deciding how you'll represent your object and the data that will define it. You'll initialize these objects. The object properties are called *data attributes* of the object.

31.2.1 Initializing an object with __init__

To initialize your object, you have to implement a special operation, the __init__ operation (notice the double underscores before and after the word init):

```
class Circle(object):
    def __init__(self):
        # code here
```

The __init__ definition looks like a function, except it's defined inside a class. Any function defined inside a class is named a *method*.

> **DEFINITION**   A method is a function defined inside a class, and defines an operation you can do on an object of that type.

The code inside the __init__ method generally initializes the data attributes that define the object. You decide that your circle class initializes a circle with radius 0 when first created.

31.2.2 Creating an object property inside __init__

A data attribute of one object is another object. Your object may be defined by more than one data attribute. To tell Python that you want to define a data attribute of the object, you use a variable named self with a dot after it. In the Circle class, you initialize a radius as the data attribute of a circle, and initialize it to 0:

```
class Circle(object):
    def __init__(self):
        self.radius = 0
```

Notice that in the definition of __init__, you take one parameter named self. Then, inside the method, you use self. to set a data attribute of your circle. The variable self is used to tell Python that you'll be using this variable to refer to any object you'll create of the type Circle. Any circle you create will have its own radius accessible through self.radius.

At this point, notice that you're still defining the class and haven't created any specific object yet. You can think of self as a placeholder variable for any object of type Circle.

Inside __init__, you use self.radius to tell Python that the variable radius belongs to an object of type Circle. Every object you create of type Circle will have its own variable named radius, whose value can differ between objects. Every variable defined using self. refers to a data attribute of the object.

> **Quick check 31.2** Write an __init__ method that contains data attribute initializations for each of the following scenarios:
> - A person
> - A car
> - A computer

31.3 Methods as object operations and behaviors

Your object has behaviors defined by operations you can do with or on the object. You implement operations via methods. For a circle, you can change its radius by writing another method:

```
class Circle(object):
    def __init__(self):
        self.radius = 0
    def change_radius(self, radius):
        self.radius = radius
```

A method looks like a function. As in the __init__ method, you use self as the first parameter to the method. The method definition says this is a method named change_radius, and it takes one parameter named radius.

Inside the method is one line. Because you want to modify a data attribute of the class, you use self. to access the radius inside the method and change its value.

Another behavior for the circle object is to tell you its radius:

```
class Circle(object):
    def __init__(self):
        self.radius = 0
    def change_radius(self, radius):
        self.radius = radius
```

```
def get_radius(self):
    return self.radius
```

Again, this is a method, and it takes no parameters besides self. All it does is return the value of its data attribute radius. As before, you use self to access the data attribute.

Quick check 31.3   Suppose you create a Door object type with the following initialization method:

```
class Door(object):
    def __init__(self):
        self.width = 1
        self.height = 1
        self.open = False
```

  - Write a method that returns whether the door is open.
  - Write a method that returns the area of the door.

31.4 Using an object type you defined

You've already been using object types written by someone else every time you've created an object: for example, int = 3 or L = []. These are shorthand notations instead of using the name of the class.

The following are equivalent in Python: L = [] and L = list(). Here, list is the name of the list class that someone implemented for others to use.

Now, you can do the same with your own object types. For the Circle class, you create a new Circle object as follows:

```
one_circle = Circle()
```

We say that the variable one_circle is bound to an object that's an instance of the Circle class. In other words, one_circle is a Circle.

> **DEFINITION**   An instance is a specific object of a certain object type.

You can create as many instances as you like by calling the class name and binding the new object to another variable name:

```
one_circle = Circle()
another_circle = Circle()
```

After you create instances of the class, you can perform operations on the objects. On a Circle instance, you can do only two operations: change its radius or get the object to tell you its radius.

Recall that the dot notation means that the operation acts on a particular object. For example,

```
one_circle.change_radius(4)
```

Notice that you pass in one actual parameter (4) to this function, whereas the definition had two formal parameters (self and radius). Python always automatically assigns the value for self to be the object on which the method is called (one_circle, in this case). The object on which the method is called is the object right before the dot. This code changes the radius of only this instance, named one_circle, to 4. All other instances of the object that may have been created in a program remain unchanged. Say you ask for the radius values as shown here:

```
print(one_circle.get_radius())
print(another_circle.get_radius())
```

This prints the following:

```
4
0
```

Here, one_circle's radius was changed to 4, but you didn't change the radius of another_circle. How do you know this? Because the radius of a circle was a data attribute and defined with self.

This is shown in figure 31.1: each object has its own data attribute for the radius, and changing one doesn't affect the other.

Figure 31.1   On the left are the data attributes of two circle objects. On the right, you can see that one data attribute changed after using dot notation on it to change the value.

> **Quick check 31.4**   Suppose you create a Door object type in the following way:
>
> ```
> class Door(object):
>     def __init__(self):
>         self.width = 1
>         self.height = 1
>         self.open = False
>     def change_state(self):
>         self.open = not self.open
>     def scale(self, factor):
>         self.height *= factor
>         self.width *= factor
> ```
>
> - Write a line that creates a new Door object and binds it to a variable named square_door.
> - Write a line that changes the state of the square_door.
> - Write a line that scales the door to be three times bigger.

31.5   Creating a class with parameters in __init__

Now, you want to make another class to represent a rectangle. The following listing shows the code.

Listing 31.1 A Rectangle **class**

```
class Rectangle(object):
    """ a rectangle object with a length and a width """
    def __init__(self, length, width):
        self.length = length
        self.width = width
    def set_length(self, length):
        self.length = length
    def set_width(self, width):
        self.width = width
```

This code presents a couple of new ideas. First, you have two parameters in __init__ besides self. When you create a new Rectangle object, you'll have to initialize it with two values: one for the length and one for the width.

You can do that this way:

```
a_rectangle = Rectangle(2,4)
```

Say you don't put in two parameters and do this:

```
bad_rectangle = Rectangle(2)
```

Then Python gives you an error saying that it's expecting two parameters when you initialize the object but you gave it only one:

```
TypeError: __init__() missing 1 required positional argument: 'width'
```

The other thing to notice in this __init__ is that the parameters and the data attributes have the same name. They don't have to be the same, but often they are. Only the attribute names matter when you want to access the values of object properties using the class methods. The parameters to the methods are formal parameters to pass data in to initialize the object, and are temporary; they last until the method call ends, while data attributes persist throughout the life of the object instance.

31.6 Dot notation on the class name, not on an object

You've been initializing and using objects by leaving out the self parameter and letting Python automatically decide what the value for self should be. This is a nice feature of Python, which allows programmers to write more-concise code.

There's a more explicit way to do this in the code, by giving a parameter for self directly, without relying on Python to detect what it should be.

Going back to the Circle class you defined, you can again initialize an object, set the radius, and print the radius as follows:

```
c = Circle()
c.change_radius(2)
r = c.get_radius()
print(r)
```

After initializing an object, a more explicit way of doing the operations on the object is by using the class name and object directly, like this:

```
c = Circle()
Circle.change_radius(c, 2)
r = Circle.get_radius(c)
print(r)
```

Notice that you're calling the methods on the class name. Additionally, you're now passing two parameters to change_radius:

- c is the object you want to do the operation on and is assigned to self.
- 2 is the value for the new radius.

If you call the method on the object directly, as in c.change_radius(2), Python knows that the parameter for self is to be c, infers that c is an object of type Circle, and translates the line behind the scenes to be Circle.change_radius(c, 2).

Quick check 31.5   You have the following lines of code. Convert the ones noted to use the explicit way of calling methods (using dot notation on the class name):

```
a = Rectangle(1,1)
b = Rectangle(1,1)
a.set_length(4)      # change this
b.set_width(4)       # change this
```

 **Summary**

In this lesson, my objective was to teach you how to define a class in Python. Here are the major takeaways:

- A class defines an object type.
- A class defines data attributes (properties) and methods (operations).
- self is a variable name conventionally used to refer to a generic instance of the object type.
- An __init__ method is a special operation that defines how to initialize an object. It's called when an object is created.
- You can define other methods (for example, functions inside a class) to do other operations.
- When using a class, the dot notation on an object accesses data attributes and methods.

Let's see if you got this…

Q31.1   Write a method for the circle class named get_area. It returns the area of a circle by using the formula $3.14 * radius^2$. Test your method by creating an object and printing the result of the method call.

Q31.2   Write two methods for the Rectangle class named get_area and get_perimeter. Test your methods by creating an object and printing the result of the method calls:

- get_area returns the area of a rectangle by using the formula length * width.
- get_perimeter returns the perimeter of a rectangle by using 2 * length + 2 * width.

32

WORKING WITH YOUR OWN OBJECT TYPES

After reading lesson 32, you'll be able to

- Define a class to simulate a stack
- Use a class with other objects you define

At this point, you know how to create a class. Formally, a class represents an object type in Python. Why do you want to make your own object types in the first place? Because an object type packages a set of properties and a set of behaviors in one data structure. With this nicely packaged data structure, you know that all objects that take on this type are consistent in the set of data that defines them, and consistent in the set of operations that they can perform.

The useful idea behind object types is that you can build upon object types you create to make objects that are more complex.

Consider this Subdivide each of the following objects into smaller objects, and those into smaller objects, until you can define the smallest object by using a built-in type (int, float, string, bool):

- Snow
- Forest

Answer:

- Snow is made up of snowflakes. Snowflakes have six sides, and are made up of crystals. Crystals are made up of water molecules arranged in a certain configuration (a list).
- A forest is made up of trees. A tree has a trunk and leaves. A trunk has a length (float) and a diameter (float). Leaves have a color (string).

32.1 Defining a stack object

In lesson 26, you used lists along with a series of appends and pops to implement a stack of pancakes. As you were doing the operations, you were careful to make sure that the operations were in line with the behavior of a stack: add to the end of the list and remove from the end of the list.

Using classes, you can create a stack object that enforces the stack rules for you so you don't have to keep track of them while the program runs.

Thinking like a programmer
Using a class, you hide implementation details from people using the class. You don't need to spell out how you'll do something, just that you want certain behaviors; for example, in a stack you can add/remove items. The implementation of these behaviors can be done in various ways, and these details aren't necessary to understand what the object is and how to use it.

32.1.1 Choosing data attributes

You name the stack object type Stack. The first step is to decide how to represent a stack. In lesson 26, you used a list to simulate the stack, so it makes sense to represent the stack by using one attribute: a list.

Thinking like a programmer

When deciding which data attributes should represent an object type, it may be helpful to do one of two things:

- Write out which data types you know and whether each would be appropriate to use. Keep in mind that an object type can be represented by more than one data attribute.
- Start with the behavior you'd like the object to have. Often, you can decide on data attributes by noticing that the behaviors you want can be represented by one or more data structures you already know.

You typically define data attributes in the initialization method for your class:

```
class Stack(object):
    def __init__( self):
        self.stack = []
```

The stack will be represented using a list. You can decide that initially a stack is empty, so you initialize a data attribute for the Stack object by using self.stack = [].

32.1.2 Implementing methods

After deciding on the data attributes that define an object type, you need to decide what behaviors your object type will have. You should decide how you want your object to behave and how others who want to use your class will interact with it.

Listing 32.1 provides the full definition for the Stack class. Aside from the initialization method, seven other methods define ways in which you can interact with a stack-type object. The method get_stack_elements returns a copy of the data attribute, to prevent users from mutating the data attribute.

The methods add_one and remove_one are consistent with the behavior of a stack; you add to one end of the list, and you remove from the same end. Similarly, the methods add_many and remove_many add and remove a certain number of times, from the same end. The method size returns the number of items in the stack. Finally, the method prettyprint_ stack prints (and therefore returns None) each item in the stack on a line, with newer items at the top.

Listing 32.1 Definition for the Stack class

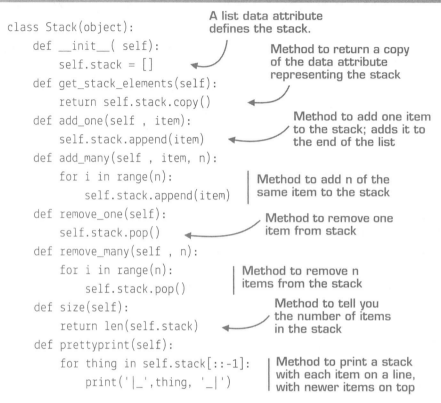

```
class Stack(object):
    def __init__( self):
        self.stack = []
    def get_stack_elements(self):
        return self.stack.copy()
    def add_one(self , item):
        self.stack.append(item)
    def add_many(self , item, n):
        for i in range(n):
            self.stack.append(item)
    def remove_one(self):
        self.stack.pop()
    def remove_many(self , n):
        for i in range(n):
            self.stack.pop()
    def size(self):
        return len(self.stack)
    def prettyprint(self):
        for thing in self.stack[::-1]:
            print('|_',thing, '_|')
```

A list data attribute defines the stack.

Method to return a copy of the data attribute representing the stack

Method to add one item to the stack; adds it to the end of the list

Method to add n of the same item to the stack

Method to remove one item from stack

Method to remove n items from the stack

Method to tell you the number of items in the stack

Method to print a stack with each item on a line, with newer items on top

One thing is important to note. In the implementation of the stack, you decided to add and remove from the end of the list. An equally valid design decision would have been to add and remove from the beginning of the list. Notice that as long as you're consistent with your decisions and the object's behavior that you're trying to implement, more than one implementation may be possible.

Quick check 32.1 Write a method for the Stack object, named add_list, which takes in a list as a parameter. Each element in the list is added to the stack, with items at the beginning of the list being added to the stack first.

32.2 Using a Stack object

Now that you've defined a Stack object type with a Python class, you can start to make Stack objects and do operations with them.

32.2.1 Make a stack of pancakes

You begin by tackling the traditional task of adding pancakes to your stack. Suppose a pancake is defined by a string representing the flavor of pancake: "chocolate" or "blueberry".

The first step is to create a stack object to which you'll add your pancakes. Listing 32.2 shows a simple sequence of commands:

- Create an empty stack by initializing a Stack object.
- Add one blueberry pancake by calling add_one on the stack.
- Add four chocolate pancakes by calling the add_many method on the stack.

The items added to the stack are strings to represent the pancake flavors. All methods you call are on the object you created, using dot notation.

Listing 32.2 Making a Stack object and adding pancakes to it

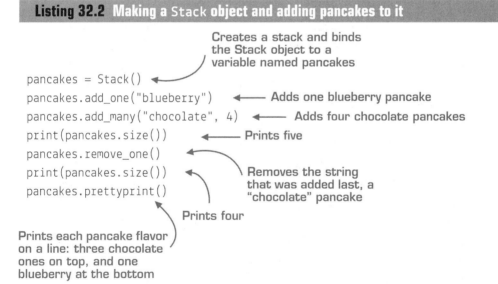

Figure 32.1 shows the steps to adding items to the stack and the value of the list data attribute, accessed by self.stack.

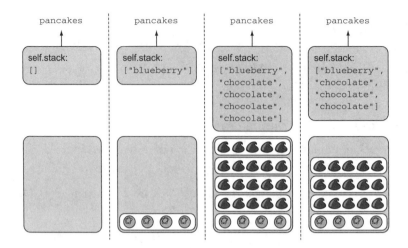

Figure 32.1 Starting from the left, the first panel shows an empty stack of pancakes. The second panel shows the stack when you add one item: one "blueberry". The third panel shows the stack after you add four of the same item: four "chocolate". The last panel shows the stack after you removed an item: the last one added, one "chocolate".

Notice that in this code snippet, every method behaves exactly like a function: it takes in parameters, does work by executing commands, and returns a value. You can have methods that don't return an explicit value, such as the prettyprint method. In this case, when you call the method, you don't need to print the result because nothing interesting is returned; the method itself prints some values.

32.2.2 Make a stack of circles

Now that you have a Stack object, you can add any other type of object to the stack, not just atomic objects (int, float, or bool). You can add objects of a type that you created.

You wrote a class that represented a Circle object in lesson 31, so now you can create a stack of circles. Listing 32.3 shows you the code to do this. This is similar to the way you added pancakes in listing 32.2. The only difference is that instead of strings representing pancake flavors, you now have to initialize a circle object before adding it to the stack. If you're running the following listing, you'll have to copy the code that defines a Circle object into the same file so that Python knows what a Circle is.

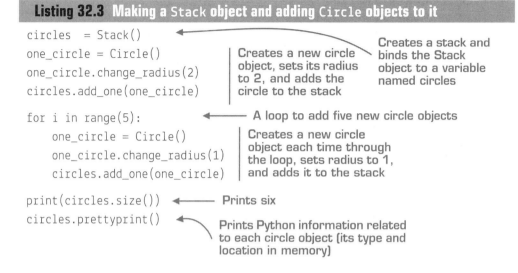

Listing 32.3 Making a `Stack` object and adding `Circle` objects to it

```
circles  = Stack()
one_circle = Circle()
one_circle.change_radius(2)
circles.add_one(one_circle)

for i in range(5):
    one_circle = Circle()
    one_circle.change_radius(1)
    circles.add_one(one_circle)

print(circles.size())
circles.prettyprint()
```

Creates a stack and binds the Stack object to a variable named circles

Creates a new circle object, sets its radius to 2, and adds the circle to the stack

A loop to add five new circle objects

Creates a new circle object each time through the loop, sets radius to 1, and adds it to the stack

Prints six

Prints Python information related to each circle object (its type and location in memory)

Figure 32.2 shows how the stack of circles might look.

You may also notice that you have a method in the `Stack` class named `add_many`. Instead of a loop that adds one circle at a time, suppose you create one circle with radius 1 and call `add_many` on the stack with this object's properties, as in the following listing, and illustrated in figure 32.3.

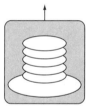

Figure 32.2 The circle with a radius of 2 is at the bottom because it's added first. Then you make a new circle with a radius of 1, five times, and add each one to the stack.

Listing 32.4 Making a `Stack` object and adding the same circle object many times

```
circles  = Stack()
one_circle = Circle()
one_circle.change_radius(2)
circles.add_one(one_circle)

one_circle = Circle()
one_circle.change_radius(1)
circles.add_many(one_circle, 5)

print(circles.size())
circles.prettyprint()
```

Same operations as listing 32.3

Creates a new circle object; sets its radius to 1

Adds the same circle object five times using a method defined in Stack class

Prints six, the total number of circles added at this point

Prints Python information related to each circle object (its type and location in memory)

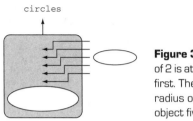

circles

Figure 32.3   The circle with a radius of 2 is at the bottom because it's added first. Then you make one circle with a radius of 1 and add this same circle object five times to the stack

Let's compare how the two stacks look from listings 32.3 and 32.4. In listing 32.3, you created a new circle object each time through the loop. When you output your stack by using the prettyprint method, the output looks something like this, representing the type of the object being printed and its location in memory:

```
|_ <__main__.Circle object at 0x00000200B8B90BA8> _|
|_ <__main__.Circle object at 0x00000200B8B90F98> _|
|_ <__main__.Circle object at 0x00000200B8B90EF0> _|
|_ <__main__.Circle object at 0x00000200B8B90710> _|
|_ <__main__.Circle object at 0x00000200B8B7BA58> _|
|_ <__main__.Circle object at 0x00000200B8B7BF28> _|
```

In listing 32.4, you created only one new circle object and added that object five times. When you output your stack by using the prettyprint method, the output now looks something like this:

```
|_ <__main__.Circle object at 0x00000200B8B7BA58> _|
|_ <__main__.Circle object at 0x00000200B8B7BA58> _|
|_ <__main__.Circle object at 0x00000200B8B7BA58> _|
|_ <__main__.Circle object at 0x00000200B8B7BA58> _|
|_ <__main__.Circle object at 0x00000200B8B7BA58> _|
|_ <__main__.Circle object at 0x000001F1E0E0CA90> _|
```

Using the memory location printed by Python, you can see the difference between these two pieces of code. Listing 32.3 creates a new object each time through the loop and adds it to the stack; it just so happens that each object has the same data associated with it, a radius of 1. On the other hand, listing 32.4 creates one object and adds the same object multiple times.

In lesson 33, you'll see how to write your own method to override the default Python print method so that you can print information related to your own objects instead of the memory location.

> **Quick check 32.2** Write code that creates two stacks. To one stack, the code adds three circle objects with radius 3, and to the other it adds five of the exact same rectangle object with width 1 and length 1. Use the classes for Circle and Rectangle defined in lesson 31.

Summary

In this lesson, my objective was to teach you how to define multiple objects and use them both in the same program. Here are the major takeaways:

- Defining a class requires deciding how to represent it.
- Defining a class also requires deciding how to use it and what methods to implement.
- A class packages properties and behaviors into one object type so that all objects of this type have the same data and methods in common.
- Using the class involves creating one or more objects of that type and performing a sequence of operations with it.

Let's see if you got this…

Q32.1 Write a class for a queue, in a similar way as that for the stack. Recall that items added to a queue are added to one end, and items removed from the queue are removed from the other end:

- Decide which data structure will represent your queue.
- Implement __init__.
- Implement methods to get the size, add one, add many, remove one, remove many, and to show the queue.
- Write code to create queue objects and perform some of the operations on them.

33

CUSTOMIZING CLASSES

After reading lesson 33, you'll be able to

- Add special Python methods to your classes
- Use special operators such as +, -, /, and * on your classes

You've been working with classes defined in the Python language since you wrote your first Python program. The most basic type of objects in the Python language, called *built-in types*, allowed you to use special operators on these types. For example, you used the + operator between two numbers. You were able to use the [] operator to index into a string or a list. You were able to use the print() statement on any of these types of objects, as well as on lists and dictionaries.

Consider this

- Name five operations you can do between integers.
- Name one operation you can do between two strings.
- Name one operation you can do between a string and an integer.

Answer:

- +, -, *, /, %
- +
- *

Each of these operations is represented in shorthand using a symbol. However, the symbol is only a shorthand notation. Each operation is actually a method that you can define to work with an object of a specific type.

33.1 Overriding a special method

Every operation on an object is implemented in a class as a method. But you may have noticed that you use several shorthand notations when you work with simple object types such as int, float, and str. These shorthand notations are things like using the + or - or * or / operator between two such objects. Even something like print() with an object in the parentheses is shorthand notation for a method in a class. You can implement such methods in your own classes so that you can use shorthand notation on your own object types.

Table 33.1 lists a few special methods, but there are many more. Notice that all these special methods begin and end with double underscores. This is specific to the Python language, and other languages may have other conventions.

Table 33.1 A few special methods in Python

Category	Operator	Method name
Mathematical operations	+	__add__
	-	__sub__
	*	__mul__
	/	__truediv__
Comparisons	==	__eq__
	<	__lt__
	>	__gt__
Others	print() **and** str()	__str__
	Create an object—for example, some_object = ClassName()	__init__

To add the capability for a special operation to work with your class, you can *override* these special methods. Overriding means that you'll implement the method in your own class and decide what the method will do, instead of the default behavior implemented by the generic Python object.

Begin by creating a new type of object, representing a fraction. A fraction has a numerator and a denominator. Therefore, the data attributes of a Fraction object are two integers. The following listing shows a basic definition of how the Fraction class might look.

Listing 33.1 Definition for the Fraction class

```
class Fraction(object):
    def __init__(self, top, bottom):          ← The initialization method
        self.top = top                          takes in two parameters.
        self.bottom = bottom                  ┤ Initializes data attributes
                                                with the parameters
```

With this definition, you can now create two Fraction objects and try to add them together:

```
half = Fraction(1,2)
quarter = Fraction(1,4)
print(half + quarter)
```

Adding 1/2 and 1/4 should give 3/4. But when you run the snippet, you get this error:

```
TypeError: unsupported operand type(s) for +: 'Fraction' and 'Fraction'
```

This tells you that Python doesn't know how to add two Fraction objects together. This error makes sense, because you never defined this operation for a Fraction object type.

To tell Python how to use the + operator, you need to implement the special method __add__ (with double underscores before and after the name add). Addition works on two objects: one is the object you're calling the method on, and the other is a parameter to the method. Inside the method, you perform the addition of two Fraction objects by referencing the numerators and denominators of both objects, as in the following listing.

Listing 33.2 Methods to add and multiply two Fraction objects

```
class Fraction(object):
    def __init__(self, top, bottom):
        self.top = top
        self.bottom = bottom
    def __add__(self, other_fraction):          ←
        new_top = self.top*other_fraction.bottom  + \
                  self.bottom*other_fraction.top
        new_bottom = self.bottom*other_fraction.bottom  ←
```

Defines special method to implement the + operator between two Fraction objects

Breaks up the line into two lines by using a backslash

Calculates the numerator from the addition

Calculates the denominator from the addition

```
    return Fraction(new_top, new_bottom)
def __mul__(self, other_fraction):
    new_top = self.top*other_fraction.top
    new_bottom = self.bottom*other_fraction.bottom
    return Fraction(new_top, new_bottom)
```

Method to
multiply two
Fraction objects

Returns a new Fraction
object, created using the new
numerator and denominator

Quick check 33.1 Write a method for the Fraction object to use the - operator between two Fraction objects.

33.2 Overriding print() to work with your class

Now that you defined the + operator between Fraction objects, you can try the same code as before:

```
half = Fraction(1,2)
quarter = Fraction(1,4)
print(half + quarter)
```

This code doesn't give an error anymore. Instead, it prints the type of the object and its memory location:

```
<__main__.Fraction object at 0x00000200B8BDC240>
```

But this isn't informative at all. You'd rather see the value of the fraction! You need to implement another special function, one that tells Python how to print an object of your type. To do this, you implement the special method __str__, as in the next listing.

Listing 33.3 Method to print a Fraction object

```
class Fraction(object):
    def __init__(self, top, bottom):
        self.top = top
        self.bottom = bottom
    def __add__(self, other_fraction):
        new_top = self.top*other_fraction.bottom  + \
```

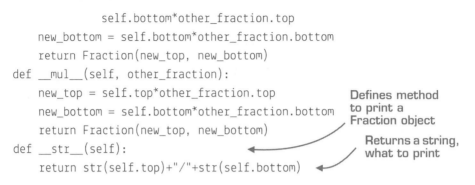

```
                        self.bottom*other_fraction.top
        new_bottom = self.bottom*other_fraction.bottom
        return Fraction(new_top, new_bottom)
    def __mul__(self, other_fraction):
        new_top = self.top*other_fraction.top
        new_bottom = self.bottom*other_fraction.bottom
        return Fraction(new_top, new_bottom)
    def __str__(self):
        return str(self.top)+"/"+str(self.bottom)
```

Defines method to print a Fraction object

Returns a string, what to print

Now, when you use print on a Fraction object, or when you use str() to convert your object to a string, it'll call the method __str__. For example, the following code prints 1/2 instead of the memory location:

```
half = Fraction(1, 2)
print(half)
```

The following creates a string object with the value 1/2:

```
half = Fraction(1, 2)
half_string = str(half)
```

> **Quick check 33.2**　Change the __str__ method for a Fraction object to print the numerator on one line, two dashes on the next, and the denominator on a third line. The line print(Fraction(1,2)) prints this:
>
> ```
> 1
> --
> 2
> ```

33.3　Behind the scenes

What exactly happens when you use a special operator? Let's look at the details, and what happens when you add two Fraction objects:

```
half = Fraction(1,2)
quarter = Fraction(1,4)
```

Consider this line:

```
half + quarter
```

It takes the first operand, half, and applies the special method __add__ to it. That's equivalent to the following:

```
half.__add__(quarter)
```

Additionally, every method call can be rewritten by using the class name and explicitly giving the method a parameter for the self parameter. The preceding line is equivalent to this:

```
Fraction.__add__(half, quarter)
```

Despite being called a *special method*, all the methods that start and end with double underscores are regular methods. They're called on an object, take parameters, and return a value. What makes them special is that there's another way to call the methods. You can either call them using a special operator (for example, a mathematical symbol) or using a fairly well-known function (for example, len() or str() or print(), among others). This shorthand notation is often more intuitive for others if they're reading code than if they were to read the formal function call notation.

Thinking like a programmer

One nice goal that you should have as a programmer is to make life easier for other programmers that may use classes you define. This involves documenting your classes, methods, and whenever possible, implementing special methods that allow others to use your class in an intuitive way.

Quick check 33.3   Rewrite each of the following lines in two ways: by calling the method on an object and by calling the method by using the class name. Assume you start with this:

```
half = Fraction(1,2)
quarter = Fraction(1,4)
```

   1 quarter * half
   2 print(quarter)
   3 print(half * half)

33.4 What can you do with classes?

You've seen the details and the syntax behind creating your own object types using Python classes. This section will show you examples of classes that you may want to create in certain situations.

33.4.1 Scheduling events

Say that you're asked to schedule a series of events. For example, you're going to a movie festival and you want to arrange the movies in your schedule.

Without using classes

If you didn't use classes, you could use one list to hold all the movies you want to see. Each element in the list is a movie to see. The relevant information regarding a movie includes its name, its start time, end time, and perhaps a critic's rating. This information could be stored in a tuple as the element of the list. Notice that almost right away the list becomes cumbersome to use. If you wanted to access the ratings of every movie, you'd rely on indexing twice—first into the list of movies and then into the tuple to retrieve the rating.

Using classes

Knowing what you know about classes, it's tempting to make every object into a class. In the scheduling problem, you could make the following classes:

- `Time` class representing a time object. An object of this type would have data attributes: hours (`int`), minutes (`int`), and seconds (`int`). Operations on this object could be to find the difference between two times, or to convert to total number of hours, minutes, or seconds.
- `Movie` class representing a movie object. An object of this type would have data attributes: name (`string`), start time (`Time`), end time (`Time`), and rating (`int`). Operations on this class would be to check whether two movies overlap in time, or whether two movies have a high rating.

With these two classes, you can abstract away some of the annoying details of scheduling a set of movies during a certain period. Now, you can create a list of `Movie` objects. If you need to index into the list (to access a rating, for example), you can use nicely named methods defined in the movie class.

Using too many classes

It's important to understand how many classes are too many. For example, you could create a class to represent an `Hour`. But this abstraction doesn't add any value because its representation would be an integer, in which case you can use the integer itself.

 **Summary**

In this lesson, my objective was to teach you how to define special methods that allow you to use multiple objects and use operators on your object types. Here are the major takeaways:

- Special methods have a certain name and use double underscores before and after the name. Other languages may take different approaches.
- Special methods have a shorthand notation.

Let's see if you got this...

Q33.1 Write a method to allow you to use the print statement on a Circle and a Stack. Your Stack's print should print each object in the same way that prettyprint does in lesson 32. Your Circle print should print the string "circle: 1" (or whatever the radius of the circle is). You'll have to implement the __str__ method in the Stack class and the Circle class. For example, the following lines

```
circles = Stack()
one_circle = Circle()
one_circle.change_radius(1)
circles.add_one(one_circle)
two_circle = Circle()
two_circle.change_radius(2)
circles.add_one(two_circle)
print(circles)
```

should print this:

```
|_ circle: 2 _|
|_ circle: 1 _|
```

34

CAPSTONE PROJECT: CARD GAME

After reading lesson 34, you'll be able to

- Use classes to build a more complex program
- Use classes others have created to improve your program
- Allow users to play a simple version of the card game War

When you make your own object types, you can organize larger programs so that they're easier to write. The principles of modularity and abstraction introduced with functions also apply to classes. Classes are used to package a set of properties and behaviors common to a set of objects so that the objects can be used consistently in a program.

A common first program with classes is to simulate playing some sort of game with the user.

THE PROBLEM   You want to simulate playing the card game War. Each round, players will take a card from one deck and compare the cards. The one with the higher card wins the round and gives their card to the other player. The winner is determined after numerous rounds, when the deck is empty. The winner is the person with fewer cards in their hand. You'll create two types of objects: a Player and a CardDeck. After defining the classes, you'll write code that simulates a game between two players. You'll first ask users for their names then create two Player objects. Both players will use the same card deck. Then you'll use methods defined in the Player and CardDeck classes to automatically simulate the rounds and determine the winner.

34.1 Using classes that already exist

Objects built into the Python language are always there for you to use in your programs; these are objects such as int, float, list, and dict. But many other classes have already been written by other programmers and can be used to enhance the functionality of your program. Instead of typing their class definition in your code file, you can use an import statement to bring in the definition of another class into your file. This way, you can create objects of that type and use that class's methods in your code.

A useful class you'll want to use in your card game is the random class. You can bring in the random class definitions with this:

```
import random
```

Now you can create an object that can perform operations with random numbers. You use dot notation on the class name, as mentioned in lesson 31, and call the method you want to use along with any parameters it expects. For example,

```
r = random.random()
```

This gives you a random number between 0 (including) and 1 (not including) and binds it to the variable r. Here's another example:

```
r = random.randint(a, b)
```

This line gives you a random integer between a and b (including) and binds it to the variable r. Now consider this line:

```
r = random.choice(L)
```

It gives you a random element from a list L and binds it to the variable r.

34.2 Detailing the game rules

The first step before beginning to code is to understand how you want your program to run, and what the specific game rules are:

- For simplicity, assume a deck contains four suits, each with cards 2 to 9. When denoting a card, use "2H" for the 2 of hearts, "4D" for the 4 of diamonds, "7S" for the 7 of spades, "9C" for the 9 of clubs, and so on.
- A player has a name (string) and a hand of cards (list).
- When the game begins, ask two players for their names and set them.
- Each round, add one card to each player's hand.

- Compare the cards just added to each player: first by the number, and then, if equal, by Spades > Hearts > Diamonds > Clubs.
- The person with the larger card removes the card from their hand, and the person with the smaller card takes the card and adds it to their hand.
- When the deck is empty, compare the number of cards the players have; the person with fewer cards wins.

You'll define two classes: one for a Player and one for a CardDeck.

34.3 Defining the Player class

A player is defined by a name and a hand. The name is a string, and the hand is a list of strings, representing the cards. When you create a Player object, you give them a name as an argument and assume that they have no cards in their hand.

The first step is to define the __init__ method to tell Python how to initialize a Player object. Knowing that you have two data attributes for a Player object, you can also write a method to return the name of the Player. This is shown in the following listing.

Listing 34.1 Definition for the Player class

```
class Player(object):
    """ a player """
    def __init__(self, name):
        """ sets the name and an empty hand """
        self.hand = []              ◄────── Sets a hand to be an empty list
        self.name = name            ◄──────────── Sets the name to the
    def get_name(self):                           string passed in when
        """ Returns the name of the player """    creating a Player object
        return self.name
```
A method to return
the player's name

Now, according to the game rules, a player can also add a card to their hand and remove a card from their hand. Notice that you check to make sure that the card added is a valid card by making sure its value is not None. To check the number of cards in players' hands and determine a winner, you can also add a method that tells you the number of cards in a hand. The following listing shows these three methods.

Listing 34.2 Definition for the Player class

```
class Player(object):
    """ a player """
    # methods from Listing 34.1
    def add_card_to_hand(self, card):
        """ card, a string
            Adds valid card to the player's hand """
        if card != None:
            self.hand.append(card)
    def remove_card_from_hand(self, card):
        """ card, a string
            Remove card from the player's hand """
        self.hand.remove(card)
    def hand_size(self):
        """ Returns the number of cards in player's hand """
        return len(self.hand)
```

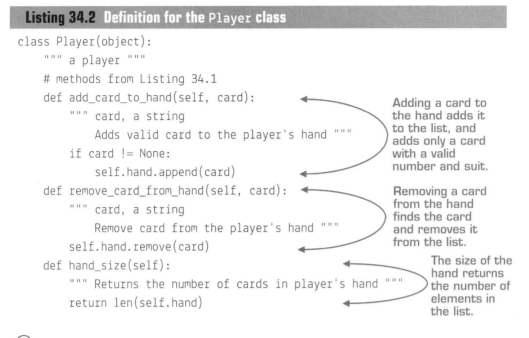

Adding a card to the hand adds it to the list, and adds only a card with a valid number and suit.

Removing a card from the hand finds the card and removes it from the list.

The size of the hand returns the number of elements in the list.

34.4 Defining the CardDeck class

A CardDeck class will represent a deck of cards. The deck has 32 cards, with the numbers 2 to 9 for each of the four deck types: spades, hearts, diamonds, and clubs. The following listing shows how to initialize the object type. There'll be only one data attribute, a list of all possible cards in the deck. Each card is denoted by a string; for example, of the form "3H" for the 3 of hearts.

Listing 34.3 Initialization for the CardDeck class

```
class CardDeck(object):
    """ A deck of cards 2-9 of spades, hearts, diamons, clubs """
    def __init__(self):
        """ a deck of cards (strings e.g. "2C" for the 2 of clubs)
            contains all cards possible """
        hearts = "2H,3H,4H,5H,6H,7H,8H,9H"
        diamonds = "2D,3D,4D,5D,6D,7D,8D,9D"
        spades = "2S,3S,4S,5S,6S,7S,8S,9S"
        clubs = "2C,3C,4C,5C,6C,7C,8C,9C"
```

Makes a string of all possible cards in the deck

```
        self.deck = hearts.split(',')+diamonds.split(',')  +  \
                      spades.split(',')+clubs.split(',')
```

Splits the long string on the
comma and adds all cards
(strings) to a list for the deck

After you decide that you'll represent a card deck with a list containing all cards in the
deck, you can start to implement the methods for this class. This class will use the random
class to pick a random card that a player will use. One method will return a random
card from the deck; another method will compare two cards and tell you which one is
higher.

Listing 34.4 Methods in the `CardDeck` class

```
import random

class CardDeck(object):
    """ A deck of cards 2-9 of spades, hearts, diamonds, clubs """
    def __init__(self):
        """ a deck of cards (strings e.g. "2C" for the 2 of clubs)
            contains all cards possible """
        hearts = "2H,3H,4H,5H,6H,7H,8H,9H"
        diamonds = "2D,3D,4D,5D,6D,7D,8D,9D"
        spades = "2S,3S,4S,5S,6S,7S,8S,9S"
        clubs = "2C,3C,4C,5C,6C,7C,8C,9C"
        self.deck = hearts.split(',')+diamonds.split(',') \
                      + spades.split(',')+clubs.split(',')
    def get_card(self):
        """ Returns one random card (string) and
            returns None if there are no more cards """
        if len(self.deck) < 1:
            return None
        card = random.choice(self.deck)
        self.deck.remove(card)
        return card
    def compare_cards(self, card1, card2):
        """ returns the larger card according to
            (1) the larger of the numbers or, if equal,
            (2) Spades > Hearts > Diamonds > Clubs """
```

Removes
the card
from the
deck list

If there are no more cards
in the deck, return None.

Picks a random card
from the deck list

Returns the value
of the card (string)

```
if card1[0] > card2[0]:          Checks the card number value,
    return card1                 returns the first card if it's higher

elif card1[0] < card2[0]:        Checks the card number value,
    return card2                 returns the second card if it's higher

elif card1[1] > card2[1]:

    return card1                 When the card number
                                 value is equal, use the suit.
else:

    return card2
```

34.5 Simulate the card game

After you define object types to help you simulate a card game, you can write code that uses these types.

34.5.1 Setting up the objects

The first step is to set up the game by creating two Player objects and one CardDeck object. You ask for the names of two players, create a new Player object for each, and call the method to set the name. This is shown in the following listing.

Listing 34.5 Initializing game variables and objects

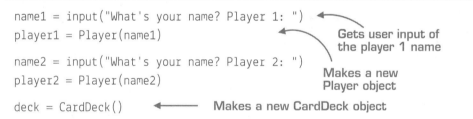

```
name1 = input("What's your name? Player 1: ")
player1 = Player(name1)                             Gets user input of
                                                    the player 1 name
name2 = input("What's your name? Player 2: ")
player2 = Player(name2)                             Makes a new
                                                    Player object
deck = CardDeck()          Makes a new CardDeck object
```

After initializing the object you'll use in the game, you can now simulate the game.

34.5.2 Simulating rounds in the game

A game consists of many rounds and continues until the deck is empty. It's possible to calculate the number of rounds players will play; if each player takes a card every round and there are 32 cards in the deck, there'll be 16 rounds. You could use a for loop to count the rounds, but a while loop is also an acceptable way of implementing the rounds.

In each round, each player gets a card, so call the get_card method on the deck twice, once for each player. Each player object then calls add_card_to_hand, which adds the random card returned from the deck to their own hand.

Then, both players will have at least a card, and there are two cases to consider:
- The game is over because the deck is empty.
- The deck still contains cards, and players must compare and decide who gives the other a card.

When the game is over, you check the sizes of the hands by calling hand_size on each player object. The player with the larger hand loses, and you exit from the loop.

If the game isn't over, you need to decide which player has the higher card by calling the compare_cards method on the deck with the two players' cards. The returned value is the higher card, and if the number values are equal, the suit decides which card weighs more. If the higher card is the same as player1's card, player1 needs to give the card to player2. In code, this translates to player1 calling remove_card_from_hand and player2 calling add_card_to_hand. A similar situation happens when the larger card is the same as player2's card. See the following listing.

Listing 34.6   Loop to simulate rounds in the game

```
name1 = input("What's your name? Player 1: ")
player1 = Player(name1)
name2 = input("What's your name? Player 2: ")
player2 = Player(name2)
deck = CardDeck()

while True:
    player1_card = deck.get_card()
    player2_card = deck.get_card()
    player1.add_card_to_hand(player1_card)
    player2.add_card_to_hand(player2_card)

    if player1_card == None or player2_card == None:
        print("Game Over. No more cards in deck.")
        print(name1, " has ", player1.hand_size())
        print(name2, " has ", player2.hand_size())
        print("Who won?")
        if player1.hand_size() > player2.hand_size():
            print(name2, " wins!")
```

Game over because at least one player has no more cards

Checks the sizes of the hands, and player2 wins because they have fewer cards

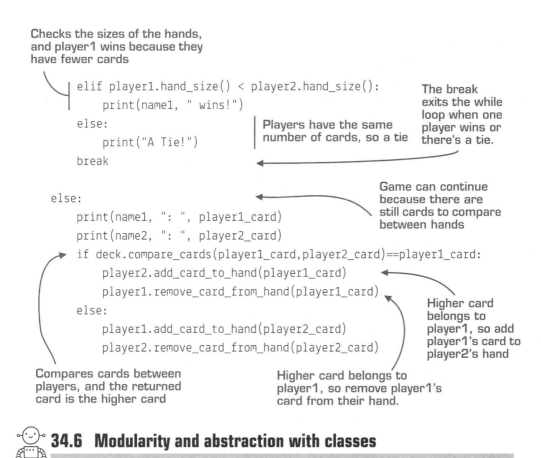

Checks the sizes of the hands, and player1 wins because they have fewer cards

```
elif player1.hand_size() < player2.hand_size():
    print(name1, " wins!")
else:
    print("A Tie!")
break
```

The break exits the while loop when one player wins or there's a tie.

Players have the same number of cards, so a tie

```
else:
    print(name1, ": ", player1_card)
    print(name2, ": ", player2_card)
    if deck.compare_cards(player1_card,player2_card)==player1_card:
        player2.add_card_to_hand(player1_card)
        player1.remove_card_from_hand(player1_card)
    else:
        player1.add_card_to_hand(player2_card)
        player2.remove_card_from_hand(player2_card)
```

Game can continue because there are still cards to compare between hands

Higher card belongs to player1, so add player1's card to player2's hand

Compares cards between players, and the returned card is the higher card

Higher card belongs to player1, so remove player1's card from their hand.

34.6 Modularity and abstraction with classes

Implementing this game is a large undertaking. Without breaking the problem into smaller subtasks, coding the game would quickly become messy.

Using objects and object-oriented programming, you've also managed to modularize your program even further. You separated your code into different objects and gave each object a set of data attributes and a set of methods.

Using object-oriented programming also allowed you to separate two main ideas: creating classes that organize your code, and using the classes to implement code that plays the game. While simulating the gameplay, you were able to use the objects of the same type consistently, leading to neat and easy-to-read code. This abstracted the details of how the object types and their methods were implemented, and you were able to use the docstrings of methods to decide which methods were appropriate during the simulation.

 **Summary**

In this lesson, my objective was to teach you how to write a larger program that uses classes others have created to improve your program, and how to create your own classes and use them to play a game.

The code for the class definitions needs to be written only once. It dictates the overall properties of your objects and operations you can do with these objects. This code doesn't manipulate any specific objects. The code for the gameplay itself (the code not including the class definitions) is straightforward, because you're creating objects and calling methods on the appropriate objects.

This structure separates code that tells others what an object is and what it can do, from code that uses these objects to achieve various tasks. In this way, you're hiding some of the unnecessary coding details that you don't need to know in order to implement the gameplay.

Using libraries to enhance your programs

For the most part, all the programs you've written have relied on combinations of built-in objects and objects that you created yourself. A large part of programming is learning to use code that others have written to your advantage. You can bring their code into your own and then use functions and classes that they've already written. You've done this a little already in some of the capstone projects.

Why would you want to do this? Often, different programmers need to do the same set of tasks. Instead of coming up with their own solutions independently, they can use libraries that contain code to help them achieve their goals. Many languages allow programmers to create libraries. The library may be included in the language, or it might be found on the internet and distributed separately. Libraries are usually bundled to contain functions and classes that are in the same vein.

In this unit, you'll see libraries and common tasks for which they can be used. You'll see three simple libraries: the `math` library contains functions that help you with mathematical operations, the `random` library contains functions that allow you to work with random numbers, and the `time` library contains functions that allow you to use the computer clock to pause your programs or to time them. You'll see two libraries that are more complex: the unittest library will help you build tests so you can check whether your code is behaving as you expect, and the tkinter library will help you add a visual layer to your programs through a graphical user interface.

In the capstone project, you'll write a program that plays a game of tag. Two players will use the keyboard and chase each other on the screen. When one gets close enough to the other, you'll print that they've been tagged.

35

USEFUL LIBRARIES

After reading lesson 35, you'll be able to

- Bring libraries from outside the standard Python package into your code
- Use the `math` library to do mathematical operations
- Use the `random` library to generate random numbers
- Use the `time` library to time programs

Programming is an activity that's usually most efficient and enjoyable when you build upon work that others have done. Some problems have already been solved, and code has likely been written to solve similar tasks to the ones that you're trying to solve. It's highly unlikely that you'll have to start a task by implementing code to do everything from scratch. In any language, libraries exist that you can use to help you code tasks in a modular way: by building upon code that's already written, tested, and debugged for correctness and efficiency.

To some extent, you've already been doing this! You've been using objects and operations built into the Python language. Imagine how tough learning to program would've been if you had to learn how to work with memory locations in the computer and to build up everything from scratch.

Consider this

Much of programming is building upon objects and ideas already there. Think about what you've learned so far. What are some examples of ways you've built upon things?

Answer:

You can use code that others have written (or even that you've written previously). You start with simple object types, and you make ones that are more complex. You build layers of abstractions by using functions and reuse functions with different inputs.

35.1 Importing libraries

Arguably, you've learned two important things so far:

- How to create your own functions
- How to create your own object types, which package together a set of properties and behaviors for an object type

More complex code requires incorporating many functions and object types whose definitions you have to include. One way to do this is to copy and paste the definitions into your code. But there's another way, which is more common and less error-prone. When you have functions and classes defined in other files, you can use an `import` statement at the top of your code. The reason you might have different functions or classes defined in different files is to keep your code organized, keeping in line with the idea of abstraction.

Suppose you have a file in which you define two classes you've already seen: `Circle` and `Rectangle`. In another file, you'd like to use these classes. You put one line in your file to bring in classes defined in another.

In a file named shapes.py, you define the `Circle` and `Rectangle` classes. In another file, you can bring in the classes by using the following:

```
import shapes
```

This process is called *importing* and tells Python to bring in all the classes defined in the file with the name shapes.py. Notice that the `import` line uses the name of the file that contains the definitions you want to import, and it omits the .py after the name of the file. For this line to work, both of these files must be in the same folder on your computer. Figure 35.1 shows the organization of code.

shapes.py
(define shapes)

test.py
(customize
shape objects)

Figure 35.1   Two files: shapes.py and test.py in the same folder. One file defines classes for `Circle` and `Rectangle`. Another file imports the classes defined in shapes.py and uses them by creating different objects of those types and changing their data attributes.

```
class Circle:
    # code
class Rectangle:
    # code
```

```
import shapes
c1 = Circle()
r1 = Rectangle(1,2)
# more code
```

Importing is a common practice that promotes code organization and decluttering. Typically, you'll want to import libraries into your code. Libraries are one or more modules, and a module is a file that contains definitions. Libraries often bundle modules of related uses together. Libraries can be built into the language (included with your installation of the language) or third-party (you download them from other online resources). In this unit, you'll use only built-in libraries.

Think of a Python library like a shop. Some shops are large, like department stores. These help you get all your items in one place, but they might not have some specialized merchandise. Other shops are small, like mall kiosks. These focus on one type of merchandise (for example, phones or perfume) and have a wider selection related to that one type of item.

When using a library, your first action is to go to its documentation to see the classes and functions defined in the library. For libraries that are built-in (a part of the language), this documentation can be found at the Python website: https://docs.python.org. This site links to the documentation for the latest version of Python, but you can view the documentation for any of the previous versions. This book uses Python version 3.5. If you don't have an internet connection to see the documentation online, you can also view the documentation through the Python console. You'll see how to do this in the next section.

35.2 Doing mathematical operations with the math library

One of the most useful libraries is the math library. The math library for Python 3.5 is documented at https://docs.python.org/3.5/library/math.html. It deals with mathematical operations on numbers, where the operations aren't built into the language. To view the math library documentation without going online, you can type the following into the IPython console:

```
import math
help(math)
```

The console shows all the classes and functions defined in the math library, along with their docstrings. You can browse the docstrings and see whether any of them would be useful in your code.

The math library consists of functions organized by type: number-theoretic and representation functions, power and logarithmic functions, trigonometric functions, angular conversion, and hyperbolic functions. It also contains two constants that you can work with: pi and e.

Suppose you'd like to simulate throwing a ball at your friend in a field. You want to see whether the throw reaches your friend, allowing for a bit of leniency because your friend can jump up to catch, if need be. Let's see how to write a program that does this simulation for you. You'll ask the user for the distance your friend is standing away from you, the speed at which you can throw the ball, and an angle at which to throw the ball. The program will tell you whether the ball will make it far enough to be caught. Figure 35.2 shows the setup.

The formula that you can use to calculate how far a ball goes when it's thrown with a certain speed at a certain angle is as follows:

```
reach = 2 * speed² * sin(angle) * cos(angle) / 9.8
```

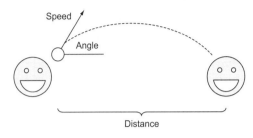

Figure 35.2 Setup for throwing a ball at a certain speed and angle so that it goes a certain distance

Listing 35.1 shows the code for this simple program. It first asks the user for the distance to the user's friend, the speed at which to throw the ball, and the angle at which to throw it. Then it uses the formula to calculate how far the ball will go. Allowing some tolerance (to account for the receiver being able to reach for it), it'll display one of three messages: it was caught, it fell short, or it went too long. To calculate the sin and cos values, you'll use functions in the math library, so you have to bring in the library using an `import` statement. Aside from implementing the formula, only one detail is left. An angle can be measured in degrees or radians. The functions in the math library assume that angles are given in radians, so you need to convert the angle from degrees to radians by using a function in the math library.

Listing 35.1 Using the math library to throw a ball at an angle

```python
import math                            ← Imports the math library functions
distance = float(input("How far away is your friend? (m) "))
speed = float(input("How fast can you throw? (m/s) "))
angle_d = float(input("What angle do you want to throw at? (degrees) "))
tolerance = 2

angle_r = math.radians(angle_d)                    ←

reach = 2*speed**2*math.sin(angle_r)*math.cos(angle_r)/9.8    ←

if reach > distance - tolerance and reach < distance + tolerance:
    print("Nice throw!")
elif reach < distance - tolerance:                 Implements the
    print("You didn't throw far enough.")          formula, using the
                                                    math library functions
else:
    print("You threw too far.")                    The library math.sin and
                                                    math.cos take radians, not
                                                    degrees, as the input, so
                                                    convert the user input.
```

> **Quick check 35.2** Modify the program so that it asks the user only for how far away the friend is and how fast to throw the ball. Then, it loops through all the angles from 0 to 90 and prints whether the ball made it.

35.3 Random numbers with the random library

The random library provides numerous operations you can do to add unpredictability to programs. This library is documented at https://docs.python.org/3.5/library/random.html.

35.3.1 Randomizing lists

Adding unpredictability and uncertainty to your programs can add more functionality and make them more interesting for your users. The unpredictability comes from a pseudo-number generator, which can help you do things like pick a random number within a certain range, pick an item at random in a list or a dictionary, or rearrange a list for you at random, among others.

For example, say you have a list of people and want to pick one at random. Try typing this code in a file and running it:

```
import random
people = ["Ana","Bob","Carl","Doug","Elle","Finn"]
print(random.choice(people))
```

It prints one of the elements, at random, in the list of named people. If you run the program more than once, you'll notice that you'll get a different output each time it's run.

You can even pick a certain number of people from the list:

```
import random
people = ["Ana","Bob","Carl","Doug","Elle","Finn"]
print(random.sample(people, 3))
```

This code ensures that the same person isn't picked more than once, and prints a list of however many elements are specified (three, in this case).

35.3.2 Simulating games of chance

Another common use of the random library is to play games of chance. You can simulate probabilities of certain events happening by using the random.random() function: the first random is the library name, and the second random is the function name, which happens to be the same as the library name. This function returns a random floating-point number between 0 (inclusive) and 1 (not inclusive).

Listing 35.2 shows a program that plays rock-paper-scissors with the user. The program first asks the user to make their choice. Then, it gets a random number by using `random.random()`. To simulate the 1/3 probability of the computer picking one of rock, paper, or scissors, you can check that the random number generated falls within one of three ranges: 0 to 1/3, 1/3 to 2/3, and 2/3 to 1.

Listing 35.2 Using the random library to play rock-paper-scissors

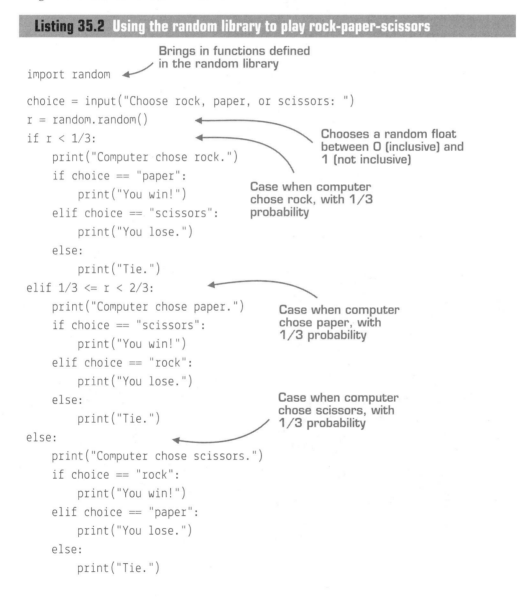

```
                        Brings in functions defined
                        in the random library
import random

choice = input("Choose rock, paper, or scissors: ")
r = random.random()                         Chooses a random float
if r < 1/3:                                 between 0 (inclusive) and
    print("Computer chose rock.")           1 (not inclusive)
    if choice == "paper":
        print("You win!")          Case when computer
    elif choice == "scissors":     chose rock, with 1/3
        print("You lose.")         probability
    else:
        print("Tie.")
elif 1/3 <= r < 2/3:
    print("Computer chose paper.")    Case when computer
    if choice == "scissors":          chose paper, with
        print("You win!")             1/3 probability
    elif choice == "rock":
        print("You lose.")
    else:                             Case when computer
        print("Tie.")                 chose scissors, with
else:                                 1/3 probability
    print("Computer chose scissors.")
    if choice == "rock":
        print("You win!")
    elif choice == "paper":
        print("You lose.")
    else:
        print("Tie.")
```

35.3.3 Replicating results by using a seed

When you have programs that don't produce the results you want, you need to test them to figure out where the problem is. Programs that deal with random numbers add a layer of complexity; a program involving a random number may work sometimes, but not others, leading to a frustrating debugging session.

Random numbers generated by the random library aren't truly random. They're pseudo-random. They appear random, but are determined by the result of applying a function on something that changes frequently or is unpredictable, such as the time in milliseconds since a specific date. The date generates the first number in the pseudo-random sequence, and each number in that sequence is generated from the previous number. The random library allows you to *seed* the random numbers generated by using random.seed(N), where N is any integer. Setting the seed allows you to start with a known number. The sequence of random numbers generated within your program will be the same every time you run the program, as long as the seed is set to the same value. The following lines generate a random integer between 2 and 17 and then between 30 and 88:

```
import random
print(random.randint(2,17))
print(random.randint(30,88))
```

If you run this program many times, the numbers printed will likely change. But you can seed the results so that the two numbers are going to be the same every time the program is run, by setting the seed:

```
import random
random.seed(0)
print(random.randint(2,17))
print(random.randint(30,88))
```

The program now prints 14 and 78 every time it's run. By changing the integer inside the seed function, you can generate a different sequence. For example, if you change random.seed(0) to random.seed(5), this program will now print 10 and 77 every time it's run. Note that these numbers may change if you're using a Python version other than 3.5.

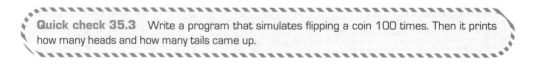

Quick check 35.3 Write a program that simulates flipping a coin 100 times. Then it prints how many heads and how many tails came up.

35.4 Timing programs with the time library

When you start dealing with programs that might take a long time to run, it'd be nice to know how long they've been running. The time library has functions that can help you do this, and its documentation is available at https://docs.python.org/3.5/library/time.html.

35.4.1 Using the clock

Computers are pretty fast, but how quickly can they do simple calculations? You can answer this question by timing a program that gets the computer to count up to one million. Listing 35.3 shows code that does this. Just before a loop that increments a counter, you save the current time on the computer clock. Then you run the loop. After the loop, you get the current time on the computer again. The difference between the start and end times tells you how long the program took to run.

Listing 35.3 Using the time library to show how long a program takes to run

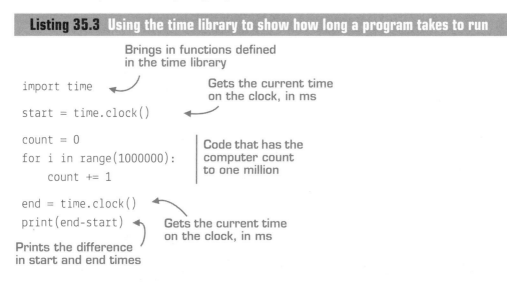

```
import time

start = time.clock()

count = 0
for i in range(1000000):
    count += 1

end = time.clock()
print(end-start)
```

Brings in functions defined in the time library

Gets the current time on the clock, in ms

Code that has the computer count to one million

Gets the current time on the clock, in ms

Prints the difference in start and end times

This program took about 0.2 seconds to run on my computer. This time will vary, depending on how new and fast your computer is and how many other applications are running. If you have video streaming in the background, the computer may dedicate resources to doing that rather than running your program, so you may see a longer time printed.

35.4.2 Pausing your program

The time library also allows you to pause your program by using a sleep function. This stops it from executing the next line until that amount of time has passed. One use for this is to show the user a loading screen. Listing 35.4 shows how to print a progress bar that shows 10% increments every half- second. The code prints the following, with a half-second pause between each line. Can you tell why the code prints multiple stars by looking at the code? You'll have to think back to the lesson on strings and string manipulations:

```
Loading...
[           ] 0 % complete
[ *         ] 10 % complete
[ **        ] 20 % complete
[ ***       ] 30 % complete
[ ****      ] 40 % complete
[ *****     ] 50 % complete
[ ******    ] 60 % complete
[ *******   ] 70 % complete
[ ********  ] 80 % complete
[ ********* ] 90 % complete
```

Listing 35.4 Using the time library to show a progress bar

Brings in functions
defined in the time
library

A loop
representing
10% increments

Prints progress
represented by
multiple * characters

```
import time

print("Loading...")
for i in range(10):
    print("[",i*"*",(10-i)*" ","]",i*10,"% complete")
    time.sleep(0.5)
```

Pauses the program for half a second

> **Quick check 35.4**   Write a program that generates 10 million random numbers and then prints how long it takes to do this.

 **Summary**

In this lesson, my goal was to teach you how to use libraries that other programmers have created to enhance your own programs. The libraries shown here are simple, but using them can lead to a more interesting user experience. Here are the major takeaways:

- Organizing code that deals with similar functionality in a separate file leads to code that's easier to read.
- Libraries store functions and classes related to one group of actions in one place.

Let's see if you got this…

Q35.1 Write a program that gets the user to roll a die against the computer. First, simulate the user rolling a six-sided die and show the result to the user. Then, simulate the computer rolling a six-sided die, add a 2-second delay, and show the result. After each roll, ask the user whether they want to roll again. When the user is done playing, show them how long they've been playing the game in seconds.

TESTING AND DEBUGGING YOUR PROGRAMS

After reading lesson 36, you'll be able to

- Use the unittest library
- Write tests for your program
- Efficiently debug your programs

It's unlikely that you'll write a perfect program on the first try. Often you'll write code, test it with a few inputs, make changes to it, and test it again, repeating this process until your program runs as expected.

Consider this

Think about your experience in programming so far. When you write a program and it doesn't work, what kinds of things do you do to fix it?

Answer:

Look at the error message, if any, and see whether there are clues like line numbers that can direct me toward the issue. Put `print` statements at certain locations. Try a different input.

36.1 Working with the unittest library

Python has many libraries that can help you create a testing structure around your program. A testing library is especially useful when you have programs that contain different functions. One testing library comes with your Python installation, and its documentation for Python 3.5 is available at https://docs.python.org/3.5/library/unittest .html.

To create a suite of tests, you create a class representing that suite. Methods inside that class represent different tests. Every test that you want to run should have test_ as a prefix, and then any name for the method. The following listing contains code that defines two simple tests and then runs them.

Listing 36.1 Simple test suite

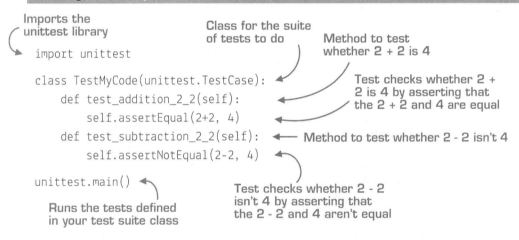

The code prints the following:

```
Ran 2 tests in 0.001s

OK
```

This is expected because the first test checks whether 2 + 2 is equal to 4, which is true. And the second test checks whether 2 - 2 isn't equal to 4, which is true. Now suppose that one of the tests is False by making the following change:

```
def test_addition_2_2(self):
        self.assertEqual(2+2, 5)
```

Now the test checks whether 2 + 2 is equal to 5, which is False. Running the test program again now prints the following:

```
FAIL: test_addition_2_2 (__main__.TestMyCode)
----------------------------------------------------------------------
Traceback (most recent call last):
  File "C:/Users/Ana/.spyder-py3/temp.py", line 5, in test_addition_2_2
    self.assertEqual(2+2, 5)
AssertionError: 4 != 5


----------------------------------------------------------------------
Ran 2 tests in 0.002s

FAILED (failures=1)
```

This message is rife with information. It tells you the following:

- Which test suite failed: TestMyCode
- Which test failed: test_addition_2_2
- Which line inside the test failed: self.assertEqual(2+2, 5)
- Why it failed, by comparing what value it got and what value it expected: 4 != 5

Comparing values in this way is a bit silly. Clearly, you'd never have to check that 2 + 2 is 4. You usually need to test code that has more substance to it; typically, you want to make sure that functions do the correct thing. You'll see how to do this in the next section.

> **Quick check 36.1**   Fill in each of the following lines:
>
> ```
> class TestMyCode(unittest.TestCase):
>     def test_addition_5_5(self):
>         # fill this in to test 5+5
>     def test_remainder_6_2(self):
>         # fill this in to test the remainder when 6 is divided by 2
> ```

36.2 Separating the program from the tests

You should decouple the code you write as part of your program from the code that you write to test the program. Decoupling reinforces the idea of modularity, in that you separate code into different files. This way, you avoid cluttering the program itself with unnecessary testing commands.

Suppose you have one file that contains the two functions shown in listing 36.2. One function checks whether a number is prime (divisible by only 1 and itself, and not equal to 1) and returns True or False. The other returns the absolute value of a number. Each of these functions has an error in its implementation. Before reading further on how to write tests, can you spot the errors?

Listing 36.2 File, named funcs.py, containing functions to test

```
def is_prime(n):
    prime = True
    for i in range(1,n):
        if n%i == 0:
            prime = False
    return prime

def absolute_value(n):
    if n < 0:
        return -n
    elif n > 0:
        return n
```

In a separate file, you can write unit tests to check whether the functions you wrote are behaving as expected. You can create different classes to organize different suites of tests corresponding to different functions. This is a good idea because you should have more than one test for each function, making sure to try a variety of inputs. Creating tests for every function you write is called *unit testing* because you're testing each function's behavior by itself.

> **DEFINITION** A unit test is a series of tests that checks whether the actual output matches the expected output for a function.

A common way of writing unit tests for a method is to use the Arrange Act Assert pattern:

- *Arrange*—Sets up objects and their values to pass to the function undergoing unit testing
- *Act*—Calls the function with the parameters set up previously
- *Assert*—Makes sure the function behavior is what was expected

The following listing shows the code for unit testing the functions in funcs.py. The class TestPrime contains tests related to the is_prime function, and the class TestAbs contains tests related to the absolute_value function.

Listing 36.3 File, named test.py, containing the tests

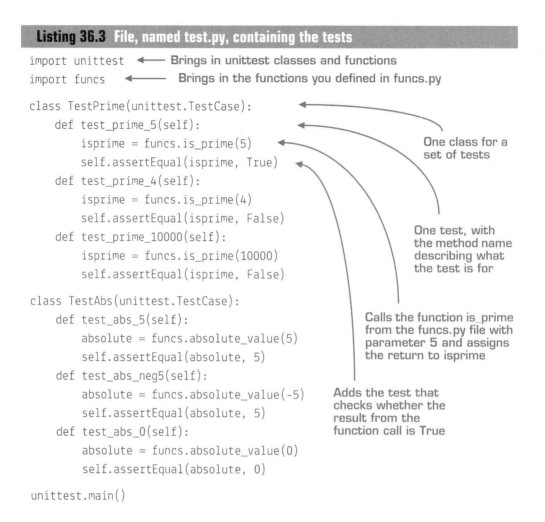

```
import unittest   ◄──── Brings in unittest classes and functions
import funcs   ◄──────── Brings in the functions you defined in funcs.py

class TestPrime(unittest.TestCase):
    def test_prime_5(self):
        isprime = funcs.is_prime(5)
        self.assertEqual(isprime, True)
    def test_prime_4(self):
        isprime = funcs.is_prime(4)
        self.assertEqual(isprime, False)
    def test_prime_10000(self):
        isprime = funcs.is_prime(10000)
        self.assertEqual(isprime, False)

class TestAbs(unittest.TestCase):
    def test_abs_5(self):
        absolute = funcs.absolute_value(5)
        self.assertEqual(absolute, 5)
    def test_abs_neg5(self):
        absolute = funcs.absolute_value(-5)
        self.assertEqual(absolute, 5)
    def test_abs_0(self):
        absolute = funcs.absolute_value(0)
        self.assertEqual(absolute, 0)

unittest.main()
```

One class for a set of tests

One test, with the method name describing what the test is for

Calls the function is_prime from the funcs.py file with parameter 5 and assigns the return to isprime

Adds the test that checks whether the result from the function call is True

Running this code shows that it ran six tests and found two errors:

```
FAIL: test_abs_0 (__main__.TestAbs)
----------------------------------------------------------------------
Traceback (most recent call last):
  File "C:/Users/Ana/test.py", line 24, in test_abs_0
    self.assertEqual(absolute, 0)
AssertionError: None != 0

======================================================================
FAIL: test_prime_5 (__main__.TestPrime)
```

```
----------------------------------------------------------------
Traceback (most recent call last):
  File "C:/Users/Ana/test.py", line 7, in test_prime_5
    self.assertEqual(isprime, True)
AssertionError: False != True

----------------------------------------------------------------

Ran 6 tests in 0.000s

FAILED (failures=2)
```

With this information, you can make changes to your functions in funcs.py to try to fix them. The information provided here tells you the tests that failed: test_abs_0 and test_prime_5. You can now go back to your function and try to fix it. This process is called *debugging* and is discussed in the next section.

> **Thinking like a programmer**
> Using descriptive names for the methods is useful for providing quick, at-a-glance, information when tests fail. You can include the function name, the inputs, and possibly a one- or two-word description of what it's testing.

It's important to make your changes incrementally. Every time you make a change, you should run the tests again by running tests.py. You do this to make sure that any changes you make to fix one issue won't cause another issue to pop up.

> **Quick check 36.2** Modify the code in listing 36.2 to fix the two errors. After each change, run tests.py to see whether you fixed the errors.

36.2.1 Types of tests

The unittest library has a variety of tests you can perform, not just to check whether one value is equal to another using assertEqual. The complete list is in the documentation for the library. Take a moment to browse through the list.

> **Quick check 36.3** Looking at the list of tests you can do, which would be most appropriate in the following situations?
>   1 To check that a value is False
>   2 To check that a value is in a list
>   3 To check that two dictionaries are equal

36.3 Debugging your code

The process of debugging code is somewhat an art form in that there's no specific formula for how to do it. The process begins after you have a set of tests that have failed. These tests offer a starting point for where to look in the code and under what specific conditions; you have a set of inputs you gave to a function, which gave you output that wasn't what you expected.

Often, a brute-force solution for debugging is most efficient; this means being systematic about looking at every line, and using a pen and paper to note values. Starting with the inputs that caused the test to fail, pretend you're the computer and execute each line. Write down what values are assigned to each variable, and ask yourself whether that's correct. As soon as you find an incorrect value being calculated from what you expect, you've likely found where an error is occurring. Now it's up to you to figure out why the error is occurring, using what you've learned.

As you're tracing through your program by going line by line, a common mistake is to assume that simple lines of code are correct, especially if you're debugging your own code. Be skeptical of every line. Pretend that you're explaining your code to someone who doesn't know anything about programming. This process is called *rubber ducky debugging*, which means you explain your code to a real (or imaginary) rubber duck, or any other inanimate object. This forces you to explain the code in plain English, not programming jargon, and gets you to tell your helper what each line of code is trying to accomplish.

36.3.1 Using tools to help you step through code

Many tools have been designed to help make your debugging process easier. A debugger is built into Spyder. The name is misleading because it doesn't do the debugging for you. Rather, it prints variable values for you with each step you take. It's still up to you to determine why a line of code is incorrect when the value for a variable isn't what you expect it to be. A debugger can be used on any code that you write.

You can use the Spyder debugger to identify the problem with the code shown in listing 36.2, using the test created in listing 36.3. You know that two tests failed: test_abs_0 and test_prime_5. You should debug each one separately.

You'll now debug test_abs_0. Figure 36.1 shows what your Spyder editor should look like after you've opened tests.py. You have the editor on the left, the IPython console on the bottom right, and the variable explorer at the top right.

The first step is to put a breakpoint in your code (#1 in figure 36.1). A breakpoint indicates a spot in the code where you'd like to stop execution so that you can inspect the value. Because the test test_abs_0 failed, put a breakpoint at the first line inside that method. You can insert a breakpoint by double-clicking the area just to the left on the line on which you want to put the breakpoint; a dot appears.

Figure 36.1   Screenshot of the debugging window

Then, you can start running the program in debugging mode. You do this by clicking the button with the blue arrow and two vertical lines (#2 in figure 36.1). The console now shows you the first few lines of the code and an arrow, ----->, indicating which line is to be executed:

```
----> 1 import unittest
      2 import funcs
      3
      4 class TestPrime(unittest.TestCase):
      5     def test_prime_5(self):
```

Click the blue double arrows (#4 in figure 36.1) to go to the breakpoint you put in. Now, the console shows where you are in the code:

```
      21            self.assertEqual(absolute, 5)
      22        def test_abs_0(self):
1--> 23            absolute = funcs.absolute_value(0)
      24            self.assertEqual(absolute, 0)
      25
```

You'd like to go into the function to see why the value for absolute isn't 0 and this test fails. Click the button with the small blue arrow that goes into three horizontal lines to "step into" the function (#3 in figure 36.1). Now you're inside the function call. Your variable explorer window should show you that the value for n is 0, and the console shows that you've just entered the function call:

```
      6     return prime
      7
----> 8 def absolute_value(n):
      9     if n < 0:
      10        return -n
```

If you click the Step Into button two more times, it takes you to the line

```
      9     if n < 0:
      10        return -n
---> 11    elif n > 0:
      12        return n
      13
```

At this point, you can see what's wrong. The if statement isn't executed because n is 0. The else statement also isn't executed because n is 0. You've likely figured out the issue and can now exit debugging by clicking the blue square. The function returns None because no case handles what the program should do when n is 0.

 **Summary**

In this lesson, my goal was to teach you the basics of testing and debugging and to give you more practice at importing and using libraries. I showed you how to use the unit-test library to organize your tests and the importance of separating the code from the testing framework. You used a debugger to step through your code.

Let's see if you got this…

Q36.1 Here's a buggy program. Write unit tests and try to debug it:

```
def remove_buggy(L, e):
    """

    L, list
    e, any object
    Removes all e from L.
    """

    for i in L:
        if e == i:
            L.remove(i)
```

37

A LIBRARY FOR GRAPHICAL USER INTERFACES

After reading lesson 37, you'll be able to

- Describe a graphical user interface
- Use a library for a graphical user interface to write a program

Every program you've written has interacted with the user in a text-based way. You've been displaying text on the screen and getting text input from the user. Although you can write interesting programs this way, the user is missing a more visual experience.

Consider this

Think about a program you use in your everyday life: a browser to go on the internet. What kinds of interactions do you have with the browser?

Answer: You open the browser window, click buttons, scroll, select text, and close the browser window.

Many programming languages have libraries that help programmers write visual applications. These applications use familiar interfaces between the user and the program: buttons, text boxes, drawing canvases, icons, and many more.

37.1 A library for graphical user interfaces

A library for a graphical user interface (GUI) is a set of classes and methods that know how to interface between the user and the operating system to display graphical control elements, called *widgets*. Widgets are meant to enhance the user experience through interaction: buttons, scrollbars, menus, windows, drawing canvases, progress bars, or dialog boxes are a few examples.

Python comes with a standard library for GUIs, called tkinter, whose documentation is available at https://docs.python.org/3.5/library/tkinter.html#module-tkinter.

Developing a GUI application usually requires three steps. Each step is demonstrated in this lesson. As with any other program, development also involves setting up unit tests and debugging. The three steps are as follows:

- Setting up the window by determining its size, location, and title.
- Adding widgets, which are interactive "things" like buttons or menus, among many others.
- Choosing behaviors for widgets to handle events such as clicking a button or selecting a menu item. Behaviors are implemented by writing event handlers in the form of functions that tell the program which actions to take when the user interacts with the specific widget.

> **Quick check 37.1** What are some actions that you could do on each of the following?
> 1 A button
> 2 A scrollbar
> 3 A menu
> 4 A canvas

37.2 Setting up a program using the tkinter library

All GUI programs typically run in a window. The window can be customized by changing its title, size, and background color. The following listing shows how to create a window of size 800 x 200 pixels, with a title of "My first GUI" and a background color of gray.

Listing 37.1 **Creating a window**

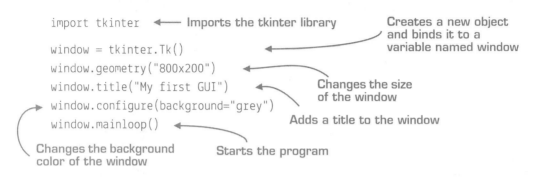

After you run this program, a new window will show up on your computer screen. If you don't see it, it might be hiding behind another window you have open, so look on your taskbar for a new icon. You can terminate your program by closing the window.

Figure 37.1 shows what the window looks like on the Windows operating system. The window may look different if you're using Linux or a Mac operating system.

Figure 37.1   An 800 x 200 pixel window with the title "My first GUI" and a background color of gray

Quick check 37.2   Write a program for each of the following:

  1   Makes a 500 x 200 window with the title "go go go" and the background color green
  2   Makes a 100 x 900 window with the title "Tall One" and the background color red
  3   Makes two 100 x 100 windows with no title, but one has the background color white and the other black

 **37.3 Adding widgets**

A blank window isn't interesting. The user has nothing to click! After you create the window, you can start adding widgets. You'll create a program that has three buttons, one text box, one progress bar, and one label.

To add a widget, you need two lines of code: one to create the widget and one to put it on the window. The following code shows the two lines by creating one button and adding it to the window object from listing 37.1. The first line creates the button and binds it to a variable named btn. The second line adds it (with pack) to the window:

```
btn = tkinter.Button(window)
btn.pack()
```

The next listing shows you how to add three buttons, one text box, and one label, assuming that you've already created a window, as in listing 37.1.

Listing 37.2 Adding widgets to the window

```
import tkinter
window = tkinter.Tk()
window.geometry("800x200")
window.title("My first GUI")
window.configure(background="grey")

red = tkinter.Button(window, text="Red", bg="red")
red.pack()

yellow = tkinter.Button(window, text="Yellow", bg="yellow")
yellow.pack()

green = tkinter.Button(window, text="Green", bg="green")
green.pack()

textbox = tkinter.Entry(window)
textbox.pack()

colorlabel = tkinter.Label(window, height="10", width="10")
colorlabel.pack()

window.mainloop()
```

Creates a new button with a red background color and with the text "Red" on it

Adds the button with those properties to the window

Creates and adds a box in which you can enter text

Creates and adds a label whose height is 10

When you run this program, you get a window that looks like the one in figure 37.2.

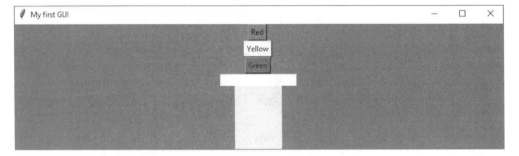

Figure 37.2   Window after adding three buttons, one text box, and one label. The top button is red and is labeled Red, the middle button is yellow and is labeled Yellow, and the bottom button is green and is labeled Green.

You can add many widgets to your programs. The ones that come with the standard tkinter library are listed in table 37.1.

Table 37.1   Widgets available in tkinter

Widget name	Description	Widget name	Description
Button	Shows a button	Menubutton	Shows menus
Canvas	Draws shapes	OptionMenu	Shows a pop-up menu
Checkbutton	Shows options via checkboxes (can select more than one option)	PanedWindow	Contains window panes that can be resized
Entry	A text field the user can type text in	Radiobutton	Shows options via radio buttons (can select only one option)
Frame	Container to put other widgets in	Scale	Shows a slider
Label	Shows single line of text or an image	Scrollbar	Adds scrollbars to other widgets
LabelFrame	Container to add space	Spinbox	Like an Entry, but can select only from some text
Listbox	Shows options via a list	Text	Shows multiple lines of text
Menu	Shows commands (contained inside Menubutton)	TopLevel	Allows for a separate window container

Quick check 37.3 Write a line that creates each of the following:

- An orange button with the text Click here
- Two radio buttons
- A checkbutton

37.4 Adding event handlers

At this point, you've created GUI windows and added widgets to them. The last step is to write code that tells the program what to do when a user interacts with the widgets. The code must somehow link the widget to the action.

When you create a widget, you give it the name of a command you want to run. The command is a function in the same program. The following listing shows an example of a code snippet that changes a window's background color when a button widget is clicked.

Listing 37.3 Event handler for a button click

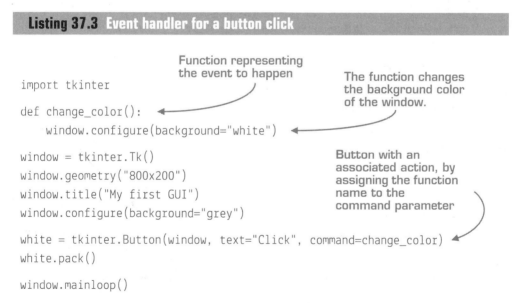

```
import tkinter

def change_color():          ←  Function representing the event to happen
    window.configure(background="white")   ←  The function changes the background color of the window.

window = tkinter.Tk()
window.geometry("800x200")
window.title("My first GUI")
window.configure(background="grey")

white = tkinter.Button(window, text="Click", command=change_color)   ←  Button with an associated action, by assigning the function name to the command parameter
white.pack()

window.mainloop()
```

Figure 37.3 shows what the screen looks like after the button is clicked. The window is originally gray, but after you click the button, it's white. Clicking the button again doesn't change the color back to gray; it stays white.

Figure 37.3   The window background color changes to white from gray after clicking the button.

You can do more interesting things with event handlers. You can apply everything you've learned so far in the book when you write GUIs. For the final example, you'll write code for a countdown timer. You'll see how to read information from other widgets, use loops in event handlers, and even use another library.

Listing 37.4 shows a program that reads a number the user enters in a text box and then displays a countdown from that number to 0, with the number changing every second. There are four widgets in the program:

- A label with instructions for the user
- A text box for the user to put in a number
- A button to start the countdown
- A label to show the changing numbers

The button is the only widget that has an event handler associated with it. The function for that event will do the following:

- Change the color of the label to white
- Get the number from the text box and convert it to an integer
- Use the number from the text box in a loop, starting from that value and ending at 0

The bulk of the work is being done inside the loop. It uses the loop variable, i, to change the text of the label. Notice that you're giving a variable name to the text parameter of the label, whose value changes every time through the loop. Then, it calls an update method to refresh the window and show the changes. Finally, it uses the `sleep` method from the `time` library to pause execution for one second. Without the `sleep` method, the countdown would go so fast that you wouldn't be able to see the changing numbers.

Listing 37.4 **Program that reads a text box and counts down that many seconds** .

Event handler function

Changes the label's color to white

Gets the value from the text box and converts it to an int

```python
import tkinter
import time

def countdown():
    countlabel.configure(background="white")
    howlong = int(textbox.get())
    for i in range(howlong,0,-1):
        countlabel.configure(text=i)
        window.update()
        time.sleep(1)
    countlabel.configure(text="DONE!")

window = tkinter.Tk()
window.geometry("800x600")
window.title("My first GUI")
window.configure(background="grey")

lbl = tkinter.Label(window, text="How many seconds to count down?")
lbl.pack()
textbox = tkinter.Entry(window)
textbox.pack()
count = tkinter.Button(window, text="Countdown!", command=countdown)
count.pack()
countlabel = tkinter.Label(window, height="10", width="10")
countlabel.pack()

window.mainloop()
```

Loops starting from the number in the text box until 0

Changes the text on the label to the value of the loop variable

Updates the window to show the updated value on the label

Waits one second using the time library

Changes the text of the label to done after reaching 0

One label with instructions for the user

A label on which to print the countdown

Text box for the user to enter a number

Button to start the countdown, with the function written in the first line as the event command

With the ability to set up a window, add widgets, and create event handlers, you can write many visually appealing and uniquely interactive programs.

Quick check 37.4   Write code that creates a button. When clicked, the button randomly chooses the color red, green, or blue, and changes the background color of the window to the chosen color.

Summary

In this lesson, my goal was to teach you how to use a graphical user interface library. The library contains classes and methods that help programmers manipulate graphical elements of the operating system. Here are the major takeaways:

- Your GUI program works inside a window.
- In the window, you can add graphical elements, called widgets.
- You can add functions that perform tasks when a user interacts with the widget.

Let's see if you got this…

Q37.1 Write a program that stores names, phone numbers, and emails of people in a phonebook. The window should have three text boxes for the name, phone, and email. Then it should have one button to add a contact, and one button to show all contacts. Finally, it should have a label. When the user clicks the Add button, the program reads the text boxes and stores the information. When the user clicks the Show button, it reads all the contacts stored and prints them on a label.

38

CAPSTONE PROJECT: GAME OF TAG

After reading lesson 38, you'll be able to

- Write a simple game by using the tkinter library
- Use classes and object-oriented programming to organize code for a GUI
- Write code that interacts with the user using the keyboard
- Use a canvas to draw shapes in your program

When you think of a program that uses a GUI, one of the most common kinds of programs that comes to mind are games. Games that are short and interactive offer quick distractions. They're even more fun to play when you write them yourself!

THE PROBLEM   Write a GUI game using the tkinter library. The game simulates a game of tag. You should create two players inside a window. The players' position and size can be randomized at the start. Both players will use the same keyboard: one will use the W, A, S, D keys, and the other will use the I, J, K, L keys to move their piece. Users decide which one will try to catch the other. Then, they'll move around the window using their respective keys to try to touch the other player. When they touch the other player, the word Tag should appear somewhere on the screen.

This is a simple game, and the code to write it won't be long. When writing GUIs or visual applications such as games, it's important to not be too ambitious at the beginning. Start with a simpler problem and build upon it as you get things working.

38.1 Identifying the parts to the problem

Given the problem, it's time to identify its parts. You'll find it easier to write the code if you do it incrementally. Ultimately, you need to accomplish three tasks:

- Create two shapes
- Move them around the window when certain keys are pressed
- Detect whether the two shapes have touched

Each of these can be written as a separate piece of code that can be tested separately.

38.2 Creating two shapes in a window

As with the other GUIs you've seen, the first step is to create a window and add any widgets your game will use to it. The next listing shows the code for this. The window will hold only one widget, a canvas. The canvas widget is a rectangular area in which you can place shapes and other graphical objects.

Listing 38.1 Initializing a window and widgets

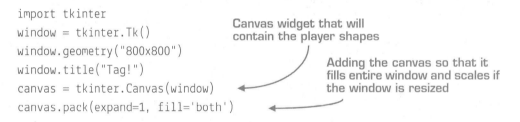

```
import tkinter
window = tkinter.Tk()
window.geometry("800x800")
window.title("Tag!")
canvas = tkinter.Canvas(window)
canvas.pack(expand=1, fill='both')
```

Canvas widget that will contain the player shapes

Adding the canvas so that it fills entire window and scales if the window is resized

Now it's time to create the shapes for the players. You'll make the player pieces rectangles. The shapes are going to be objects added to the canvas, not the window itself. Because you'll be creating more than one player, it's a good idea to think in a modular way. You'll create a class for the player, which will initialize the player piece on the canvas.

To make the game more interesting, you can use random numbers to set up the starting position and size of the shape. Figure 38.1 shows how you'll construct the rectangle. You'll choose a random coordinate for the top-left corner, x1 and y1. Then, you'll choose a random number for the size of the rectangle. The x2 and y2 coordinates are calculated by adding the size to x1 and y1.

The random aspect of creating the rectangle means that every time you create a new player, the rectangle will be placed at a random position in the window and will be a random size.

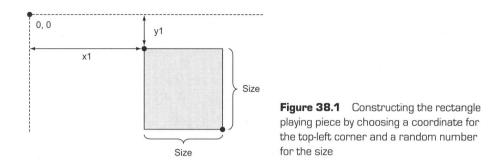

Figure 38.1 Constructing the rectangle playing piece by choosing a coordinate for the top-left corner and a random number for the size

Listing 38.2 shows the code for creating the player's rectangle piece. The code creates a class named Player. You'll use a rectangle to denote the player's piece. Any object on a canvas is denoted by a tuple of four integers, x1, y1, x2, y2, where (x1, y1) is the top-left corner, and (x2, y2) is the bottom-right corner of the shape.

Listing 38.2 A class for the player

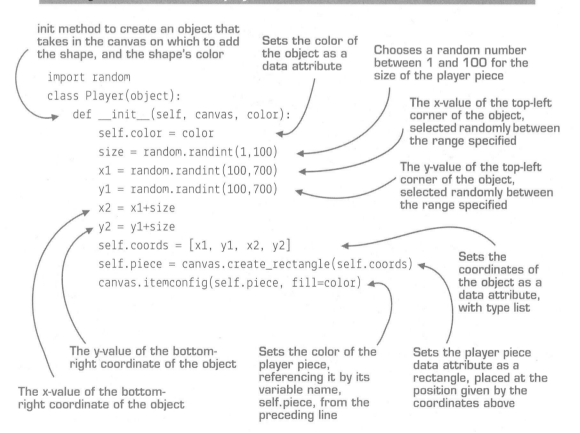

init method to create an object that takes in the canvas on which to add the shape, and the shape's color

Sets the color of the object as a data attribute

Chooses a random number between 1 and 100 for the size of the player piece

```
import random
class Player(object):
    def __init__(self, canvas, color):
        self.color = color
        size = random.randint(1,100)
        x1 = random.randint(100,700)
        y1 = random.randint(100,700)
        x2 = x1+size
        y2 = y1+size
        self.coords = [x1, y1, x2, y2]
        self.piece = canvas.create_rectangle(self.coords)
        canvas.itemconfig(self.piece, fill=color)
```

The x-value of the top-left corner of the object, selected randomly between the range specified

The y-value of the top-left corner of the object, selected randomly between the range specified

Sets the coordinates of the object as a data attribute, with type list

The y-value of the bottom-right coordinate of the object

The x-value of the bottom-right coordinate of the object

Sets the color of the player piece, referencing it by its variable name, self.piece, from the preceding line

Sets the player piece data attribute as a rectangle, placed at the position given by the coordinates above

After creating the window, you can add the players to the canvas with the following code, which creates two `Player` objects on the same canvas, one yellow and one blue:

```
player1 = Player(canvas, "yellow")
player2 = Player(canvas, "blue")
```

If you run the code, you'll get a window that looks something like figure 38.2. You have two shapes of different colors at a random position and with a random size. Nothing happens when the mouse is clicked or when a key is pressed.

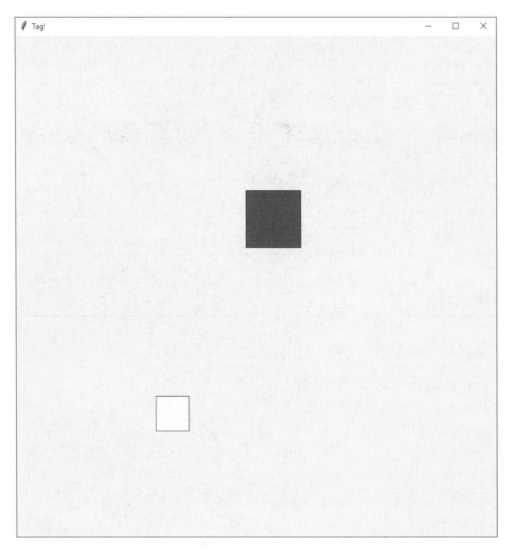

Figure 38.2   The game after creating two player objects. The position and size of each square varies each time the program is run.

 **38.3   Moving shapes inside the canvas**

Each shape responds to the same type of event, keypresses:

- To move the shape up, press W for one shape and I for the other.
- To move the shape left, press A for one shape and J for the other.
- To move the shape down, press S for one shape and K for the other.
- To move the shape right, press D for one shape and L for the other.

You'll have to create a function that acts as the event handler for any keypress on the canvas. Inside the function, you'll move one player or the other, depending on which button is pressed. The following listing shows the code. In this code, move is a method you'll define in the Player class. It'll move the player's position with "u" for up, "d" for down, "r" for right, and "l" for left.

Listing 38.3   Event handler function when any key is pressed on the canvas

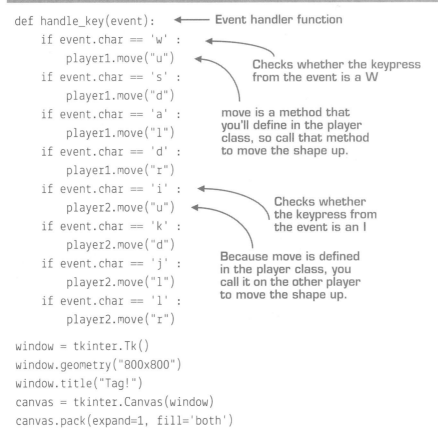

```
def handle_key(event):              ◄─── Event handler function
    if event.char == 'w' :
        player1.move("u")           ◄─── Checks whether the keypress
    if event.char == 's' :               from the event is a W
        player1.move("d")
    if event.char == 'a' :          move is a method that
        player1.move("l")           you'll define in the player
    if event.char == 'd' :          class, so call that method
        player1.move("r")           to move the shape up.
    if event.char == 'i' :          ◄───
        player2.move("u")           ◄─── Checks whether
    if event.char == 'k' :               the keypress from
        player2.move("d")                the event is an I
    if event.char == 'j' :          Because move is defined
        player2.move("l")           in the player class, you
    if event.char == 'l' :          call it on the other player
        player2.move("r")           to move the shape up.

window = tkinter.Tk()
window.geometry("800x800")
window.title("Tag!")
canvas = tkinter.Canvas(window)
canvas.pack(expand=1, fill='both')
```

```
player1 = Player(canvas, "yellow")
player2 = Player(canvas, "blue")
canvas.bind_all('<Key>', handle_key)
```

For the canvas, any keypress event will call the handle_key function.

Notice how nicely modular this code is. It's easy to understand what's going on, because you've removed the logic behind moving the shape into the player class. All that you do in the event handler function is decide which player to move and in which direction, denoted by "u" for up, "d" for down, "l" for left, and "r" for right.

Inside the Player class, you can write code that handles moving the shape by changing the values of the coordinates. Listing 38.4 shows the code. For each of the directions that the player can move, you modify the coordinate data attribute. Then, you update the canvas coordinates for the shape to the new coordinates. Two players can't move simultaneously. After a player starts moving, it'll stop moving as soon as the other player presses a key.

Listing 38.4 How to move a shape inside the canvas

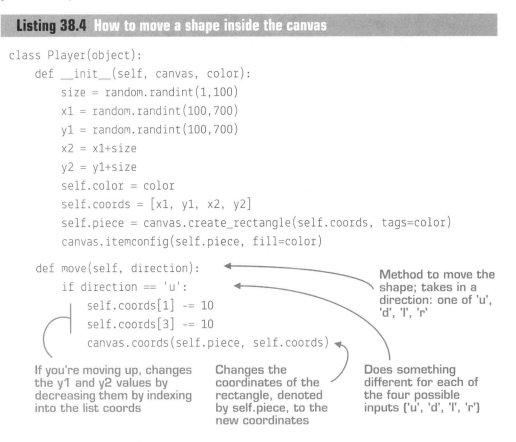

```
class Player(object):
    def __init__(self, canvas, color):
        size = random.randint(1,100)
        x1 = random.randint(100,700)
        y1 = random.randint(100,700)
        x2 = x1+size
        y2 = y1+size
        self.color = color
        self.coords = [x1, y1, x2, y2]
        self.piece = canvas.create_rectangle(self.coords, tags=color)
        canvas.itemconfig(self.piece, fill=color)

    def move(self, direction):
        if direction == 'u':
            self.coords[1] -= 10
            self.coords[3] -= 10
            canvas.coords(self.piece, self.coords)
```

Method to move the shape; takes in a direction: one of 'u', 'd', 'l', 'r'

If you're moving up, changes the y1 and y2 values by decreasing them by indexing into the list coords

Changes the coordinates of the rectangle, denoted by self.piece, to the new coordinates

Does something different for each of the four possible inputs ('u', 'd', 'l', 'r')

```
if direction == 'd':
    self.coords[1] += 10
    self.coords[3] += 10
    canvas.coords(self.piece, self.coords)
if direction == 'l':
    self.coords[0] -= 10
    self.coords[2] -= 10
    canvas.coords(self.piece, self.coords)
if direction == 'r':
    self.coords[0] += 10
    self.coords[2] += 10
    canvas.coords(self.piece, self.coords)
```

This code is used by any player object created. It follows the abstraction and modularity principles because it's under the Player class, which means you have to write it only once but it can be reused by any of the objects.

Now when you run the program, the set of keys W, A, S, D will move the yellow shape around the window, and the keys I, J, K, L will move the blue shape. You can even ask someone to play with you to test the code. You'll notice that if you hold a key down, the shape will move continuously, but as soon as you press another key, the shape will stop and move according to the other keypress (until another key is pressed). Chasing the shapes around is fun, but nothing happens when they touch.

 ## 38.4 Detecting a collision between shapes

The last piece to the game is to add the code logic for detecting whether two shapes collide. After all, this is a game of tag, and it'd be nice to be notified when one shape has touched the other one. The code logic will consist of making two method calls on the canvas. It'll be implemented inside the same event function that deals with keypresses in the canvas. This is because after every keypress, you'd like to see whether a collision has occurred.

Listing 38.5 shows the code for detecting the collision between two shapes. By design, in the tkinter library, every shape added to the canvas is assigned an ID. The first shape added gets an ID of 1, the second of 2, and so on. The first shape you added to the canvas was the yellow one. The idea behind the code is that you'll get the coordinates of the first shape in the canvas by calling the method bbox, which finds the bounding box around the shape. In the case of the rectangle, the bounding box is the rectangle itself, but in other cases, the bounding box is a rectangle that the shape barely fits in. Then, you call the find_overlapping method on the canvas, with the coordinates of the bounding box as a parameter. The method returns a tuple that tells you all IDs that are within that box. Because the coordinates given as a parameter are those of the bounding box for one shape, the method will give back a tuple of (1, 2) whenever the shapes are overlapping. All that's left to do is to check whether the shape with ID of 2 is in the returned tuple. If it is, then add text to the canvas.

Listing 38.5 Detecting a collision

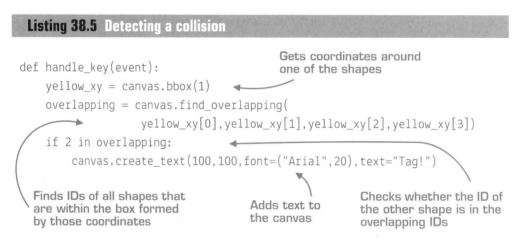

```
def handle_key(event):
    yellow_xy = canvas.bbox(1)
    overlapping = canvas.find_overlapping(
                  yellow_xy[0],yellow_xy[1],yellow_xy[2],yellow_xy[3])
    if 2 in overlapping:
        canvas.create_text(100,100,font=("Arial",20),text="Tag!")
```

Gets coordinates around one of the shapes

Finds IDs of all shapes that are within the box formed by those coordinates

Adds text to the canvas

Checks whether the ID of the other shape is in the overlapping IDs

As soon as one shape touches the other one, the screen will look something like figure 38.3.

38.5 Possible extensions

Many possibilities for extensions exist with this game. Your coding in this lesson is a great start. Here are some ideas:

- Instead of closing the window and restarting it to play again, add a button to ask the user to play again. When they do, choose another random position and size for your shapes.
- Allow the shape to escape. If the shapes aren't touching after having touched once, remove the text from the canvas.
- Allow the players to customize their shapes by changing the color or changing the shape to a circle.

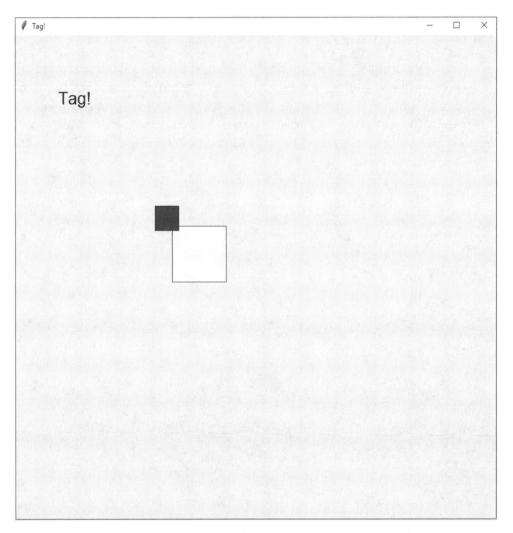

Figure 38.3   When one shape overlaps with the bounding box of the other shape, the text *Tag!* is printed on the canvas.

 **Summary**

In this lesson, my goal was to teach you how to use more advanced GUI elements to make a game. You used a canvas to add shapes to the GUI, and you added an event handler that moved shapes around depending on which key was pressed. You also saw how to detect collisions between shapes in a canvas. You saw how to write neat, organized, and easy-to-read code by using classes and functions for major parts of the code that you know will be reused.

ANSWERS TO LESSON EXERCISES

This appendix contains the answers to the exercises found in the lessons. The answers to the Quick checks are very straightforward, but the answers to some of the Summary exercises may be achieved in several different ways. I have provided a possible solution for each, but your answers may vary slightly from the ones that I have provided.

Lesson 2

Answers to quick checks

Quick check 2.1

Problem—Make mac-and-cheese.

Vague statement—Dump box of mac-and-cheese in boiling water for 12 minutes.

Specific statement—Pour 6 cups of water in a pot, turn up stovetop temp and wait for water to boil, pour in noodles, let them cook for 12 minutes, drain noodles, add packet of cheese, and stir.

Quick check 2.2

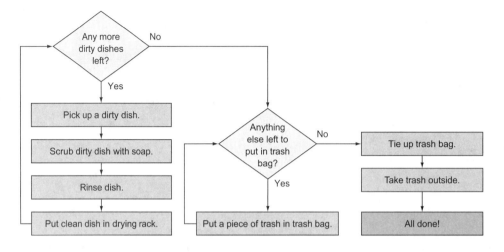

Quick check 2.3
1   Keep value of interest on the left: $c^2 = a^2 + b^2$
2   Take the square root: $c = \sqrt{(a^2 + b^2)}$

Quick check 2.4
```
# initialize times to fill pool (in fraction hours)
# convert times to minutes
# convert times to rates
# add rates
# solve for minutes when using both hoses
```

Lesson 3

Answers to quick checks

Quick check 3.1
1   Peek
2   Print
3   Peek
4   Print

Quick check 3.2
1   Will see -12
2   Will see 19
3   Won't see any output on the console

Lesson 4

Answers to quick checks

Quick check 4.1

1 Not allowed
2 Not allowed
3 Allowed
4 Allowed

Quick check 4.2

Phone attributes—Rectangular, glossy, black, lights up, 4 in x 2 in, has buttons. Operations—Click buttons, makes noise, throw it, make a call, type an email.

Dog attributes—Furry, four paws, one mouth, two eyes, one nose, two ears. Operations—Bark, scratch, run, jump, whine, lick.

Mirror attributes—Reflective, fragile, sharp. Operations—Breaks, shows reflection.

Credit card attributes—3 in x 2 in, thin, flexible, has numbers and letters. Operations—Swipe, use to open doors, use to buy stuff.

Quick check 4.3

1 Yes
2 No
3 No
4 No
5 Yes
6 Yes

Quick check 4.4

1 Yes
2 No
3 No (descriptive but not meaningful, unless you're writing a program about unicorns)
4 No (too long)

Quick check 4.5

1 `apples = 5`
2 `oranges = 10`
3 `fruits = apples + oranges`
4 `apples = 20`
5 `fruits = apples + oranges`

Answers to summary questions

Q4.1

```
x = b - a = 2 - 2 = 0
```

Q4.2

You still get an error. This is because the Python interpreter doesn't understand what to do with the last line. The interpreter is expecting a name to the left of the equal sign, but a + x isn't a name.

Lesson 5

Answers to quick checks

Quick check 5.1

```
1  six = 2 + 2 + 2
2  neg = six * (-6)
3  neg /= 10
```

Quick check 5.2

```
1  half = 0.25 * 2
2  other_half = 1.0 - half
```

Quick check 5.3

```
1  cold = True
2  rain = False
3  day = cold and rain
```

Quick check 5.4

```
1  one = "one" or one = 'one'
2  another_one = "1.0" or another_one = '1.0'
3  last_one = "one 1"or last_one = 'one 1'
```

Quick check 5.5

```
1  float
2  int
3  bool
4  string
5  string
6  int
7  int
8  string
9  NoneType
```

Quick check 5.6

```
1  Statement and expression
2  Statement and expression
3  Statement
4  Statement
```

Quick check 5.7

```
1  str(True)
   'True'
```

```
2  float(3)
   3.0
3  str(3.8)
   '3.8'
4  int(0.5)
   0
5  int("4")
   4
```

Quick check 5.8

```
1  float
   1.25
2  float
   9.0
3  int
   8
4  int
   201
5  float
   16.0
6  float
   1.0
7  float
   1.5
8  int
   2
9  int
   0
```

Lesson 6

Answers to quick checks

Quick check 6.1

1 7 hours and 36 minutes
2 0 hours and 0 minutes
3 166 hours and 39 minutes

Quick check 6.2

1 13
2 0
3 12
4 meters = 1000*km
5 print("miles")
6 print(miles)

```
 7   print("km")
 8   print(km)
 9   print("meters")
10   print(meters)
```

Quick check 6.3

```
1   stars = 50
2   stripes = 13
3   ratio = stars/stripes  ratio is a float
4   ratio_truncated = int(ratio)  ratio_truncated is an int
```

Quick check 6.4

```
minutes_to_convert = 789
hours_decimal = minutes_to_convert/60
hours_part = int(hours_decimal)
minutes_decimal = hours_decimal-hours_part
minutes_part = round(minutes_decimal*60)
print("Hours")
print(hours_part)
print("Minutes")
print(minutes_part)
```

Output:

```
Hours
13
Minutes
9
```

Answers to summary questions

Q6.1

```
fah = 75
cel = (fah-32)/1.8
print(cel)
```

Q6.2

```
miles = 5
km = miles/0.62137
meters = 1000*km
print("miles")
print(miles)
print("km")
print(km)
print("meters")
print(meters)
```

Lesson 7

Answers to quick checks

Quick check 7.1

1   Yes
2   Yes
3   No
4   No
5   Yes

Quick check 7.2

1   Forward: 5 Backward: -8
2   Forward: 0 Backward: -13
3   Forward: 12 Backward: -1

Quick check 7.3

1   'e'
2   ' '

  (the space character)

3   'L'

  'x'

Quick check 7.4

1   't'
2   'nhy tWp np'
3   ' '

  (empty string, because the start index is further in the string than the stop index, but the step is 1)

Quick check 7.5

1   'Python 4 ever&ever'
2   'PYTHON 4 EVER&ever'
3   'PYTHON 4 EVER&EVER'
4   'python 4 ever&ever'

Answers to summary questions

Q7.1

```
s = "Guten Morgen"
s[2:5].upper()
```

Q7.2

```
s = "RaceTrack"
s[1:4].captalize()
```

Lesson 8

Answers to quick checks

Quick check 8.1

1 14
2 9
3 -1
4 15
5 6
6 8

Quick check 8.2

1 True
2 True
3 False

Quick check 8.3

1 1
2 2
3 1
4 0

Quick check 8.4

1 'raining in the spring time.'
2 'Rain in the spr time.'
3 'Raining in the spring time.'
4 (No output) but b is now 'Raining in the spring tiempo.'

Quick check 8.5

1 'lalaLand'
2 'USA vs Canada'
3 'NYcNYcNYcNYcNYc'
4 'red-circlered-circlered-circle'

Answers to summary questions

Q8.1

There are many other ways of achieving this!

```
s = "Eat Work Play Sleep repeat"
s = s.replace(" ", "ing ")
s = s[7:22]
s = s.lower()
print(s)
```

Lesson 9

Answers to summary questions

Q9.1

1. You're trying to access an index in the string that's beyond the size of the string.
2. You're trying to call the command with an object when the command doesn't need anything in the parentheses.
3. You're trying to call the command with only one object when the command needs two in the parentheses.
4. You're trying to call the command with an object of the wrong type. You must give it a string object, not an integer object.
5. You're trying to call the command with a variable name and not a string object. This would work if you initialized h to be a string before you use it.
6. You're trying to multiply two strings when you're only allowed to add two strings or multiply a string by an integer.

Lesson 10

Answers to quick checks

Quick check 10.1

1. Yes
2. Yes
3. No
4. Yes

Quick check 10.2

1. 4
2. 2
3. 1
4. 0

Quick check 10.3

1. (1, 2, 3)
2. '3'
3. ((1,2), '3')
4. True

Quick check 10.4

1. ('no', 'no', 'no')
2. ('no', 'no', 'no', 'no', 'no', 'no')
3. (0, 0, 0, 1)

   4 (1, 1, 1, 1)

Quick check 10.5

   1 (s, w) = (w, s)

   2 (no, yes) = (yes, no)

Answers to summary questions

Q10.1

There are many ways you can do this. Here's one way:

```
word = "echo"
t = ()
count = 3

echo = (word,)
echo *= count
cho = (word[1:],)
cho *= count
ho = (word[2:],)
ho *= count
o = (word[3:],)
o *= count

t = echo + cho + ho + o
print(t)
```

Lesson 11

Answers to quick checks

Quick check 11.1

   1 12

   2 [Nothing printed]

   3 Nice is the new cool

Quick check 11.2

   1 sweet = "cookies"

   2 savory = "pickles"

   3 num = 100

   4 print(num, savory, "and", num, sweet)

   5 print("I choose the " + sweet.upper() + "!")

Quick check 11.3

   1 input("Tell me a secret: ")

   2 input("What's your favorite color? ")

   3 input("Enter one of: # or $ or % or & or *: ")

Quick check 11.4

```
1  song = input("Tell me your favorite song: ")
   print(song)
   print(song)
   print(song)
2  celeb = input("Tell me the first & last name of a celebrity: ")
   space = celeb.find(" ")
   print(celeb[0:space])
   print(celeb[space+1:len(celeb)])
```

Quick check 11.5

```
user_input = input("Enter a number to find the square of: ")
num = float(user_input)
print(num*num)
```

Answers to summary questions

Q11.1

```
b = int(input("Enter a number: "))
e = int(input("Enter a number: "))
b_e = b**e
print("b to the power of e is", b_e)
```

Q11.2

```
name = input("What's your name? ")
age = int(input("How old are you? "))
older = age+25
print("Hi " + name + "! In 25 years you will be " + str(older) + "!")
```

Lesson 13

Answers to quick checks

Quick check 13.1

1 No
2 Yes
3 No
4 No
5 No

Quick check 13.2

1 You live in a treehouse.
2 [Can't be converted.]
3 [Can't be converted.]
4 The word youniverse is in the dictionary.

   5 The number 7 is even.

   6 Variables a and b are equal

Quick check 13.3

   1 `num is less than 10`
       `Finished`
   2 `Finished`
   3 `Finished`

Quick check 13.4

   1
```
word = input("Tell me a word: ")
print(word)
if " " in word:
    print("You did not follow directions!")
```
   2
```
num1 = int(input("One number: "))
num2 = int(input("Another number: "))
print(num1+num2)
if num1+num2 < 0:
    print("Wow, negative sum!")
```

Quick check 13.5

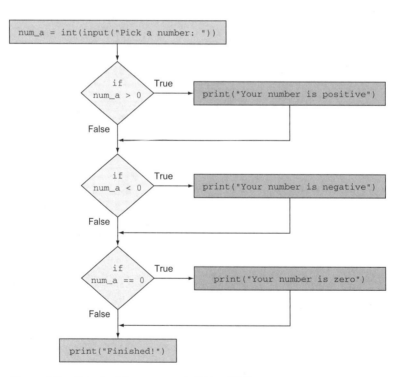

Figure A.1 Flowchart for program in listing 13.3

Quick check 13.6

num_a	num_b	Answer (nested)	Answer (unnested)
-9	5	num_a: is negative Finished	num_a: is negative Finished
9	5	Finished	Finished
-9	-5	num_a: is negative num_b is negative Finished	num_a: is negative num_b is negative Finished
9	-5	Finished	num_b is negative Finished

Quick check 13.7

One possible solution shown in listing 13.5.

Answers to summary questions

Q13.1

If *x* is an odd number then *X* + 1 is an even number.

Q13.2

```
var = 0
if type(var) == int:
    print("I'm a numbers person.")
if type(var) == str:
    print("I'm a words person.")
```

Q13.3

```
words = input("Tell me anything: ")
if " " in words:
    print("This string has spaces.")
```

Q13.4

```
print("Guess my number! ")
secret = 7
num = int(input("What's your guess? "))
if num < secret:
    print("Too low.")
if num > secret:
    print("Too high.")
if num == secret:
    print("You got it!")
```

Q13.5

```
num = int(input("Tell me a number: "))
if num >= 0:
    print("Absolute value:", num)
if num < 0:
    print("Absolute value:", -num)
```

Lesson 14

Answers to quick checks

Quick check 14.1

1   Do you need milk and have a car? If yes, drive to the store to buy milk.
2   Is variable a zero and variable b zero and variable c zero? If yes, then all variables are zero.
3   Do you have a jacket or a sweater? Take one of these; it's cold outside.

Quick check 14.2

1   True
2   True
3   False

Quick check 14.3

num_a	num_b
0	0
0	-5
-20	0
-1	-1
-20	-988

Quick check 14.4

num is -3	Output: num is negative
num is 0	Output: num is zero
num is 2	Output: num is positive
num is 1	Output: num is positive

Quick check 14.5

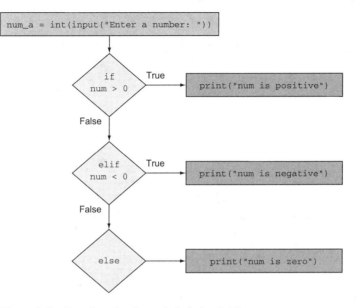

```
num_a = int(input("Enter a number: "))
```

```
if
num > 0
```
True → `print("num is positive")`

False

```
elif
num < 0
```
True → `print("num is negative")`

False

```
else
```
→ `print("num is zero")`

Figure A.2 Flowchart for the code in listing 14.3

Quick check 14.6

num	With if-elif-else	With if
20	num is greater than 3 Finished.	num is greater than 3 Finished.
9	num is less than 10 Finished.	num is less than 10 num is greater than 3 Finished.
5	num is less than 6 Finished.	num is less than 6 num is less than 10 num is greater than 3 Finished.
0	num is less than 6 Finished.	num is less than 6 num is less than 10 Finished.

Answers to summary questions

Q14.1

```
num1 = int(input("One number: "))
num2 = int(input("Another number: "))
if num1 < num2:
    print("first number is less than the second number")
elif num2 < num1:
    print("first number is greater than the second number")
else:
    print("numbers are equal")
```

Q14.2

```
words = input("Enter anything: ")
if "a" in words and "e" in words and "i" in words and "o" in words and "u" in words:
    print("You have all the vowels!")
if words[0] == 'a' and words[-1] == 'z':
    print("And it's sort of alphabetical!")
```

Lesson 16

Answers to quick checks

Quick check 16.1

```
1  for i in range(8):
       print("crazy")
2  for i in range(100):
       print("centipede")
```

Quick check 16.2

```
1  0, 1
2  0, 1, 2, 3, 4
3  0, 1, 2, 3, 4, 5, 6, ..., 99
```

Answers to summary questions

Q16.1

```
num = int(input("Tell me a number: "))
for i in range(num):
    print("Hello")
```

It's not possible to write without a for loop because you don't know the number the user will give you.

Lesson 17

Answers to quick checks

Quick check 17.1

  1   0, 1, 2, 3, 4, 5, 6, 7, 8

  2   3, 4, 5, 6, 7

  3   -2, 0, 2

  4   5, 2, -1, -4

  5   [Nothing]

Quick check 17.2

```python
vowels = "aeiou"
words = input("Tell me something: ")
for letter in words:
    if letter in vowels:
        print("vowel")
```

Answers to summary questions

Q17.1

```python
counter = 0
for num in range(2, 100, 2):
    if num%6 == 0:
        counter += 1
print(counter, "numbers are even and divisible by 6")
```

Q17.2

```python
count = int(input("How many books on Python do you have? "))
for n in range(count,0,-1):
    if n == 1:
        print(n, "book on Python on the shelf", n, "book on Python")
        print("Take one down, pass it around, no more books!")
    else:
        print(n, "books on Python on the shelf", n, "books on Python")
        print("Take one down, pass it around,", n-1, " books left.")
```

Q17.3

```python
names = input("Tell me some names, separated by spaces: ")
name= ""
for ch in names:
    if ch == " ":
        print("Hi", name)
        name = ""
```

```
    else:
        name += ch
# deal with the last name given (does not have a space after it)
lastspace = names.rfind(" ")
print("Hi", names[lastspace+1:])
```

Lesson 18

Answers to quick checks

Quick check 18.1

```
password = "robot fort flower graph"
space_count = 0
for ch in password:
    if ch == " ":
        space_count += 1
print(space_count)
```

As a side note, the preceding code can also be written using a command on strings, count, with password.count(" ").

Quick check 18.2

```
secret = "snake"
word = input("What's my secret word? ")
guesses = 1
while word != secret:
    word = input("What's my secret word? ")
    if guesses == 20 and word != secret:
        print("You did not get it.")
        break
    guesses += 1
```

Answers to summary questions

Q18.1

```
# corrected code
num = 8
guess = int(input("Guess my number: "))
while guess != num:
    guess = int(input("Guess again: "))
print("Right!")
```

Q18.2

```
play = input("Play? y or yes: ")
while play == 'y' or play == "yes":
```

```
    num = 8
    guess = int(input("Guess a number! "))
    while guess != num:
        guess = int(input("Guess again: "))
    print("Right!")
    play = input("Play? y or yes: ")
print("See you later!")
```

Lesson 20

Answers to quick checks

Quick check 20.1

1 Independent
2 Dependent
3 Independent

Quick check 20.2

1 In: Pen, paper, name, address, envelope, stamp, wedding date, fiancée
  Out: Wedding invitation ready to be mailed
2 In: Phone number, phone
  Out: No output
3 In: Coin
  Out: Heads or tails
4 In: Money
  Out: A dress

Quick check 20.3

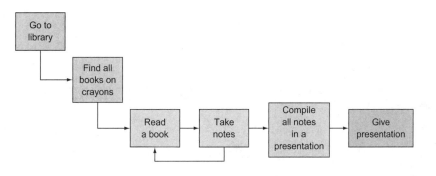

Quick check 20.4

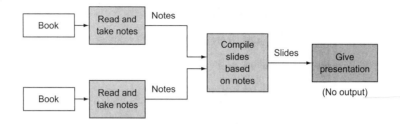

Answers to summary questions

Q20.1

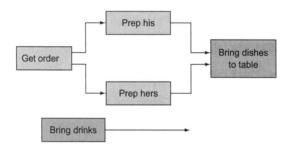

Lesson 21

Answers to quick checks

Quick check 21.1

```
1  def set_color(name, color):
2  def get_inverse(num):
3  def print_my_name():
```

Quick check 21.2

```
1  3
2  0
3  4
```

Quick check 21.3

1 Yes (when 2 and 3 are variables types that can be added together)
2 Yes
3 No (indentation error)

Quick check 21.4

These are only a few possibilities; many others exist:

1 `get_age` or `get_tree_age`
2 `translate` or `dog_says`
3 `cloud_to_animal` or `take_picture`
4 `age` or `get_age` or `years_later`

Quick check 21.5

1 Length of variable sign (return type is an integer)
2 True (return type is a Boolean)
3 `"and toes"` (return type is a string)

Quick check 21.6

1 `return (money_won, guessed)`
2

- `(100, True)`
- `(1.0, False)`
- Doesn't print anything
- Doesn't print anything

  `False`

  `8.0`

Quick check 21.7

1 Nothing is printed
2 `Hector is eating`
3 `Hector is eating 8 bananas`
4 `Hector is bananas is eating 8 bananas`
5 `None`

Answers to summary questions

Q21.1

1
```
def calculate_total(price, percent):
    tip = price*percent/100
    total = price + tip
    return total
```
2 `calculate_total(20, 15)`
3
```
my_price = 78.55
my_tip = 20
total = calculate_total(my_price, my_tip)
print("Total is:", total)
```

Lesson 22

Answers to quick checks

Quick check 22.1

    1 -11
       -11.0
    2 -3
       -3.0
    3 24
       1.5
    4 32
       2.0

Quick check 22.2

    1 42
    2 6
    3 12
    4 21

Quick check 22.3

```
--------------------------------------------------
def sandwich(kind_of_sandwich):
    print("--------")
    print(kind_of_sandwich ())
    print("--------")
def blt():
    my_blt = " bacon\nlettuce\n tomato"
    return my_blt
def breakfast():
    my_ec = " eggegg\n cheese"
    return my_ec

print(sandwich(blt))                    <-------- here
                                        GLOBAL SCOPE
                                            sandwich:    (some code)
                                            blt:         (some code)
                                            breakfast:   (some code

--------------------------------------------------
def sandwich(kind_of_sandwich):         <-------- here
    print("--------")
    print(kind_of_sandwich ())
    print("--------")
def blt():
```

```
      my_blt = " bacon\nlettuce\n tomato"
      return my_blt
def breakfast():
      my_ec = " eggegg\n cheese"
      return my_ec

print(sandwich(blt))
```

```
                                    GLOBAL SCOPE
                                        sandwich:      (some code)
                                        blt:           (some code)
                                        breakfast:     (some code

                                    SCOPE OF sandwich(blt)
                                    kind_of_sandwich: blt
```

```
def sandwich(kind_of_sandwich):
    print("--------")
    print(kind_of_sandwich ())              <-------- here
    print("--------")
def blt():
      my_blt = " bacon\nlettuce\n tomato"
      return my_blt
def breakfast():
      my_ec = " eggegg\n cheese"
      return my_ec

print(sandwich(blt))
```

```
                                    GLOBAL SCOPE
                                    sandwich:      (some code)
                                    blt:           (some code)
                                    breakfast:     (some code

                                    SCOPE OF sandwich(blt)
                                    kind_of_sandwich: blt
```

```
def sandwich(kind_of_sandwich):
    print("--------")
    print(kind_of_sandwich ())
    print("--------")
def blt():                                  <-------- here
      my_blt = " bacon\nlettuce\n tomato"
      return my_blt
def breakfast():
    my_ec = " eggegg\n cheese"
    return my_ec
```

```
print(sandwich(blt))
```

```
GLOBAL SCOPE
sandwich:      (some code)
blt:           (some code)
breakfast:     (some code

SCOPE OF sandwich(blt)
   kind_of_sandwich: blt

   SCOPE OF blt()
```

```
def sandwich(kind_of_sandwich):
   print("--------")
   print(kind_of_sandwich ())
   print("--------")
def blt():
   my_blt = " bacon\nlettuce\n tomato"
   return my_blt                                 <-------- here
def breakfast():
   my_ec = " eggegg\n cheese"
   return my_ec

print(sandwich(blt))
```

```
GLOBAL SCOPE
sandwich:      (some code)
blt:           (some code)
breakfast:     (some code

SCOPE OF sandwich(blt)
kind_of_sandwich: blt
```

```
SCOPE OF blt()
Returns:  bacon
          lettuce
          tomato
```

```
def sandwich(kind_of_sandwich):
   print("--------")
   print(kind_of_sandwich ())
   print("--------")                             <-------- here
def blt():
   my_blt = " bacon\nlettuce\n tomato"
   return my_blt
def breakfast():
   my_ec = " eggegg\n cheese"
```

```
        return my_ec
print(sandwich(blt))
```

```
GLOBAL SCOPE
sandwich:     (some code)
   blt:             (some code)
breakfast:    (some code

SCOPE OF sandwich(blt)
kind_of_sandwich: blt
returns: None
```

Quick check 22.4

```
def grumpy():
    print("I am a grumpy cat:")
    def no_n_times(n):
        print("No", n,"times...")
        def no_m_more_times(m):
            print("...and no", m,"more times")
            for i in range(n+m):
                print("no")
        return no_m_more_times
    return no_n_times

grumpy()(4)(2)
```

```
<---------- here
GLOBAL SCOPE
grumpy:    (some code)
```

```
def grumpy():                              <---------- here
    print("I am a grumpy cat:")
    def no_n_times(n):
        print("No", n,"times...")
        def no_m_more_times(m):
            print("...and no", m,"more times")
            for i in range(n+m):
                print("no")
        return no_m_more_times
    return no_n_times

grumpy()(4)(2)
```

```
GLOBAL SCOPE
grumpy:     (some code)

SCOPE OF grumpy()
```

```
def grumpy():
```

```
    print("I am a grumpy cat:")
    def no_n_times(n):
        print("No", n,"times...")
        def no_m_more_times(m):
            print("...and no", m,"more times")
            for i in range(n+m):
                print("no")
        return no_m_more_times
    return no_n_times                        <---------- here
grumpy()(4)(2)
```

```
                                        GLOBAL SCOPE
                                        grumpy:    (some code)

                                        SCOPE OF grumpy()
                                        no_n_times():  (some code)
                                        Returns: no_n_times
```

```
def grumpy():
    print("I am a grumpy cat:")
    def no_n_times(n):
        print("No", n,"times...")
        def no_m_more_times(m):
            print("...and no", m,"more times")
            for i in range(n+m):
                print("no")
        return no_m_more_times
    return no_n_times

grumpy()(4)(2)                                 <---------- here
                            this line is now no_n_times(4)(2)

                                        GLOBAL SCOPE
                                        grumpy:      (some code)
```

```
def grumpy():
    print("I am a grumpy cat:")
    def no_n_times(n):                         <---------- here
        print("No", n,"times...")
        def no_m_more_times(m):
            print("...and no", m,"more times")
            for i in range(n+m):
                print("no")
        return no_m_more_times
    return no_n_times
```

```
grumpy()(4)(2)
```
                                        GLOBAL SCOPE
                                        grumpy: (some code)

                                        SCOPE OF no_n_times(4)
                                        n:
                                        no_m_more_times: (some code)

```
def grumpy():
    print("I am a grumpy cat:")
    def no_n_times(n):
        print("No", n,"times...")
        def no_m_more_times(m):
            print("...and no", m,"more times")
            for i in range(n+m):
                print("no")
        return no_m_more_times                 <---------- here
    return no_n_times
```

```
grumpy()(4)(2)
```
                                        GLOBAL SCOPE
                                        grumpy: (some code)

                                        SCOPE OF no_n_times(4)
                                        n: 4
                                        no_m_more_times: (some code)
                                        Returns: no_m_more_times

----
```
def grumpy():
    print("I am a grumpy cat:")
    def no_n_times(n):
        print("No", n,"times...")
        def no_m_more_times(m):
            print("...and no", m,"more times")
            for i in range(n+m):
                print("no")
        return no_m_more_times
    return no_n_times
```
```
grumpy()(4)(2)
```                                        <---------- here
                                    this line is now no_m_more_times(2)

                                        GLOBAL SCOPE

```
                                        grumpy:     (some code)
----------------------------------------------------------------
def grumpy():
    print("I am a grumpy cat:")
    def no_n_times(n):
        print("No", n,"times...")
        def no_m_more_times(m):                 <---------- here
            print("...and no", m,"more times")
            for i in range(n+m):
                print("no")
        return no_m_more_times
    return no_n_times

grumpy()(4)(2)
                            GLOBAL SCOPE
                            grumpy:     (some code)

                            SCOPE OF no_m_more_times(2)
                            m:     2
----------------------------------------------------------------
def grumpy():
    print("I am a grumpy cat:")
    def no_n_times(n):
        print("No", n,"times...")
        def no_m_more_times(m):
            print("...and no", m,"more times")
            for i in range(n+m):
                print("no")                     <---------- here
        return no_m_more_times
    return no_n_times

grumpy()(4)(2)
GLOBAL SCOPE
                                grumpy:     (some code)

                                SCOPE OF no_m_more_times(2)
                                m:     2
                                Returns: None
----------------------------------------------------------------
def grumpy():
    print("I am a grumpy cat:")
    def no_n_times(n):
        print("No", n,"times...")
        def no_m_more_times(m):
```

```
            print("...and no", m,"more times")
            for i in range(n+m):
                print("no")
        return no_m_more_times
    return no_n_times

grumpy()(4)(2)                                    <---------- here
and done with this line
GLOBAL SCOPE

                                        grumpy:    (some code)
```

Answers to summary questions

Q22.1

```
def area(shape, n):
    # write a line to return the area
    # of a generic shape with a parameter of n
    return shape(n)
  1  area(circle, 10)
  2  area(square, 5)
  3  area(circle, 4/2)
```

Q22.2

```
def person(age):
    print("I am a person")
    def student(major):
        print("I like learning")
        def vacation(place):
            print("But I need to take breaks")
            print(age,"|",major,"|",place)
        return vacation
    return student
  1  person(29)("CS")("Japan")
  2  person(23)("Law")("Florida")
```

Lesson 24

Answers to quick checks

Quick check 24.1

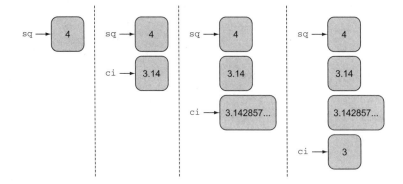

Figure A.3   Visualization of the sequence of statements

Quick check 24.2

1   Either immutable object (tuple, because the names of cities won't change) or mutable (list, because you may add/remove cities as needed)
2   Immutable object, an int (a mutable object would be overkill because age is only one item, so the overhead of changing it isn't worth making it mutable)
3   Mutable object, a dictionary to store an item and its cost
4   Immutable object, a string

Answers to summary questions

Q24.1

one is an immutable object.

age is a mutable object.

Lesson 25

Answers to quick checks

Quick check 25.1

1 Tuple
2 Tuple
3 Tuple
4 List
5 List

Quick check 25.2

1 tape
2 mouse
3 Error, index out of bounds
4 stapler

Quick check 25.3

```
1
4
0
8
2
error
```

Quick check 25.4

1 `[1, '1']`
2 `[0, ['zero']]` (Notice the second element is another list.)
3 `[]`
4 `[1,2,3,4,5]`
  `[0,1,2,3,4,5]`

Quick check 25.5

```
[3,1,4,1,5,9]
[3,1,4,1,5]
[3,1,4,1]
```

Quick check 25.6

1 `[1, 2, 3, 4, 7, 11, 13, 17]`
2 `[1, 2, 3, 4, 6, 11, 13, 17]`
3 `[1, 2, 3, 4, 6, 11, 13, 1]`
4 `[3, 2, 3, 4, 6, 11, 13, 1]`

Answers to summary questions

Q25.1

```
1  menu = []
   menu.append("pizza")
   menu.append("beer")
   menu.append("fries")
   menu.append("wings")
   menu.append("salad")
2  menu[0] = menu[-1]
   menu[-1] = ""
   menu.pop(1)
   menu[-1] = "pizza"
3  menu.pop()
   menu.pop()
   menu.pop()
   menu.append("quinoa")
   menu.append("steak")
```

Q25.2

```
def unique(L):
    L_unique = []
    for n in L:
        if n not in L_unique:
            L_unique.append(n)
    return L_unique
```

Q25.3

```
def unique(L):
    L_unique = []
    for n in L:
        if n not in L_unique:
            L_unique.append(n)
    return L_unique

def common(L1, L2):
    unique_L1 = unique(L1)
    unique_L2 = unique(L2)
    length_L1 = len(unique_L1)
    length_L2 = len(unique_L2)
    if length_L1 != length_L2:
        return False
    else:
        for i in range(length_L1):
            if L1[i] not in L2:
```

```
        return False
    return True
```

Lesson 26

Answers to quick checks

Quick check 26.1

```
['g', 'n', 'i', 'm', 'm', 'a', 'r', 'g', 'o', 'r', 'p']
['a', 'g', 'g', 'i', 'm', 'm', 'n', 'o', 'p', 'r', 'r']
['r', 'r', 'p', 'o', 'n', 'm', 'm', 'i', 'g', 'g', 'a']
['a', 'g', 'g', 'i', 'm', 'm', 'n', 'o', 'p', 'r', 'r']
['a', 'g', 'g', 'i', 'm', 'm', 'n', 'o', 'p', 'r', 'r']
```

Quick check 26.2

1 board = [[empty, empty, empty], [x, x, x], [o, o, o]]
2 board = [[x, o, x, o], [o, o, x, x], [o, empty, x, x]]

Quick check 26.3

1 " abcdefghijklmnopqrstuvwxyz".split(" ")
2 "spaces and more spaces".split(" ")
3 "the secret of life is 42".split("s")

Quick check 26.4

1 Stack
2 Stack
3 Queue
4 Neither (because the first luggage out may never get picked up)

Answers to summary questions

Q26.1

```
cities = "san francisco,boston,chicago,indianapolis"
city_list = cities.split(",")
city_list.sort()
print(city_list)
```

Q26.2

```
def is_permutation(L1, L2):
    L1.sort()
    L2.sort()
    return L1 == L2
```

Lesson 27

Answers to quick checks

Quick check 27.1

1 `employee_database = {}`
   Key: string for the name
   Value: tuple of (phone number as a string, home address as a string)
2 `snow_accumulation = {}`
   Key: string for the city
   Value: tuple (int year 1990, float for snow in 1990, int year 2000, float for snow in 2000)
3 `valuables = {"tv": 2000, "sofa": 1500}`
   Key: string for the item name
   Value: int for the value

Quick check 27.2

1 Three entries. Maps integers to integers.
2 Three entries. Maps strings to integers.
3 Three entries. Maps integers to lists.

Quick check 27.3

```
{}
{'LA': 3884}
{'NYC': 8406, 'LA': 3884}
{'NYC': 8406, 'LA': 3884, 'SF': 837}
{'NYC': 8406, 'LA': 4031, 'SF': 837}
```

Quick check 27.4

```
3.14
1.41
(there will be an error)
```

Quick check 27.5

(Order doesn't matter, as you'll see in the next section.)

```
25
51
35
```

Answers to summary questions

Q27.1

```
songs = {"Wannabe": 3, "Roar": 4, "Let It Be": 5, "Red Corvette": 5, "Something": 1}

for s in songs.keys():
```

```
    if songs[s] == 5:
        print(s)
```

Q27.2
```
def replace(d, v, e):
    for k in d:
        if d[k] == v:
            d[k] = e
```

Q27.3
```
def invert(d):
    d_inv = {}
    for k in d:
        v = d[k]
        if v not in d_inv:
            d_inv[v] = [k]
        else:
            d_inv[v].append(k)
    return d_inv
```

Lesson 28

Answers to quick checks

Quick check 28.1

1 Same ID
2 Same ID
3 Same ID (Technically, this should be a different ID because immutable objects don't have aliases. But Python is optimizing behind the scenes by referencing the object that already exists with the same value instead of creating another one. These optimizations aren't guaranteed to happen all the time.)

Quick check 28.2

1 Same ID
2 Same ID
3 Different ID (You're creating another object that happens to have the same elements, not an alias.)

Quick check 28.3

1 Yes
2 Yes
3 Yes
4 Yes
5 No

Quick check 28.4

1 `order = sorted(chaos)`
2 `colors.sort()`
3 `cards = deck`
4 `deck.sort()`

Answers to summary questions

Q28.1

```
def invert_dict(d):
    new_d = {}
    for k in d.keys():
        new_d[d[k]] = k
    return new_d
```

Q28.2

```
def invert_dict_inplace(d):
    new_d = d.copy()
    d = {}
    for k in new_d.keys():
        d[d_new[k]] = k
```

Lesson 30

Answers to quick checks

Quick check 30.1

1 Yes, with an integer
2 Yes, with a tuple (or a list)
3 No (would need to decide which properties and behaviors to define a person—for example, a name, an age, height, weight, can they walk, talk?)
4 No (would need to decide which properties and behaviors to define a chair—for example, number of legs, height, depth, what can you do with a chair?)

Quick check 30.2

1 A width and a height
2 A width, a height, a depth, number of ports, number of pixels, and so forth
3 Number of legs, seat back or not, cushioned or not
4 Name, age, height, weight, hair color, eye color, and so forth

Quick check 30.3

1 Find the area or the perimeter
2 Turn it on/off, get its diagonal, connect a cable to a port
3 Have a person sit on a chair, cut off a leg, add a cushion

4   Change name, increment the age, change hair color

Quick check 30.4

1   String
2   List
3   Dictionary
4   String

Lesson 31

Answers to quick checks

Quick check 31.1

1   `class Person(object):`
2   `class Car(object):`
3   `class Computer(object):`

Quick check 31.2

```
class Person(object):
    def __init__(self):
        self.name = ""
        self.age = 0


class Car(object):
    def __init__(self):
        self.length = 0
        self.width = 0
        self.height = 0


class Computer(object):
    def __init__(self):
        self.on = False
        self.touchscreen = False
```

Quick check 31.3

```
class Door(object):
    def __init__(self):
        self.width = 1
        self.height = 1
        self.open = False
    def get_status(self):
        return self.open
    def get_area(self):
```

```
        return self.width*self.height
```

Quick check 31.4
```
square_door = Door()
square_door.change_state()
square_door.scale(3)
```

Quick check 31.5
```
a = Rectangle(1,1)
b = Rectangle(1,1)
Rectangle.set_length(a, 4)
Rectangle.set_width(b, 4)
```

Answers to summary questions

Q31.1
```
def get_area(self):
    """ returns area of a circle """
    return 3.14*self.radius**2

# testing method
a = Circle()
print(a.get_area()) # shoould be 0
a.change_radius(3)
print(a.get_area()) # should be 28.26
```

Q31.2
```
def get_area(self):
    """ returns area of a rectangle """
    return self.length*self.width

def get_perimeter(self):
    """ returns perimeter of a rectangle """
    return self.length*2 + self.width*2
```

Lesson 32

Answers to quick checks

Quick check 32.1
```
def add_list(self, L):
    for e in L:
        self.stack.append(e)
```

Quick check 32.2

```
circles  = Stack()
for i in range(3):
    one_circle = Circle()
    one_circle.change_radius(3)
    circles.add_one(one_circle)
rectangles  = Stack()
one_rectangle = Rectangle(1, 1)
rectangles.add_many(one_rectangle, 5)
```

Answers to summary questions

Q32.1

```
class Queue(object):
    def __init__(self):
        self.queue = []
    def get_queue_elements(self):
        return self.queue.copy()
    def add_one(self, item):
        self.queue.append(item)
    def add_many(self, item, n):
        for i in range(n):
            self.queue.append(item)
    def remove_one(self):
        self.queue.pop(0)
    def remove_many(self, n):
        for i in range(n):
            self.queue.pop(0)
    def size(self):
        return len(self.queue)
    def prettyprint(self):
        for thing in self.queue[::-1]:
            print('|_',thing, '_|')

# testing the class by making objects and doing operations
a = Queue()
a.add_one(3)
a.add_one(1)
a.prettyprint()
a.add_many(6,2)
a.prettyprint()
a.remove_one()
a.prettyprint()
b = Queue()
b.prettyprint()
```

Lesson 33

Answers to quick checks

Quick check 33.1

```python
def __sub__(self, other_fraction):
    new_top = self.top*other_fraction.bottom - \
            self.bottom*other_fraction.top
    new_bottom = self.bottom*other_fraction.bottom
    return Fraction(new_top, new_bottom)
```

Quick check 33.2

```python
def __str__(self):
        toreturn = str(self.top) + "\n--\n" + str(self.bottom)
        return toreturn
```

Quick check 33.3

1 `quarter.__mul__(half)`
   `Fraction.__mul__(quarter, half)`
2 `quarter.__str__()`
   `Fraction.__str__(quarter)`
3 `(half.__mul__(half)).__str__()`
   `Fraction.__str__(Fraction.__mul__(half, half))`

Answers to summary questions

Q33.1

```python
class Circle(object):
    def __init__(self):
        self.radius = 0
    def change_radius(self, radius):
        self.radius = radius
    def get_radius(self):
        return self.radius
    def __str__(self):
        return "circle: "+str(self.radius)

class Stack(object):
    def __init__( self):
        self.stack = []
    def get_stack_elements(self):
        return self.stack.copy()
    def add_one(self , item):
        self.stack.append(item)
    def add_many(self , item, n):
```

```
        for i in range(n):
            self.stack.append(item)
    def remove_one(self):
        self.stack.pop()
    def remove_many(self , n):
        for i in range(n):
            self.stack.pop()
    def size(self):
        return len(self.stack)
    def prettyprint(self):
        for thing in self.stack[::-1]:
            print('|_',thing, '_|')
    def __str__(self):
        ret = ""
        for thing in self.stack[::-1]:
            ret += ('|_ '+str(thing)+ ' _|\n')
        return ret
```

Lesson 35

Answers to quick checks

Quick check 35.1
```
import fruits
import activities
```

Quick check 35.2
```
import math

distance = float(input("How far away is your friend? (m) "))
speed = float(input("How fast can you throw? (m/s) "))

tolerance = 2

# 0 degrees means throw horizontal and 90 degrees means straight up
for i in range(0,91):
    angle_r = math.radians(i)
    reach = 2*speed**2*math.sin(angle_r)*math.cos(angle_r)/9.8
    if reach > distance - tolerance and reach < distance + tolerance:
        print("angle: ", i, "Nice throw!")
    elif reach < distance - tolerance:
        print("angle: ", i, "You didn't throw far enough.")
    else:
        print("angle: ", i, "You threw too far.")
```

Quick check 35.3

```
import random

heads = 0
tails = 0
for i in range(100):
    r = random.random()
    if r < 0.5:
        heads += 1
    else:
        tails += 1
print("Heads:", heads)
print("Tails:", tails)
```

Quick check 35.4

```
import time
import random

count = 0
start = time.clock()
for i in range(10000000):
    count += 1
    random.random()

end = time.clock()
print(end-start)       # prints about 4.5 seconds
```

Answers to summary questions

Q35.1

```
import time
import random

def roll_dice():
    r = str(random.randint(1,6))
    # put bars around the number so it looks like a dice
    dice = " _ \n|" + r + "|"
    print(dice)
    return r

start = time.clock()

p = "roll"
while p == "roll":
    print("You rolled a dice...")
    userroll = roll_dice()
    print("Computer rolling...")
```

```
    comproll = roll_dice()
    time.sleep(2)
    if userroll >= comproll:
        print("You win!")
    else:
        print("You lose.")
    p = input("Type roll to roll again, any other key to quit: ")
end = time.clock()
print("You played for", end-start, "seconds.")
```

Lesson 36

Answers to quick checks

Quick check 36.1
```
class TestMyCode(unittest.TestCase):
    def test_addition_5_5(self):
        self.assertEqual(5+5, 10)
    def test_remainder_6_2(self):
        self.assertEqual(6%2, 0)
```

Quick check 36.2
```
def is_prime(n):
    prime = True
    for i in range(2,n):
        if n%i == 0:
            prime = False
    return prime

def absolute_value(n):
    if n < 0:
        return -n
    elif n >= 0:
        return n
```

Quick check 36.3
1 assertFalse(x, msg=None)
2 assertIn(a, b, msg=None)
3 assertDictEqual(a, b, msg=None)

Quick check 36.4
1 Breakpoint at line isprime = funcs.is_prime(5)
2 Click blue arrow with two vertical lines, click button with two arrows
3 Step into function and notice that loop starts at 1, not 2

Answers to summary questions

Q36.1

```
import unittest

def remove_buggy(L, e):
    """

    L, list
    e, any object
    Removes all e from L.
    """

    for i in L:
        if e == i:
            L.remove(i)

def remove_fixed(L, e):
    """

    L, list
    e, any object
    Removes all e from L.
    """

    for i in L.copy():
        if e == i:
            L.remove(i)

class Tests(unittest.TestCase):
    def test_123_1(self):
        L = [1,2,3]
        e = 1
        remove_buggy(L,e)
        self.assertEqual(L, [2,3])
    def test_1123_1(self):
        L = [1,1,2,3]
        e = 1
        remove_buggy(L,e)
        self.assertEqual(L, [2,3])

unittest.main()
```

Lesson 37

Answers to quick checks

Quick check 37.1

1 A button: click it
2 A scrollbar: hold mouse button and drag
3 A menu: hover over an item and click it
4 A canvas: draw lines, circles, rectangles, erase

Quick check 37.2

1
```
import tkinter
window = tkinter.Tk()
window.geometry("500x200")
window.title("go go go")
window.configure(background="green")
window.mainloop()
```

2
```
import tkinter
window = tkinter.Tk()
window.geometry("100x900")
window.title("Tall One")
window.configure(background="red")
window.mainloop()
```

3
```
import tkinter
window1 = tkinter.Tk()
window1.geometry("100x100")
window1.configure(background="white")
window2 = tkinter.Tk()
window2.geometry("100x100")
window2.configure(background="black")
window1.mainloop()
window2.mainloop()
```

Quick check 37.3

```
btn = tkinter.Button(window, text="Click here", bg="orange")
radio_btn1 = tkinter.Radiobutton()
radio_btn2 = tkinter.Radiobutton()
check_btn = tkinter.Checkbutton()
```

Quick check 37.4

```
import tkinter
import random

def changecolor():
    r = random.choice(["red", "green", "blue"])
    window.configure(background=r)
```

```
window = tkinter.Tk()
window.geometry("800x600")
window.title("My first GUI")

btn = tkinter.Button(window, text="Random color!", command=changecolor)
btn.pack()

window.mainloop()
```

Answer to summary questions

Q37.1

```
import tkinter

window = tkinter.Tk()
window.geometry("200x800")
window.title("PhoneBook")

phonebook = {}

def add():
    name = txt_name.get()
    phone = txt_phone.get()
    email = txt_email.get()
    phonebook[name] = [phone, email]
    lbl.configure(text = "Contact added!")

def show():
    s = ""
    for name, details in phonebook.items():
        s += name+"\n"+details[0]+"\n"+details[1]+"\n\n"
    lbl.configure(text=s)

txt_name = tkinter.Entry()
txt_phone = tkinter.Entry()
txt_email = tkinter.Entry()

btn_add = tkinter.Button(text="Add contact", command=add)
btn_show = tkinter.Button(text="Show all", command=show)

lbl = tkinter.Label()

txt_name.pack()
txt_phone.pack()
txt_email.pack()
btn_add.pack()
btn_show.pack()
lbl.pack()
window.mainloop()
```

PYTHON CHEAT SHEET

Variable names

- Case-sensitive
- Can't start with a number
- Can't be a Python keyword
- OK—name, my_name, my_1st_name, name2
- Not OK—13_numbers, print

Strings

Description	Operator	Example	Output
Equality	==	'me' == 'ME' 'you' == 'you'	False True
Inequality	!=	'me' != 'ME' 'you' != 'you'	True False
Less than	<	'A' < 'a' 'b' < 'a'	True False
Less than or equal	<=	'Z' <= 'a' 'a' <= 'a'	True True
Greater than	>	'a' > 'B' 'a' > 'z'	True False

Strings (continued)

Description	Operator	Example	Output
Greater than or equal	>=	'a' >= 'a' 'a' >= 'z'	True False
Contains	in	'Go' in 'Gopher' 'py' in 'PYTHON'	True False
Length	len	len('program') len('')	7 0

String indexing for s = "Python Cheat Sheet"

Indexing/slicing	Result
s[0]	'P'
s[-1]	't'
s[6]	' '
s[2:10]	'thon Che'
s[7:15:2]	'CetS'
s[4:8:-1]	' '
s[13:3:-2]	'SteCn'
s[::]	'Python Cheat Sheet'
s[::-1]	'teehS taehC nohtyP'

Lists for L = ['hello', 'hi', 'welcome']

Slice	Result
Indexing/slicing	Same as for strings
L[0][0]	'h'
len(L)	3
L.append([])	['hello', 'hi', 'welcome', []]
'hi' in L	True
L[1] = 'bye'	['hello', 'bye', 'welcome']
L.remove('welcome')	['hello', 'hi']

Mutable vs. immutable

- Immutable—integer, float, string, Boolean.
- Mutable—list, dictionary.
- Be careful about mutating while iterating.

Dictionaries

- Keys can't be mutable objects.
- Values can be mutable or immutable.

INTERESTING PYTHON LIBRARIES

Libraries you've seen

Name	Description
math	Mathematical operations
random	Operations with pseudo-random numbers
time	Operations that use the clock
unittest	Framework for adding tests
tkinter	Working with graphical user interfaces

Other interesting libraries

Name	Description
numpy	Advanced mathematical operations: • Make multidimensional arrays of data and matrices • Populate arrays with all zeros, random numbers, and so forth • Do array mathematical operations on elements or pairs • Reshape arrays
scrapy	For web scraping: • Crawl websites and extract data • Can export data in multiple standard formats (CSV, JSON, XML)

Other interesting libraries (continued)

Name	Description
matplotlib	Making plots and graphs: • Make bar graphs, line graphs, histograms, boxplots, pie charts, scatter plots, pie charts • Make images, contours, stream plots • Add text, labels, axes, legends, change data markers
pygame	2D game development: • Can add images, draw shapes, load cursors • Manage events based on joystick, mouse, or keyboard input • Manipulate sounds, images, and timing • Transform images by scaling, rotating, or flipping
scipy	Scientific computing tools and algorithms: • Solve integrals, differential equations, and optimizations • Can cluster data, do signal processing (and distortions on images), and various statistical analyses
smtplib	Email: • Set up data and compose an email message with headers • Authenticate and encrypt
pillow	Working with images: • Create thumbnails, convert formats, print • Process images (resize, rotate, change contrast and brightness, perform distortions)
wxpyton	Working with graphical user interfaces (alternative to tkinter)
pyqt	Working with graphical user interfaces (alternative to tkinter)
nltk	Natural Language Toolkit: • Analyze words, sentences, text • Mark a word as corresponding to a part of speech • Extract names from text into categories (person, place, time, quantity, and so forth)
basemap	Plot 2D data on maps: • Extension of matplotlib • Plot coast lines, continents, countries • Draw points and contours • Read point data to draw polygons
sqlalchemy	Databases: • Interface for interacting with a database in an object-oriented way
pandas	Data analysis: • Work with tabular data, time-series data, matrix data, statistical data

INDEX